GAINING
SENTENCE
POWER

GAINING SENTENCE POWER

Dorothy Rubin
TRENTON STATE COLLEGE

Macmillan Publishing Co., Inc.

NEW YORK

Collier Macmillan Publishers

LONDON

A portion of this book is reprinted from the Vital Arts—Reading and Writing, copyright © 1979 by Dorothy Rubin.

Macmillan Publishing Co., Inc.
866 Third Avenue, New York, New York 10022

Collier Macmillan Canada, Ltd.

Library of Congress Cataloging in Publication Data

Rubin, Dorothy.
  Gaining sentence power.

  includes index.
  1. English language—Sentences. I. Title.
PE1375.R8   428.2   80-22004
ISBN 0-02-404190-4

Printing: 1 2 3 4 5 6 7 8   Year: 1 2 3 4 5 6 7

Preface

The ability to write clearly and effectively is not a luxury but a necessity. Writing is essential to many aspects of social, practical, and professional communication, and those who have difficulty in expressing themselves in writing are handicapped in our society. When writing is judged, the writer is also judged. The individual's personality, creativity, schooling, and intelligence are literally "on the line."

GAINING SENTENCE POWER is a text workbook written to help improve writing skills. Because the basic unit of writing is the sentence, GAINING SENTENCE POWER is primarily concerned with the development of sentence competency, as well as such related skills as word usage, punctuation, capitalization, and spelling. GAINING SENTENCE POWER includes many opportunities to write because writing improves writing. Answers and sample sentences are provided for every practice in the body of the text, for knowledge of achievement is essential to growth and progress.

Although a number of the students who open this book will have worked with many of its principles before, I hope that my presentation of the principles in simple units and understandable terms will provide new insights to familiar writing problems. The emphasis in GAINING SENTENCE POWER is on the rapid, enduring, and enjoyable acquisition of fundamentals. The contents progress from the simple sentence through the compound-complex sentence to more advanced sentence writing skills. Readers are given numerous opportunities to write the various types of sentences and to combine, expand, and shorten sentences.

The text is divided into four units. The first is devoted to the simple sentence, the second to the compound sentence, the third to complex and compound-complex sentences, as well as to sentence combining and sentence variety. The fourth unit takes up advanced sentence and writing skills. Each unit is divided into lessons, and each lesson is divided into four parts. The four components of each lesson are related to each other but involve the students in a variety of skills instead of in an endurance test of unvarying concentration. The first lesson, for example, introduces the simple sentence, nouns, the general use of punctuation marks, and the spelling of noun plurals; the second lesson continues with sentence patterns, the subject of a sentence, capitalization, and more on the spelling of noun plurals. The separate parts of the lessons are cumulative; that is, a topic such as punctuation is pursued throughout the book as part of each lesson until the student has met, and met again, every punctuation mark and its use. The student is never subjected, however, to a single, gruelling marathon in punctuation.

Each lesson part provides a simple, concise explanation of the specific skill it presents and supports each explanation with numerous examples analyzed as necessary. Practice in using the particular skills follows. Answers to the practices are given at the end of each lesson. At the end of each unit, word puzzles and review crossword puzzles add to the challenge, and two review tests, presented without answers, may be used as quizzes or in-class assignments. Repetition of practice in each skill and access to the answers insure the overlearning essential to fixing a principle in the mind.

In addition to the primary content of the book there are five appendixes. The first contains a list of some troublesome verbs, and the second a list of the principal parts of some common irregular verbs. The third appendix consists of a diagnostic test for each of the skill areas presented in the book, and the fourth provides extra practice exercises for each lesson. These additional practices are not answered in the book and so may be used as quizzes or in-class assignments. The fifth appendix is a comprehensive handbook-glossary for reference that gives definitions and explanations for every term or principle in the text.

The organization of GAINING SENTENCE POWER will adapt to a variety of courses and student needs. Someone who wants to follow a single topic from start to finish without interruption can do so by turning from lesson part to lesson part. The answers to the main exercises are in the book, and the content is self-pacing. A student taking a conventional class and a student enrolled in a learning lab or self-help program will gain equally from the text.

D.R.

With love to my understanding, helpful, and supportive husband, Artie, my delightful daughters, Carol and Sharon, and my precious granddaughter, Jennifer.

I would like to thank Anthony English for being the personification of a perfect editor. His valuable suggestions, creative editing, intelligent insights, and uncanny wit have made working with him an extreme pleasure and privilege. I would also like to thank John Travis for being such a considerate and helpful production editor.

Contents

UNIT III

GAINING
SENTENCE
POWER

Simple Sentences
Word Usage: Nouns
Punctuation
Spelling: Noun Plurals
Answers to Practices

Lesson 1

Simple Sentences

1. A simple sentence contains a word or a group of words that names something (subject) and says something about the thing named (predicate). It expresses a complete meaning or thought. *Examples:* Jack works. José is a sophomore in college. The rain ended a twenty-day drought.

2. A simple sentence consists of one single statement, command, wish, question, or exclamation. *Examples:* Sharon is an excellent student. Don't go. Stay here. Were I only able to support myself. How old are you? How fantastic that we can all share an apartment!

3. A simple sentence may be as brief as one word if it expresses a complete thought. In each of the following sentences, you must realize that the subject, *you*, is understood. Also, notice how the punctuation helps give meaning. *Examples:* Go. Stop. Help! Wait. Hurry! Stay. Scream!

4. A simple sentence may have a single subject and single verb or a compound (two or more) subject and compound verb. *Examples:* Jim plays soccer. Jennifer swims. Sharon and Seth play tennis. The faculty and students play basketball together. Tony and George swim and jog every day. My brother jogs, swims, and bicycles every day. He goes to bed late and sleeps late.

5. A group of words that does not express a complete thought is called a sentence fragment (incomplete part). Examples: *Into the woods, And in a minute, the children, When they arrive.*

SPECIAL NOTE

Sentence fragments (incomplete parts) do not express a complete thought; therefore they cannot stand alone as sentences. Although the group of words *When they arrive* has a subject (a word or a group of words about which something is said) and a predicate (a word or a group of words that says something about the subject), it cannot stand alone as a sentence because the thought signaled by "when" has not been completed.

Practice A. Underline the sentences in the following list.

1. Stay here.
2. The students.
3. In the study.
4. Jump.
5. Help me.
6. The gasoline shortage.
7. We can't afford a car.
8. I don't have enough.
9. Let's do it.
10. Beyond the school, when we arrived.
11. To get closer.
12. No one can go.
13. Such as a giraffe.
14. Because of you.
15. Such people as you.
16. Stop that.
17. Above which a fire was burning.
18. As well as our meal tickets.
19. They tried to stop us.
20. When the cheer leaders arrived on the field and went into their cheer sequences.

Check answers at the end of Lesson 1.

Practice B. Choose one word or a group of words from column I and a group of words from column II to construct a simple sentence that makes the *best* sense. Put the letter from column II to the left of the number in column I.

	Column I	*Column II*
_____	1. A black overcast sky	a. went to the same school.
_____	2. Did	b. blocked all entrances.
_____	3. The strikers	c. is overcrowded.
_____	4. Our dormitory at college	d. is taking over my room.
_____	5. My car	e. are identical twins.
_____	6. The company	f. have slowed down construction.
_____	7. My spreading plant	g. threatened the festivities.
_____	8. Herb and Jack	h. is closing one of its plants.
_____	9. My parents	i. needs a complete overhaul.
_____	10. Frequent fires and un-explained accidents	j. you see Mary in class today?

Check answers at the end of Lesson 1.

Practice C. Fill in each blank to make a simple sentence.

1. The _____ runs.

2. The students _____ .

3. My pet _____ .

4. "Good grief, _____ you _____ to that lecture?"

5. My best _____ is _____ .

6. The _____ and _____ went _____ .

7. The _____ and _____ went _____
   and _____ .

8. My pet _____ and _____ all day.

9. Reading and writing _____ important skills.

10. Help _____ finish _____ the _____ .

Check sample answers at the end of Lesson 1.

Practice D.   Underline all sentence fragments in the following paragraphs.

1. Many people work by day and sleep by night. Studies show. Night workers are not as efficient as day workers. Night workers also have many more serious physical illnesses than day workers. The research done. Has been on workers with routine jobs. Research has not been done on night workers with creative jobs.

2. The race was finally ready to begin. The faculty looked smugly at the students. The students laughing at the faculty's self-confidence. How could they win? Some of the faculty were old enough to be grandfathers. The whistle blew. The race had begun.

3. We entered the dark room very cautiously. Suddenly a ray of light came into the room. Almost blinding us. We were terrified! There had been three murders in this room. We did not intend to be the next victims. Even though being stuck here now. We heard a loud pounding noise. Only our hearts. We couldn't seem to move. Someone was definitely in the room with us. Who was there?

4. In the years between 1543 and 1800 European science made re-markable progress. National governments capable of maintaining law and order and replacing feudalism. Art and science were patronized by kings. And by the prosperous new middle class. Geographical discoveries and the changes affecting everyday life were encouraging men to be skeptical of old notions. And to seek new ideas. As well as new lands.

Check answers at the end of Lesson 1.

Practice E.   Write a simple sentence for all sentence fragments found in Practice D. (You may combine sentence fragments to make a simple sentence, and you may change word forms, add words, or leave out words as long as the idea is not changed.)

1. _____

_____

_____

_____

2. _____

_____

_____

_____

3. _____

_____

_____

_____

4. _____

_____

_____

_____

Check sample sentences at the end of Lesson 1.

Practice F. Write three simple sentences.

1. _____

_____

2. _____

_____

3. _____

_____

Check sample sentences at the end of Lesson 1.

Word Usage: Nouns

Nouns are words such as *cat, dog, house, mother, candy, rock, goodness, cleanliness,* and *beauty.* Nouns name persons, animals, places, things, or ideas.

1. A **proper noun** names a particular person, place, or thing. Proper nouns are capitalized. *Examples:* George Washington, Grand Canyon, India, Empire State Building.

2. All other nouns are called **common nouns**. Common nouns are not capitalized. *Examples:* man, place, country, city, animals, strength, love.

3. A **collective noun** names a group, a class, or a collection and is considered as a unit or whole. *Examples:* class, group, clergy, party, flock, breed, gang, jury, crowd, company, family, choir.

4. Certain clues help you to determine that a word is a noun.

    a. Position, which has to do with word order, is an important clue. Words such as *the, a, an, one, some, each, this, that, his, her, those, my, our, your,* and so on, signal that a noun follows. *Examples:* My *brother* is a friendly person. A *stranger* waved to me. The *students* decided to vote on it.

    b. Another important clue has to do with word changes. Nouns change their form for both number and possession. *Examples:* one apple (singular), two apples (plural); cat's fur (singular possessive), cats' fur (plural possessive).

    c. Certain endings are also a clue that the word is a noun. Endings such as *-tion, -sion, -ence, -ance, -er, -or, -ness, -ship, -ment, -ism, -ity,* signal that the word is probably a noun. *Examples:* Courtship, imperialism, author, painter, hardness, impotence, charity.

5. Following are sentences that show three ways in which nouns may be used:

The *man* works. (subjective case)	*Man is the* **subject** of the sentence. It is about *man* that something is said.
The child threw the *ball.* (objective case)	*Ball* is the **object** of *threw. Ball* is what the child threw. *Child* is the **subject** of the sentence. *Ball is receiving the action.* An **object** receives the action.
John's house is large. (possessive case)	*John's* is a **proper noun** showing ownership. The house belongs to John. *House* is the **subject** of the sentence.

Practice A. Change the nonsense word in each sentence to a noun that would make sense in the sentence.

1. The glob went to my school.

2. How many jibs do you own?

3. My drobe broke yesterday.

4. Why can't Loy go?

5. Chait is not being fair.

6. Stop that flebe!

7. The dembes are not prepared.

8. A doam should not be subjected to such behavior.

9. Please tell Blaf to attend the party tomorrow.

10. The groibes are postponing exams until next week.

Check sample answers at the end of Lesson 1.

Practice B. Underline the nonsense word(s) in the following nonsense sentences that are nouns.

1. The gribble grobbed.   2. Plaib the deme.

3. Naim the veib.   4. A saze doiled the neim.

5. A nome nims the beib.   6. Chailism pliesed.

7. The chansess bu the foim.   8. The daminence doined.

9. Slabe that werity.   10. An aristance blanned.

Check answers at the end of Lesson 1.

Practice C. For each given clue, write a noun that would follow.

1. A _____   2. The _____

3. An _____   4. Two _____

5. One _____   6. His _____

7. Each _____   8. Some _____

9. My _____   10. Several _____

Check sample answers at the end of Lesson 1.

Practice D. For each of the endings given, write a noun that uses that ending.

1. ness _____   2. ity _____

3. ance _____   4. tion _____

5. ence _____   6. sion _____

7. or _____   8. er _____

9. ism _____   10. ment _____

Check sample answers at the end of Lesson 1.

Practice E. Write a simple sentence for each of the words that you gave in Practice D.

1. _____

2. _____

3. _____

4. _____

5. _____

6. _____

7. _____

8. _____

9. _____

10. _____

Check sample sentences at the end of Lesson 1.

Punctuation

In speaking, your voice, facial gestures, and body movements help clarify meaning. In writing, punctuation marks are the signals that help to convey clear meaning. Punctuation marks help the reader to know whether the sentence is a statement, a question, a command, or a sentence of strong emotion. Read the following sentences.

1. That is a good idea.
2. Who is he?
3. That is wonderful!
4. Go.

Sentence 1 is a statement. Statement (declarative) sentences are the most often written sentences. The **period** (.) is used at the end of these sentences. Sentence 2 is a question (interrogative) sentence. A **question mark** (?) ends such a sentence. Sentence 3 is one that expresses strong emotion (exclamatory). **An exclamation mark** (!) ends such sentences. Sentence 4 is a sentence expressing a command (imperative). A period is most often used to end such sentences; however, an exclamation mark may be used to show special or strong emphasis. (An imperative sentence usually has an *understood* subject rather than a stated one. The sentence *Go* includes the understood subject *you* and means *You go*.)

SPECIAL NOTE

An interjection, which is considered a part of speech, is a word usually used with an exclamation mark to express an emotion. An interjection is independent of the rest of the sentence. *Examples:* Oh! Aha! Hurrah! Goodness!

PEANUTS ®   By Charles M. Schulz

©1958 United Feature Syndicate Inc.

Practice A. Put the proper punctuation at the end of the following sentences.

1. What does she want

2. Don't go with her

3. Help

4. She is very nice

5. May I go now

6. How old are you

7. We went to the picnic without them

8. Which is the best

9. Leave immediately

10. Imagine that

Check answers at the end of Lesson 1.

Practice B. Write simple sentences according to the instructions given in the parentheses.

1. (Write a declarative sentence.) _____

_____

2. (Write an interrogative sentence.) _____

_____

3. (Write an imperative sentence.) _____

_____

4. (Write an exclamatory sentence.) _____

_____

5. (Write an imperative sentence that expresses strong emphasis.) _____

_____

Check sample sentences at the end of Lesson 1.

Spelling: Noun Plurals

1. To indicate a plural (more than one), an -s is added to nouns such as *tree, airplane, truck, wagon, puzzle, boy, girl, cow, table.*

2. To indicate a plural, an -es is usually added to nouns that end in -s, -ss, -sh, -ch, or -x, making an extra syllable: *bus, buses, busses; glass, glasses; bush, bushes; bench, benches; box, boxes.*

3. Proper nouns (names) follow the regular rules for -s and -es *plurals. Examples:* Jack, three Jacks; Mr. and Mrs. Smith, the Smiths; Helen and Ruth Jones, the Joneses; Charles, three Charleses; Ms. and Mr. Burns, the Burnses; José, three Josés; Flores, three Floreses.

4. Nouns that end in -y with a vowel before the y add -s to make the word plural: *boy, boys; key, keys.* Nouns that end in -y with a consonant before the y, change the y to i and add -es to form the plural: *baby, babies; story, stories.*

Practice A. Make each of the following words plural. Add -s or -es to the end of each word.

1. dress_____   2. church_____   3. lamp_____

4. brush_____   5. fox_____   6. lunch_____

7. clock_____   8. window_____   9. pass_____

10. box_____   11. lock_____   12. ball_____

13. kiss_____   14. list_____   15. tree_____

16. class_____   17. punch_____   18. ranch_____

19. ax_____   20. plant_____   21. crash_____

22. fish_____   23. mess_____   24. wish_____

25. tax_____   26. marsh_____   27. splash_____

28. witch_____   29. watch_____   30. stitch_____

31. pinch_____   32. princess_____   33. six_____

34. wash_____   35. Jim_____   36. Burns_____

37. Jones_____   38. Flores_____   39. Brown_____

40. James_____

Check answers at the end of Lesson 1.

Practice B. Write three simple sentences incorporating a number of the noun plurals from Practice A in each of the sentences.

1._____

_____

2._____

_____

3._____

_____

Check sample sentences at the end of Lesson 1.

Practice C. Make each of the following words plural.

1. candy_____   2. hobby_____

3. turkey_____   4. laundry_____

5. enemy_____   6. policy_____

7. decoy_____   8. day_____

9. journey_____   10. democracy_____

11. play_____   12. joy _____

13. berry_____   14. alley_____

15. pony_____   16. tray_____

17. spy_____   18. study_____

19. monkey_____   20. lady_____

Check answers at the end of Lesson 1.

Practice D. Write three simple sentences incorporating a number of the noun plurals from Practice C.

1._____

_____

2._____

_____

3._____

_____

Check sample sentences at the end of Lesson 1.

LESSON 1 ANSWERS

Simple Sentences (pp. 1–4)

Practice A: 1, 4, 5, 7, 8, 9, 12, 16, 19

Practice B: 1. g   2. j   3. b   4. c   5. i   6. h   7. d   8. e   9. a   10. f

Practice C (sample answers):   1. train; man, etc.*   2. study; play; work hard; etc.   3. is a snake; is a dog; etc.   4. did, go   5. subject, math; friend, Arthur; etc.   6. men, women, swimming; girls, boys, hiking; etc. 7. boys, girls, fishing, swimming; etc.   8. eats, plays; eats, sleeps; etc.   9. are 10. me, wiping, dishes; us, painting, house; etc.

Practice D: Sentence fragments are: 1. Studies show; The research done; Has been on workers with routine jobs   2. The students laughing at the faculty's self-confidence;   3. Almost blinding us; Even though being stuck here now; Only our hearts;   4. National governments capable of maintaining law and order and replacing feudalism; And by the prosperous new middle class; And to seek new ideas; As well as new lands.

Practice E.   (sample sentences)   1. Studies show interesting results. The research done has been on workers with routine jobs.   2. The students laughed at the faculty's self-confidence.   3. Suddenly a ray of light came into the room almost blinding us.   However, we were stuck here now.   Only our hearts were pounding.   4. National governments were capable of maintaining law and order and replacing feudalism.   Art and science were patronized by kings and by the prosperous new middle class.   Men were encouraged to seek new ideas as well as new lands.

Practice F.   (sample sentences):   1. The grocery store was closed.   2. I speak English, French, and Spanish.   3. We are going bowling and dancing.

Word Usage: Nouns (pp. 4–7)

Practice A: (sample answers)   1. murderer   2. tapes   3. bike   4. Jim 5. Charles   6. crying   7. students   8. person   9. Bret   10. instructors

Practice B: 1. gribble   2. deme   3. veib   4. saze; neim   5. nome; beib 6. Chailism   7. chansess; foim   8. daminence   9. werity   10. aristance

Practice C: (sample answers)   1. dragon   2. truth   3. alligator   4. students   5. teacher   6. brother   7. person   8. people   9. friend   10. instructors

Practice D: (sample answers)   1. kindness   2. clarity   3. radiance 4. constitution   5. patience   6. mission   7. author   8. writer   9. capitalism 10. pavement

Practice E: (sample sentences)   1. I will always be grateful for his *kindness* to me.   2. His writing needs more *clarity*.   3. I will never forget the *radiance* of her smile.   4. We need to uphold the *constitution*.   5. His *pa-*

---

* *Etc.* means *and so on.*

tience is unsurpassed.   6. What is my *mission*?   7. She is a good *author*.
8. Tony is a creative *writer*.   9. Our economic system is based on *capitalism*.
10. Someone slipped on the wet *pavement*.

Punctuation (pp. 7–8)

Practice A: 1. (?)   2. (.)   3. (!)   4. (.)   5. (?)   6. (?)   7. (.)   8. (?)
9. (.)   10. (!).

Practice B: (sample sentences)   1. My classmates and I play bridge during our class breaks.   2. Why did you do that?   3. Stop that.   4. That is
beautiful!   5. Don't go!

Spelling: Noun Plurals (pp. 8–10)

Practice A: 1. dresses   2. churches   3. lamps   4. brushes   5. foxes
6. lunches   7. clocks   8. windows   9. passes   10. boxes   11. locks   12. balls
13. kisses   14. lists   15. trees   16. classes   17. punches   18. ranches   19. axes
20. plants   21. crashes   22. fish (fishes when referring to different species)
23. messes   24. wishes   25. taxes   26. marshes   27. splashes   28. witches
29. watches   30. stitches   31. pinches   32. princesses   33. sixes   34. washes
35. Jims   36. Burnses   37. Joneses   38. Floreses   39. Browns   40. Jameses.

Practice B: (sample sentences)   1. The witch changed for foxes into
fishes and ate them for lunches.   2. The Jameses and the Browns live on
large ranches and pay lots of taxes.   3. The witches gave the princesses three
wishes.

Practice C: 1. candies   2. hobbies   3. turkeys   4. laundries   5. enemies
6. policies   7. decoys   8. days   9. journeys   10. democracies   11. plays
12. joys   13. berries   14. alleys   15. ponies   16. trays   17. spies   18. studies
19. monkeys   20. ladies

Practice D: (sample sentences)   1. Monkeys were used as decoys to
elude the spies.   2. The ponies refused to eat the berries off the trays.
3. The ladies looked silly carrying the live turkeys.

Lesson 2

Sentence Patterns

The words in English sentences must be arranged in a certain order for the sentences to make sense. The arrangement *Ball the hit he* does not make sense, and it is not a sentence. The arrangement *He hit the ball* does make sense, and it is a sentence in English. From the above, we can say that a sentence is an orderly arrangement of words that makes sense.

All writing in English is based on a few basic sentence patterns, that is, the way that words can be arranged and still make sense. The sentence patterns you choose are based on the message you wish to convey.

This lesson and the following ones in this unit present seven basic sentence patterns. All basic sentence patterns presented in this unit are **simple sentences**. More complicated sentences can be made from these basic patterns by combining sentence patterns and/or by adding words that limit or describe.

Sentence Pattern 1 (N/P V)

English is primarily a subject-predicate language; the subject alone is a noun or a pronoun, and the predicate alone is a verb. Sentence Pattern 1 is the only one that can be made with only a subject and a verb.

Examples:

N/P	V	N/P	V
Arthur	works.	Rain	falls.
Helen	reads.	Susan	cries.
Tom	flies.	Moods	change.
Faucets	drip.	Plants	grow.
Sharon	runs.	Wounds	hurt.
Seth	jogs.	They	walk.

13

SPECIAL NOTE

In the sentence patterns, N refers to a *noun*, P refers to a *pronoun*, and V refers to a *verb*. N/P means that the word can be either a noun or a pronoun. (A pronoun is a word such as *he* or *she* that is used in the place of a noun.)

The N/P V pattern can be expanded by adding words that describe or limit the bare subject or the bare predicate. A word that describes or limits is called a **modifier**. Most sentences in Sentence Pattern 1 contain modifiers. *Examples:*

1. Arthur works hard.
2. Helen reads very quickly.
3. Leaky faucets drip.
4. My plants grow in a pot.
5. Seth jogs to work.
6. My moods change a lot.

Practice A. Write five simple sentences that conform to Sentence Pattern 1.

1. _____
2. _____
3. _____
4. _____
5. _____

Check sample sentences at the end of Lesson 2.

Practice B. Change all of the sentences in Practice A to interrogative sentences.

1. _____
2. _____
3. _____
4. _____
5. _____

Check sample sentences at the end of Lesson 2.

Practice C. Underline all the sentences in the following list that do not conform to Sentence Pattern 1.

1. Carol runs.

2. Seth swims every day.

3. Sharon plays tennis every day.

4. The trees rustle in the wind.

5. The robbers wore masks.

6. No one bought lunch yesterday.

7. Who yawned?

8. The students laughed very loudly.

9. Please return that.

10. How many came?

Check answers at the end of Lesson 2.

Practice D.   Underline all those in the following list that are not sentences.

1. He beat.

2. She wore.

3. I sneezed.

4. John waits.

5. Rain falls.

6. Butter melts.

7. Students cheer.

8. Ducks quack.

9. Morty became.

10. He employed.

Check answers at the end of Lesson 2.

Word Usage:
The Subject of a Sentence

The **subject** of a sentence is a word or group of words about which something is said. The subject of a sentence can be a person, an animal, a place, a thing, an idea, and so on.

1. Simple Subject — A **simple subject** is either a noun or a pronoun alone. (A pronoun is a word such as *he* or *she* that is used in the place of a noun.)   *Examples:* Biology is the science of living things. She likes to jog every morning. (*Biology* is the subject in the first sentence. It is about a noun *biology* that something is said. *She* is the subject in the second sentence, and it is about the pronoun *she* that something is said. *Biology* and *she* are both *simple subjects.*)

2. Compound Subject — A **compound subject** consists of two or more simple subjects (words about which something is said). The simple subjects may be two or more nouns or pronouns.   *Examples:* Joe, Bill, and I went swimming. Crushed stone and tar can be used as a base for driveways. (The words *Joe, Bill,* and *I* are the compound subjects in the first sentence. *Stone* and *tar* form the compound subject in the second sentence.)

3. Complete Subject — The **complete subject** consists of the simple subject (noun or pronoun) and the words that modify (describe or limit) the subject.   *Example:* The big red tomato tasted very good. (the simple subject is *tomato*.) The complete subject is *the big red tomato.* The words *the, big,* and *red* all describe and limit the subject *tomato.* You know that what is being said concerns a tomato that must be both big and red.)

Practice A.   Circle the simple subject in each sentence.

1. I am riding my bicycle to school rather than driving.

2. The gasoline shortage has changed many people's habits.

3. My best friend is moving closer to the campus.

4. People think twice about driving to the corner store.

5. Some people have to wait in gasoline lines for three hours.

6. The exhausted men worked all night to finish the job.

7. Most fruits contain a large quantity of natural sugar.

8. Most professional athletes must train every day to keep in shape.

9. Human babies are helpless for a longer time than other animal babies.

10. Expert help is on the way.

Check answers at the end of Lesson 2.

Practice B.   Circle the compound subject in each sentence.

1. Faculty, students, and administrators met to discuss the recent rash of vandalism on campus.

2. Dick, George, and I are rooming together next semester.

3. Turtles and lizards are reptiles.

4. Egypt and Israel signed a peace treaty in 1979.

5. Mr. and Mrs. Jones filed a malpractice suit.

6. Juniors and seniors usually have a good chance of getting the course schedule that they have requested.

7. The men and women in our organization are working together to clean up our neighborhood.

8. Professors and students are trying to work out an agreeable method of faculty evaluation.

9. Measurement and evaluation are not the same.

10. My science professor and my math instructor are both giving their finals on the same day.

Check answers at the end of Lesson 2.

Practice C. Circle the complete subject in each sentence.

1. The happy couple waved farewell to their relatives.

2. The overloaded bridge collapsed.

3. The small, frightened cat jumped out the window.

4. The tired men and women decided to stop and rest.

5. My big brother and my little sister look alike.

6. The bearded man and the bearded woman are husband and wife.

7. The snakelike line of cars extended for two miles.

8. The mystery of Big Foot still exists.

9. Professional athletes cannot compete in the Olympics.

10. My friend Speedy lost his license because of speeding.

Check answers at the end of Lesson 2.

Practice D. Complete each sentence by inserting a simple or a compound subject.

1. _____ are in bloom this time of year.

2. _____ , _____ , and _____ are three of my favorite science courses.

3. _____ give off a foul odor when they are frightened.

4. _____ look like walking pincushions.

5. The sudden loud _____ awakened the baby.

6. The _____ for the common cold has still not been invented.

7. _____ , _____ , and _____ are qualities I value in a friend.

8. The _____ frightened us.

9. A sudden _____ brought hurricanelike winds to the island.

10. My best _____ and my sister are married.

Check sample answers at the end of Lesson 2.

Capitalization

Following is a list of items that are capitalized:

The first word of a sentence — Help is on the way.
Names of persons — John Smith, Seth Johnson
Titles of persons — Mr., Mrs., Ms., Dr., Rev., Capt.
Days of the week — Monday, Tuesday, Wednesday
Months of the year — January, February, March
Titles of Books — *Tom Sawyer*
Titles of Plays — *Macbeth, A Doll's House*
Titles of magazines and journals — *Psychology Today, The English Journal*
Titles of poems — "Fog," "The Raven"
Titles of movies — *Citizen Kane, Rocky*
Titles of stories — "The Killers," "The Monkey's Paw"
Names of countries — the United States of America, England, France, Germany
Names of cities — New York, San Francisco, Atlanta
Names of streets, avenues, and roads — Stuart Rd., Nineteenth Street, Fifth Ave.
Names of languages — French, Spanish, Russian
Names of companies — the Great Atlantic and Pacific Co., Autodynamics, Inc.
Names of institutions — the Smithsonian Institution, the Ford Foundation

SPECIAL NOTES

a. All words in titles are capitalized except for such short words as *a, an, the, of, to,* which are not capitalized in a title unless they begin the title. (All verbs in titles, including short verbs such as *Is, Am,* and *Be,* are capitalized.)

b. The term *Reverend* (*Rev.*) is usually preceded by *the* and followed by a *title* or a *full name. Examples:* the Rev. Dr. Jones; the Rev. James Jackson.

Practice A. Circle all words in the following sentences that should have capital letters.

1. on mondays and tuesdays, we go swimming with herb, jack, and kim.

2. laura, donna, and terry usually go to florida during the month of january.

3. anthony read robert frost's poem, "the death of the hired man."

4. every day, she reads *newsday* and *sports illustrated.*

5. the rev. dr. smith delivered an excellent sermon.

6. mr. and mrs. brown went to hear president brown speak.

7. they live on jackson street near columbia university in new york city.

8. england, france, and germany are all european nations.

9. my mother, who is bilingual, speaks spanish and french.

10. we have to read tolstoy's *war and peace* for our literature class.

Check answers at the end of Lesson 2.

Practice B. Here is a list of words or phrases. In the blank after each word or phrase, write *No* if the word or phrase should not be capitalized; write *Yes* if the word or any part of the phrase should be capitalized, and circle the letters that should be capitals.

1. the rev. Dr. Smith _____   2. asia _____

3. baseball_____   4. jack _____

5. a literature course _____   6. russian roulette_____

7. autodynamics, inc._____   8. wednesday _____

9. strawberry bush _____   10. father brown _____

Check answers at the end of Lesson 2.

Practice C. In each of the following sets of items, one is incorrectly capitalized. Underline the *incorrectly* capitalized one, and circle the letters that should or should not be capitals.

1. *The Way Of All Flesh*; *The Scarlet Letter*

2. the Institute for Advanced Study; The Institute For Foreign Affairs

3. the Rev. Paul Piersine; father's Day

4. "The Lamb"; "Ode To The West Wind"

5. "There is no Frigate Like a Book"; "Believe Me If All Those Endearing
   Young Charms"

Check answers at the end of Lesson 2.

Spelling: Noun Plurals

1. Nouns that end in -*o* with a consonant before the *o* usually add -*es* or -*s* to make the word plural. *Examples:* potato — potatoes; hero — heroes; piano — pianos; solo — solos; dynamo — dynamos; auto — autos. Nouns that end in -*o* with a vowel before the *o* add -*s* to make the word plural. *Examples:* radio — radios; folio — folios; cameo — cameos. The plural of some nouns ending in -*o* may be formed with either -*s* or -*es*. *Examples:* volcanos or volcanoes; halos or haloes; mottoes or mottos; cargoes or cargos; banjos or banjoes; zeros or zeroes.

2. Nouns that end in -*f* or -*fe* usually are made plural by changing the *f* or *fe* to *ves*. *Examples:* shelf — shelves; knife — knives. Some nouns ending in -*f* or -*fe* form the plural by adding -*s*. *Examples:* Chief — chiefs; roof — roofs; dwarf — dwarfs; gulf — gulfs; safe — safes. The plural of some nouns ending in -*f* may be formed by either -*s* or -*ves*. *Examples:* wharves or wharfs; scarves or scarfs.

3. Nouns that end in *-ff* usually add *-s* to the word to form the plural. *Examples:* staff — staffs; sheriff — sheriffs; cuff — cuffs; muff — muffs.

4. Following are some nouns that do not conform to rule patterns: foot — feet; man — men; child — children; goose — geese; mouse — mice; ox — oxen; tooth — teeth.

5. Some nouns are the same in both the singular and the plural: deer — deer; sheep — sheep; salmon — salmon; grouse — grouse; bison — bison.

6. Hyphenated compound words from their plurals by adding *-s* or *-es* to the important word in the hyphenated compound word. Usually, the first word is the important word in the compound. *Examples:* mother-in-law — mothers-in-law; attorney-at-law — attorneys-at-law; lady-in-waiting — ladies-in-waiting; jack-in-the-box — jacks-in-the-box or jack-in-the-boxes; jack-of-all-trades — jacks-of-all-trades or jack-of-all-trades; attorney-general — attorneys-general or attorney-generals.

SPECIAL NOTES

a. If you are unsure of the spelling of a word, consult your dictionary.

b. When a dictionary gives two spellings for a word, the first spelling is the one most commonly used.

Practice A. Give the plural of the following words.

1. calf _____   2. domino_____

3. hero _____   4. potato_____

5. tomato_____   6. tooth _____

7. goose_____   8. ox_____

9. man _____   10. child_____

11. roof _____   12. chief_____

13. shelf_____   14. leaf_____

15. thief_____   16. wife_____

17. sheriff_____   18. elf_____

19. radio _____   20. mosquito _____

21. echo _____   22. veto_____

23. torpedo_____   24. Negro _____

25. piano_____   26. solo_____

27. self _____   28. volcano_____

29. buffalo_____   30. embargo_____

31. brother-in-law_____   32. attorney-at-law_____

33. cuff_____   34. bailiff_____

35. lady-in-waiting _____

Check answers at the end of Lesson 2.

Practice B. Underline the noun plural in each group that is misspelled.

1. a) sheriffs, b) churches, c) salmons, d) cookies.

2. a) attorneys-at-law, b) jacks-in-the-boxes, c) matrons of honor, d) attorneys-general.

3. a) potatoes, b) volcanos, c) dwarves, d) safes.

4. a) autos, b) flys, c) roofs, d) chiefs.

5. a) cameos, b) vetos, c) passers-by, d) bamboos.

6. a) son-in-laws, b) Charleses, c) mosquitoes, d) echoes.

7. a) swine, b) donkeys, c) fishes, d) deers.

8. a) Jones, b) Browns, c) Jerries, d) radios.

9. a) courts-martial, b) theorys, c) Floreses, d) solos.

10. a) loaves, b) pianos, c) quizzes, d) elfs.

Check answers at the end of Lesson 2.

Practice C. Correctly spell each word that is misspelled in Practice B.

1. _____   2. _____

3. _____   4. _____

5. _____   6. _____

7. _____   8. _____

9. _____   10. _____

Check answers at the end of Lesson 2.

LESSON 2 ANSWERS

Sentence Patterns (pp. 13-15)

Practice A: (sample sentences)   1. The penguin walks on two feet. 2. Jack studies hard.   3. No one cares.   4. Rain falls.   5. The wind blows.

Practice B: (sample sentences)   1. Do the penguins walk on two feet. 2. Does Jack study hard?   3. Does no one care?   4. Does rain fall?   5. Does the wind blow?

Practice C: 3, 5, 6, 9

Practice D: 1, 2, 9, 10 (These do not express a complete meaning or thought.)

Word Usage: The Subject of a Sentence (pp. 15-17)

Practice A: 1. I   2. shortage   3. friend   4. People   5. people   6. men 7. fruits   8. athletes   9. babies   10. help

Practice B: 1. Faculty, students, administrators   2. Dick, George, I 3. Turtles, lizards   4. Egypt, Israel   5. Mr., Mrs. Jones   6. Juniors, seniors 7. men, women   8. Professors, students   9. Measurement, evaluation 10. professor, instructor

Practice C: 1. The happy couple   2. The overloaded bridge   3. The small, frightened cat   4. The tired men and women   5. My big brother and my little sister   6. The bearded man and the bearded woman   7. The snake-like line of cars   8. The mystery of Big Foot   9. Professional athletes 10. My friend Speedy

Practice D: (sample answers)   1. Tulips (the name of any flower that blooms at a certain time of year is correct)   2. Biology, geology, anthropology (the names of any sciences are correct).   3. Skunks   4. Porcupines 5. noise   6. cure   7. Trustworthiness, truthfulness, kindness   8. noise 9. storm   10. friend

Capitalization (pp. 18-19)

Practice A: 1. On, Mondays, Tuesdays, Herb, Jack, Kim   2. Laura, Donna, Terry, Florida, January   3. Anthony, Robert Frost's, The Death, Hired Man   4. Every, *Newsday, Sports Illustrated*   5. The Rev. Dr. Smith 6. Mr., Mrs. Brown, President Brown   7. They, Jackson Street, Columbia University, New York City   8. England, France, Germany, European   9. My, Spanish, French   10. We, Tolstoy, *War, Peace.*

Practice B: 1. Yes — Rev.   2. Yes — Asia   3. No   4. Yes — Jack   5. No 6. Yes — Russian   7. Yes — Autodynamics, Inc.   8. Yes — Wednesday   9. No 10. Yes — Father Brown

Practice C: 1. The Way of All Flesh   2. the Institute for Foreign Affairs   3. Father's Day   4. "Ode to the West Wind"   5. "There Is No Frigate Like a Book"

Spelling: Noun Plurals (pp. 19–21)

Practice A:

1. calves	2. dominoes	3. heroes
4. potatoes	5. tomatoes	6. teeth
7. geese	8. oxen	9. men
10. children	11. roofs	12. chiefs
13. shelves	14. leaves	15. thieves
16. wives	17. sheriffs	18. elves
19. radios	20. mosquitoes	21. echoes
22. vetoes	23. torpedoes	24. Negroes
25. pianos	26. solos	27. selves
28. volcanoes	29. buffaloes or buffalos*	30. embargoes
31. brothers-in-law	32. attorneys-at-law	33. cuffs
34. baliliffs	35. ladies-in-waiting	

Practice B: The following are *incorrectly* spelled: 1. salmons   2. jacks in the boxes   3. dwarves   4. flys   5. vetos   6. son-in-laws   7. deers   8. Jones   9. theorys   10. elfs

Practice C: 1. salmon   2. jacks-in-the box   3. dwarfs   4. flies   5. vetoes   6. sons-in-law   7. deer   8. Joneses   9. theories   10. elves

---

* The plural of *buffalo* may also be spelled *buffalo*.

Sentence Patterns
Word Usage: Verbs
Capitalization
Spelling: Abbreviations
Answers to Practices

Lesson 3

Sentence Patterns

1. Sentence Pattern 2 (N/P V N/P)

Most sentences in English conform to this pattern. The first noun or pronoun in the N/P V N/P pattern is the *subject* of the sentence, and the second noun or pronoun is the *direct object* of the verb.

Examples:

N/P	V	N/P
José	plays	football.
Jack	builds	houses.
Carol	knits	sweaters.
Jennifer	eats	cookies.
He	chews	gum.
She	scolded	him.

These sentences can also be expanded with modifiers.   *Examples:*

José plays football every day.
Carol knits sweaters for John.

SPECIAL NOTES

a. The **direct object** of a verb is the person or thing that receives the action of the verb. It usually answers the question *what* or *whom.*   *Examples:*
Tony hit the ball. (The ball is what Tony hit. The ball receives the action.)
The dog bit Mary. (Mary is whom the dog bit. Mary receives the action.)
b. Remember that N refers to a *noun,* P refers to a *pronoun,* V refers to a *verb,* and N/P means that the word can be either a noun or a pronoun.

2. Sentence Pattern 3 (N/P V N/P N)

Sentence Pattern 3 consists of a noun or a pronoun, which is the *subject* of the sentence, a verb, another noun or pronoun, which is the *indirect object,* and the final noun, which is the *direct object.*
Examples:

N/P	V	N/P (Indirect object)	N (Direct Object)
Jerry	gives	Jim	the notes.
Barbara	reads	the baby	a story.
Harry	bought	Clara	a present.
The bird	brings	its young	worms.
He	gave	her	the message.

The ideas expressed by using Sentence Pattern 3 can be expressed by using Sentence Pattern 2.   *Examples:*

N/P	V	N/P
Jerry	gives	the notes to Jim.
Barbara	reads	a story to the baby.
Harry	bought	a present for Clara.
The bird	brings	worms to its young.
He	gave	the message to her.

SPECIAL NOTES

a. These sentences contain both an object and an indirect object:
  (1) The child threw John the ball.
  (2) We bought her a gift.
b. The **indirect object** of a verb is the person or thing indirectly affected by the action of the verb.

3. Sentence Pattern 4 (N/P LV N/P)

Although Sentence Pattern 4 appears to be similar to Sentence Pattern 2, it is not. Sentence Pattern 4 contains a linking verb. Verbs such as *be, become, smell, sound, taste, feel, look, seem* and *appear* are called **linking verbs** because they often link a subject with a word that in effect renames the subject.
Examples:

N/P	LV (Linking Verb)	N/P
The flowers	are	tulips.
Jack	is	my brother.
Seth	became	a tennis player.
She	is	my mother.
That	is	mine.

4. Sentence Pattern 5 (N/P LV Adj.)

Sentence Pattern 5 also uses a linking verb, but in Sentence Pattern 5 the linking verb is used to link the subject with a word that describes the subject. A word that describes a noun or a pronoun is called an **adjective**.

Examples:

N/P	LV (Linking Verb)	Adj. (Adjective)
The flower	is	pretty.
My allergy	is	worse.
My fingers	became	numb.
They	seem	happy.

Practice A. Write five simple sentences that conform to Sentence Pattern 2.

1. _____

2. _____

3. _____

4. _____

5. _____

Check sample sentences at the end of Lesson 3.

Practice B. Write five simple sentences that conform to Sentence Pattern 3.

1. _____

2. _____

3. _____

4. _____

5. _____

Check sample sentences at the end of Lesson 3.

Practice C. Write five simple sentences that conform to Sentence Pattern 4.

1. _____

2. _____

3. _____

4. _____

5. _____

Check sample sentences at the end of Lesson 3.

Practice D. Write five simple sentences that conform to Sentence Pattern 5.

1. _____

2. _____

3. _____

4. _____

5. _____

Check sample sentences at the end of Lesson 3.

Practice E. Here are ten simple sentences. In the blank at the end of each sentence, write which sentence pattern the simple sentence conforms to.

1. The athletes in our school jog every day. _____

2. Seth and Sharon are good tennis players. _____

3. My college is very conservative. _____

4. Our gym instructor gave George a poor grade. _____

5. This concoction tastes good. _____

6. Mr. Brown is our math instructor. _____

7. The airplane flew at a high altitude above the clouds. _____

8. The pilot handled the plane very well. _____

9. Please give Herbert my regards. _____

10. Tony is a creative writer. _____

Check answers at the end of Lesson 3.

Word Usage: Verbs

The verb is a telling word. It expresses action, existence (a state of being), or occurrence (anything that happens or takes place). The verb can be one word, such as *bake, run,* or *go,* or a group of words (verb phrase) such as *am going, have seen, can play,* or *will be going.* *Examples:* Mother *bakes* a cake. I *am going* to the library. We *will be staying* at Lauren's house for a few days.

1. English verbs are either regular or irregular. A **regular verb** changes its form by adding the endings *-s* or *-es, -d* or *-ed,* and *-ing.* *Examples:* I *hated* having to phone her so late. We *played* basketball all afternoon. She is *practicing* her piece on the piano. An archaeologist *searches* for fossils.

2. An **irregular verb** changes its form by adding *-s* or *-es,* and *-ing,* but not *-d* or *-ed.* An irregular verb does not have a regular pattern for its past form. *Examples:* (1) He *brings* his guitar with him everywhere he goes. (2) He is *bringing* a guitar to the party. (3) I *brought* my guitar to the party. (4) He *flies* to Bermuda every year. (5) He is *flying* to Bermuda next week.

(6) We *flew* to the Bahamas for our vacation. (7) She *sings* with great emotion. (8) She is *singing* with great emotion. (9) They *sang* with great emotion. (See Appendix II for a list of some irregular verbs and their principal parts.)

SPECIAL NOTE

In the verb phrases *am going, have seen, will be going, may help,* and *did know,* the words *am, have, will be, may,* and *did* are called **auxiliaries**. Auxiliaries are helping verbs. When they accompany a verb, they give the tense (time) of the verb, person, number, and so on. *Examples:* They *will* go to the concert tomorrow. She *is* going to be here. They *have* not eaten yet. He *has* eaten already.

3. **Transitive verbs** are verbs that can take an object, that is, verbs that carry over an action from a subject to an object. *Examples:* Sharon *drinks* milk. I *can fly* a plane. They *are raking* the leaves.

4. **Intransitive verbs** are verbs that cannot take an object; that is, they cannot carry over an action from a subject to an object. Intransitive verbs express a state that is limited to the subject of the sentence. *Examples:* Birds *fly*. She *is* a lawyer. She *seems* nice. Linking verbs such as *be, become, smell, sound, taste, feel, look,* and so on, are intransitive verbs.

5. The verb *fly* in *Birds fly* is an intransitive verb because it cannot take an object. However, in the sentence *I can fly a plane* the verb *fly* is a transitive verb because it can take an object. The verb *is* in *She is a lawyer* and the verb *became* in *John became a doctor* are both intransitive verbs that cannot take objects. *Lawyer* and *doctor* are not objects of the verbs *is* and *became.*

6. Verbs like nouns have some special endings. Endings such as *ize, ate, en,* and *ify* signal that the word is a verb. For example, *economy* (noun) becomes *economize* (verb); *height* (noun) becomes *heighten* (verb); and *constitution* (noun) becomes *constitute* (verb). Adjectives can also be changed into verbs. For example, *beautiful* (adjective) becomes *beautify; hard* (adjective) becomes *harden*; and *clear* (adjective) becomes *clarify*.

7. In writing, the verb is usually the key word in the sentence, and it gives momentum to the sentence. Writers need to choose verbs for their sentences that clarify meaning and that add sparkle to their sentences. For example, read the following two sentences. Isn't sentence b more descriptive than sentence a?

Sentence a: The horse came out of the stable.
Sentence b: The horse galloped out of the stable.

SPECIAL NOTE

See other sections on verbs in this book for more information on verbs and how they are used in sentences.

Practice A. Change the nonsense word in each sentence to a verb that would make sense in the sentence.

1. I crebed the weeds. _____

2. We lail such things. _____

3. Jane dibs. _____

4. Chate that! _____

5. We weited the new things. _____

6. All the students in our section regated against the resolution. _____

7. The hungry men and women grimmed the food. _____

8. All seniors rog their costumes to the party. _____

9. The police ferred the spectators. _____

10. Beibe me. _____

Check sample answers at the end of Lesson 3.

Practice B. Underline the nonsense word that is a verb in each of the following nonsense sentences.

1. A cavy haille derred the zaim.

2. The duner bims the naim.

3. She ceims.

4. Blime that.

5. Some rewers grome the greibe.

6. An aberite loked the veim.

7. Olame the reiter.

8. Five crants squilled the buve.

9. The bein ti the dert hamt.

10. Someone wuns a veim.

Check answers at the end of Lesson 3.

Practice C. Write a simple sentence using the words given in parentheses for each sentence.

1. (run, students) _____

_____

2. (house, dormitory) _____

_____

3. (is, outing) _____

_____

4. (are, courses) _____

_____

5. (is going, He) _____

_____

6. (are arriving, they) _____

_____

7. (seems, Jim) _____

_____

8. (convened, leaders) _____

_____

9. (protested, many) _____

_____

10. (navigates, she) _____

_____

Check sample sentences at the end of Lesson 3.

Capitalization

The following items are capitalized:

Historical periods — the Stone Age, the Renaissance.

Names of Wars — the War of the Roses, World War II.

Documents — the Constitution, the Declaration of Independence.

Buildings — the Empire State Building.

The pronoun — I.

The first word of every line of poetry (except for the poetry of some modern poets, who do not capitalize the first word of every line of poetry).   *Example:*

> A little learning is a dangerous thing;
> Drink deep, or taste not the Pierian spring.

Names of God — Lord, Father, and pronouns used for God.

Titles of school course offerings — Education 201, Geography 511.

The first word of a direct quotation — Carol said, "She is a lovely person."

The title *president* and the words *presidential* or *presidency* when they refer to the President of the United States.

The interjection — O.

The first and last words of the salutation in a letter.   *Examples:*
   Dear Sir:
   Dear Mr. Smith:
   Dear Arthur,
The first word only of the closing of a letter.
   Examples: Yours sincerely, Yours truly, Your friend,
One or more words in a compound word may begin with a capital letter.
   Examples: Pulitzer prize, Russian roulette, French dressing, Middle
   American, Good Friday.
Certain abbreviations — A.D., B.C., Jr., Sr., Esq., U.S. (A.M. and P.M.
   may be written with or without capitals.)

Do not capitalize:
   Seasons — summer, winter, fall, spring.
   Games — football, basketball, tennis.
   School subjects unless they are names of languages or titles of specific
      course offerings (see preceding) — geometry, history, mathematics,
      English, French.
   Names of relatives, unless they are used as part of the person's name —
      mother, father, brother, sister, aunt, Aunt Flo, Uncle Jack.
   A direction unless it names a definite area or is part of a name — east,
      west, north, south, northeast, southwest, North America, East Ber-
      lin. He went west. He lives in the West.
   Words that are used in a general sense rather than as a name or part
      of a title — general, president, highway, hospital, street, bank.
   Titles used alone unless they stand for a specific person of high
      rank — The instructor said . . . , The Vice-President said . . . .
   The second part of a hyphenated word unless the second part of the
      hyphenated word is a noun.   *Examples:* Ninety-second Street;
      Polish-American.
   The first word of a quoted sentence from which words have been
      omitted at the beginning.   *Example:* ". . . but you can't fool all
      of the people all of the time."
   A quoted sentence part that has been inserted in a sentence and that
      fits in the sentence.   *Example:* He seemed to "melt under her
      stare."

SPECIAL NOTE

The interjection *oh* is followed by an exclamation mark, a comma, or no mark;
however, the poetic exclamation *O* is *not* followed by punctuation.   *Examples:*

   O powerful western fallen star!
   O shades of night—O moody, tearful night!
   O great star disappear'd—O the black murk that hides the star!
   O cruel hands that hold me powerless—O helpless soul of me!
   O harsh surrounding cloud that will not free my soul.
                                                                        —Walt Whitman

Practice A. Circle each word in the following sentences that should be capitalized.

1. president lincoln was a famous president.

2. yolanda and charlie live on long island on jackson street next to the grant building.

3. my favorite subjects in school were english and psychology.

4. i took anthropology 102 to learn more about the samoan tribe as well as other tribes.

5. aunt susan is my favorite aunt and uncle arthur is my favorite uncle.

6. the climate in the northeast is different from that in the northwest.

7. we were told to go north for three miles and then to turn left at the chrysler building.

8. spring and fall are my favorite seasons because summer is usually too hot for me and winter is usually too cold.

9. we visited southeast asia last summer.

10. the officer gave us permission to visit the army post.

11. senator jones said, "i am pleased with how former members have handled the matter."

12. after the election of the new president, incumbent president smith congratulated her.

13. going south on highway 73 can be dangerous because the south-bound lanes of the highway are under construction.

14. i am glad that drake hospital is close to our home, because i like to live close to a hospital.

15. as i was walking down mason street toward my bank, i saw a man running out of the first national bank across the street.

Check answers at the end of Lesson 3.

Practice B. Here are fifteen items. Read each carefully to determine whether it should be capitalized and, if it has been capitalized, whether it has been correctly capitalized. In the given blank write *yes* if it is correct, and *no* if it is not. If it is not correct, correct it.

1. o _____

2. Dear sir: _____

3. Good friday _____

4. spring _____

 5. South America _____

 6. language arts _____

 7. history 101 _____

 8. The War Of The Roses _____

 9. aunt Marie _____

10. an Uncle _____

11. the Drake building _____

12. Fifty-Second Street _____

13. John Jones, jr. _____

14. Yours Truly, _____

15. Chinese-American _____

Check answers at the end of Lesson 3.

Practice C. Here are five sentences. Read each carefully. Determine whether it has been correctly capitalized. If a sentence has not been correctly capitalized, write *no* in the given blank, and correctly capitalize it. If a sentence has been correctly capitalized write *yes* in the blank.

 1. Life is "Too much with us." _____

 2. ". . . is an apt statement, but it will not hold here." _____

 3. This summer we are going west. _____

 4. Jennifer said, "I am visiting my grandparents during the semester break." _____

 5. Frank said That he was going to study during the semester break, but no one believed him. _____

Check answers at the end of Lesson 3.

Practice D. The instructions for each of the following is given in the parentheses.

 1. (Write a sentence containing a direct quotation.) _____

_____

 2. (Write a sentence containing the name of a person with a title.) _____

_____

 3. (Write a sentence containing a direction.) _____

_____

4. (Write a sentence containing an indirect quotation.) _____

_____

5. (Write a sentence containing at least three items that require capitalization.)

_____

_____

_____

Check sample answers at the end of Lesson 3.

Spelling: Abbreviations

An abbreviation is a shortened form of a word or phrase. A period often follows an abbreviation. Following are some abbreviations that are used often: *Examples:*

   a. P.S. (postscript)   I needed to add a *P.S.* to my letter to Carol because I had already signed my name, and I had something more to say.
   b. A.M. (before noon)   It is 10:00 *A.M.*, and he is still asleep.
   c. P.M. (afternoon)   At 10:00 *P.M.* we listen to the news.
   d. B.C. (before Christ)   We studied about persons living in the fifth century, *B.C.*
   e. A.D. (Latin: *anno Domini* = in the year of the Lord) The tricentennial will be in *A.D.* 2076.
   f. etc. (and so on *or* and so forth)   Terry said that he likes cookies, candy, ice cream, *etc.*
   g. e.g. (for example)   They were discussing a number of different automobiles, *e.g.*, Fords, Chevrolets, and Cadillacs.
   h. i.e. (that is)   The beagle, dachshund, collie, and fox terrier are dogs, *i.e.*, four-legged animals that bark and wag their tails.
   i. Inc. (Incorporated)   Many companies such as Land, *Inc.*, Time, *Inc.*, and Dresses, *Inc.*, have *Inc.* in their titles because they are corporations.
   j. Co. (Company)   The King *Co.* always uses the abbreviation *Co.* in its title.

SPECIAL NOTE

B.C. and A.D. are sometimes replaced with B.C.E. (before the Common Era), and CE (Common Era).

Practice A.   Match the word or phrase to its correct abbreviation.

Abbreviations	Word or Phrase
_____ 1. A.M.	a. and so on
_____ 2. i.e.	b. for example
_____ 3. e.g.	c. before noon
_____ 4. B.C.	d. Incorporated
_____ 5. etc.	e. that is
_____ 6. A.D.	f. afternoon
_____ 7. P.S.	g. before Christ
_____ 8. Inc.	h. postscript
_____ 9. P.M.	i. in the year of the Lord
_____ 10. Co.	j. Company

Check answers at the end of Lesson 3.

Practice B.   Write a sentence using each of the following abbreviations.

1. e.g. _____

_____

2. P.M. _____

_____

3. i.e. _____

_____

4. etc. _____

_____

5. B.C. _____

_____

Check sample sentences at the end of Lesson 3.

LESSON 3 ANSWERS

Sentence Patterns (pp. 25–28)

Practice A: (sample sentences)   1. My boyfriend kissed me.   2. I ate three sandwiches.   3. My cat scratched me.   4. My horse kicked me.   5. The doctor examined me.

Practice B: (sample sentences)   1. My mother gave me a huge hug. 2. The charming prince gave the princess a kiss.   3. The instructor gave us a surprise quiz.   4. We gave the instructor our own surprise.   5. We gave him a poor rating.

Practice C: (sample sentences)   1. Henry is a lawyer.   2. Sharon is a lovely young lady.   3. George became a doctor.   4. Everyone is a person of worth.   5. The Smiths are a married couple.

Practice D: (sample sentences)   1. He is handsome.   2. That is good 3. The food smells delicious.   4. That looks good.   5. She seems happy.

Practice E: 1. Sentence Pattern 1 (N/P V)   2. Sentence Pattern 4 (N/P LV N/P)   3. Sentence Pattern 5 (N/P LV Adj.)   4. Sentence Pattern 3 (N/P V N/P N)   5. Sentence Pattern 1 (N/P V)   6. Sentence Pattern 4 (N/P LV N/P)   7. Sentence Pattern 1 (N/P V)   8. Sentence Pattern 2 (N/P V N/P) 9. Sentence Pattern 3 (N/P V N/P N)   10. Sentence Pattern 4 (N/P LV N/P)

Word Usage: Verbs (pp. 28–31)

Practice A: (sample answers) 1. picked   2. discuss   3. drinks   4. Stop 5. washed   6. voted   7. attacked   8. wore   9. dispersed   10. Help

Practice B: 1. derred   2. bims   3. ceims   4. Blime   5. grome   6. loked 7. Olame   8. squilled   9. ti   10. wuns

Practice C: (sample sentences) 1. The students run our school.   2. The dormitory can house about one hundred students.   3. This is a fun outing. 4. Here are the courses for next semester.   5. He is going with us.   6. They are arriving tomorrow.   7. Jim seems nice.   8. The leaders convened the meeting.   9. Many protested the unnecessary brutality.   10. She navigates the ship very well.

Capitalization (pp. 31–35)

Practice A: 1. President Lincoln   2. Yolanda, Charlie, Long Island, Jackson Street, Grant Building   3. My, English   4. I, Anthropology, Samoan   5. Aunt Susan, Uncle Arthur   6. The, Northeast, Northwest 7. We, Chrysler Building   8. Spring   9. We, Southeast Asia   10. The 11. Senator Jones, I   12. After, President Smith   13. Going, Highway 14. I, Drake Hospital, I   15. As I, Mason Street, I, First National Bank.

Practice B: 1. No — O   2. No — Dear Sir: 3. No — Good Friday
4. Yes   5. Yes   6. Yes   7. No — History 101   8. No — the War of the
Roses   9. No — Aunt Marie   10. No — an uncle   11. No — the Drake
Building   12. No — Fifty-second Street   13. No — John Jones, Jr.   14. No —
Your truly   15. Yes

Practice C: 1. No — Life is "too much with us."   2. Yes   3. Yes
4. Yes   5. No — Frank said that he was going to study during the semester
break, but no one believed him.

Practice D: (sample answers)   1. Sharon said, "I like what I am doing."
2. The Rev. Dr. Baines is an excellent speaker.   3. The Johnsons are going
south this winter.   4. Carol said that she was going to visit her parents this
winter.   5. Dr. Brown lives on Fifty-sixth Street in Minneapolis.

Spelling: Abbreviations (pp. 35–36)

Practice A: 1. c   2. e   3. b   4. g   5. a   6. i   7. h   8. d   9. f   10. j.

Practice B (sample sentences):   1. In my class there are a number of persons with the same last name, e.g., Mary Brown, John Brown, and George
Brown.   2. At 9:34 P.M. on July 14, 1977, New York City had a blackout.
3. Hypertension is the "invisible killer," i.e., many persons who have died
from the effects of hypertension were unaware that they had high blood
pressure.   4. The first day of classes, the instructors spoke about many things
of interest to us: grading, tests, assignments, etc.   5. We studied about life
in the fourth century B.C.

Lesson 4

Sentence Patterns

Sentence Pattern 6 (N/P V N/P N)

Sentence Pattern 6 appears to be similar to Sentence Pattern 3; however, it is not. In Sentence Pattern 6 the first noun or pronoun is the *subject* of the sentence, the second noun or pronoun is the *direct object*, and the third noun *renames the direct object*.

Examples:

N/P	V	N/P	N
Terry	considered	Jim	a liar.
The judges	voted	Carol	the winner.
The major	appointed	Marsha	the representative.
The people	called	the murderer	a monster.
The instructors	named	John	the chairperson.
The members	considered	their club	a haven.
They	appointed	her	treasurer.

Sentence Pattern 7 (N/P V N/P Adj.)

Sentence Pattern 7 is similar to Sentence Pattern 6 except that a word that describes or limits (adjective) is used to complete the meaning of the direct object and the verb. In Sentence Pattern 7 the first noun or pronoun is the *subject* of the sentence, the second is the *direct object*, and the adjective *describes the direct object*.

Examples:

N/P	V	N/P	Adj.
The pitcher	considered	the ball	low.
The students	thought	the instructor	dull.
The instructor	found	the students	bored.
The instructor	made	his lectures	livelier.
The campers	found	the campsite	empty.
The workers	considered	their boss	mean.
People	consider	the twins	prosperous.
We	found	them	dull.

Practice A. Write five simple sentences that conform to Sentence Pattern 6.

1. _____

2. _____

3. _____

4. _____

5. _____

Check sample sentences at the end of Lesson 4.

Practice B. Write five simple sentences that conform to Sentence Pattern 7.

1. _____

2. _____

3. _____

4. _____

5. _____

Check sample sentences at the end of Lesson 4.

Practice C. Here are ten simple sentences. In the blank at the end of each sentence, write which sentence pattern the simple sentence conforms to.

1. My dormitory is old. _____

2. Sally gave Jim a hug. _____

3. Jim blushed. _____

4. Darlene rushed to class. _____

5. The students elected Arthur their representative. _____

6. The freshmen found the orientation dull. _____

7. The first day of classes is always hectic. _____

8. All my friends consider college a necessity in this day and age. _____

9. Everyone, except Arthur, considers Arthur a genius. _____

10. I became ill at the party. _____

Check answers at the end of Lesson 4.

Word Usage:
The Predicate of a Sentence

The **predicate** of a sentence is a word or group of words that tells something about the subject.

1. Simple Predicate — A **simple predicate** is the verb alone. *Examples:* The horses *galloped* across the field. Jennifer *is* a beautiful child. The men and the women *are working* hard. (*Galloped, is,* and *are working* are simple predicates. They all tell something about the subjects of the sentences.)

2. Compound Predicate — A **compound predicate** consists of two or more simple predicates (verbs). *Examples:* The motorcycle *swerved* and *hit* a tree. He *won* his case but *was* not happy. (*Swerved* and *hit* form a compound predicate in the first sentence. *Won* and *was* form the compound predicate in the second sentence.)

SPECIAL NOTE

The motorcycle swerved and hit a tree and *He won his case but was not happy* are simple sentences. Although each sentence has two verbs, it is not a compound sentence because each sentence consists of only one simple sentence. A compound sentence is made up of two or more simple sentences.

3. Complete predicate — The **complete predicate** consists of the simple predicate (verb) and the words that **modify** (describe or limit) the verb. *Examples:* The defense lawyer *rested his case.* Pat's brother *is a forest ranger.* (*Rested* and *is* are the simple predicates. *Rested his case* and *is a forest ranger* are the complete predicates.)

Practice A. Circle the simple predicate in each sentence.

1. The hungry children ate heartily.

2. The ambulance rushed to the scene of the accident.

3. Help is on the way.

4. We are studying for finals.

5. Go away.

Check answers at the end of Lesson 4.

Practice B. Circle the compound predicate in each sentence.

1. The marching strikers waved their posters and shouted their demands.

2. Jack and Herb played tennis and swam.

3. The wide-awake baby laughed, cried, and babbled.

4. The running man shouted and waved to the driver in the departing bus.

5. She was frightened by the large dog but acted very bravely.

Check answers at the end of Lesson 4.

Practice C. Circle the complete predicate in each sentence.

1. Geology is the study of the earth's crust.

2. Anthropology is the study of mankind.

3. A biographer writes the life stories of famous people.

4. I studied and passed Astronomy 1 in my freshman year.

5. Our instructor explained the work to us.

Check answers at the end of Lesson 4.

Practice D. The instructions for each of the following is given in the parentheses.

1. (Write a simple sentence with a compound subject and a compound predicate.) _____

_____

2. (Write a simple sentence with a compound subject and a simple predicate.) _____

_____

3. (Write a simple sentence with a simple subject and a simple predicate.)

_____

_____

4. (Write a simple sentence with a simple subject and a compound predicate.) _____

_____

Check sample sentences at the end of Lesson 4.

Compound Words

In the English language many words combine with other words to form new words. A **compound** word is made up of separate words that combine to form a new word. Compound words may appear as one-word compounds, as two-word compounds, as multiword compounds, or as hyphenated compounds.

1. **One-word compound words** are probably the ones with which you are the most familiar. These are composed of separate words that join together without a hyphen to form a new word. *Examples:* hayride, girlfriend, treadmill, payroll, sunshine, grandfather, lawsuit, upstairs, bandwagon, folktale, railroad, homecoming, homeland.

2. **Two-word compounds** are composed of two separate words, and they are written as two separate words to form a new word. *Examples:* hay fever, stage fright, hot dogs, bus depot, girl scout, river bank, majority leader, potato salad, home rule, lone wolf.

3. **Multiword compounds** are made up of more than two words to form a new word. *Examples:* maid of honor, tug of war, make light of, Bill of Rights, Piece by piece, course of study, rural free delivery, hybrid tea rose, man of the cloth.

4. **Hyphenated compounds** are the joining of two or more words with a hyphen between the words. *Examples:* good-bye, thank-you, pinch-hit, public-address-system, right-of-way, man-of-war, good-for-nothing, henpecked, bull's-eye, down-to-earth.

5. Some compound words are made up of partly hyphenated words. *Examples:* man-o'-war bird, red-legged grasshopper, blue-ribbon jury.

6. Often adjectives, which are words that are used to describe a noun or pronoun, are made up of hyphenated compound words. *Examples:* ice-cream cone, blue-eyed, ice-cold, heavy-hearted, broken-down, light-footed, light-handed, lily-white, long-winded, long-standing, long-suffering, long-lived.

SPECIAL NOTES

a. The trend seem to be to omit the hyphen; however, if you are not sure whether a word contains a hyphen, check your dictionary. It's important to note also that not all dictionaries are in agreement on this; that is, in some dictionaries a word may contain a hyphen, whereas in others it may not.

b. The compound word *ice cream* is written without a hyphen when it is a noun; it is written with a hyphen when it is an adjective. *Example:* ice-cream cone.

c. The compound word *ice skate* is written without a hyphen when it is a noun; it is written with a hyphen when it is a verb. *Example:* to ice-skate.

d. The meaning of the sentence may change based on whether the word is presented as a compound or not. For example, the sentence *He is a great uncle* is different from the sentence *He is a great-uncle.*

e. When two words are combined to be used as an adjective, they are usually hyphenated. *Examples:* brown-eyed, long-legged, red-nosed, hard-nosed, strong-armed, heavy-hearted, thick-skinned, thick-headed, bright-eyed.

Practice A. Here are twenty nouns. Combine these to make ten different words.

Nouns: bed, air, life, shelf, line, door, room, boat, jacket, port, way, pocket, basket, book, flood, back, post, time, man, light.

_____   _____

_____   _____

_____   _____

_____   _____

_____   _____

Check sample answers at the end of Lesson 4.

Practice B. Here are some words that are verbs, nouns, adjectives, and adverbs. Combine these in any way to make twenty-five compound words.

Words: go, run, play, turn, pick, sit, lift, ground, thought, pass, ball, top, yard, tooth, stream, cart, goods, pack, boy, police, court, charge, pepper, piece, home, story, candy, rat, page, rock, ghost, hot, nursing, around, up, hill, after, soft, hard, by, down, over, cover, line.

_____   _____

_____   _____

_____   _____

_____   _____

_____   _____

_____   _____

_____   _____

_____   _____

_____   _____

_____   _____

_____   _____

_____   _____

_____

Check sample answers at the end of Lesson 4.

Practice C. Write two sentences expressing different meanings using the words in parentheses.

1. (holdup; hold up)_____

_____

_____

2. (great-niece; great niece) _____

_____

_____

3. (lowdown; low-down) _____

_____

_____

4. (second-class; second class) _____

_____

_____

5. (live wire; live wire) _____

_____

_____

Check sample sentences at the end of Lesson 4.

Practice D.   Write a compound word for each of the following letters of the alphabet.

1. (a) _____   2. (b) _____
3. (c) _____   4. (d) _____
5. (e) _____   6. (f) _____
7. (g) _____   8. (h) _____
9. (i) _____   10. (j) _____

Check sample answers at the end of Lesson 4.

Practice E.   Use the clues in parentheses to form a compound word.

1. A part of the body plus drink containers (you wear these).

   _____

2. A part of the body plus something you can hang clothes on (a newspaper uses this). _____

3. A part of the body plus something you eat out of (helps clean you).

   _____

4. A part of the body plus a tool pointed at one or both ends (restaurants
   have this). _____

5. A part of the body plus something round that bounces (a game).

   _____

6. A part of the body plus the opposite of "in" (beggars want this).

_____

7. A part of the body plus something you can eat (a tree).

_____

8. Two parts of the body — one is part of the mouth and the other is part of the eye (you don't want this)._____

9. A part of the body plus something that is knotted (men wear this).

_____

10. A part of the body plus being cheerful (these have a lovely fragrance).

_____

Check answers at the end of Lesson 4.

_____

Spelling: Contractions

A **Contraction** is usually a combination of two words or a shortening of a compound word. In the writing of contractions, one or more letters are omitted, and an apostrophe is put in the place of the omitted letters. The apostrophe signals that a letter or letters have been omitted. _Examples: Who is there? Who's there? It is John. It's John. He is here. He's here. I cannot go now. I can't go now. There is no room. There's no room. I do not know him. I don't know him. Pat has not eaten yet. Pat hasn't eaten yet. I will go there tomorrow. I'll go there tomorrow. We have eaten already. We've eaten already. I am going now. I'm going now. He will not do it. He won't do it. She would not speak to me. She wouldn't speak to me. Let us play. Let's play. He does not know the song. He doesn't know the song. Are you not ready yet? Aren't you ready yet?_

SPECIAL NOTE

Do not confuse the possessives such as _whose, its, theirs_ with the contractions _who's, it's, there's._

Practice A. Give the two words that were combined to form the following contractions.

1. I'll _____   2. He's _____

3. I've _____   4. Who's _____

5. What's _____   6. Couldn't _____

7. Weren't _____   8. Won't _____

9. Don't _____   10. Isn't _____

11. Hasn't _____   12. Let's _____

13. I'm _____   14. There's _____

Check answers at the end of Lesson 4.

Practice B.   **Write contractions for the following words.**

1. There is _____   2. I will _____

3. I have _____   4. She is _____

5. We will _____   6. They have _____

7. Who is _____   8. Let us _____

9. Does not _____   10. I am _____

11. You are _____   12. You have _____

13. We have _____   14. Would not _____

15. It is _____

Check answers at the end of Lesson 4.

LESSON 4 ANSWERS

Sentence Patterns (pp. 39–41)

Practice A: (sample sentences)   1. Marion considered Don a friend. 2. Jane named Jim the phantom robber.   3. Jim called Jane a liar.   4. We voted Jennifer the class representative.   5. My friend, a Vietnam veteran, considers school another battleground.

Practice B: (sample sentences)   1. Jim, the veteran, considers school important.   2. However, he considers some lectures meaningless.   3. He finds many students very immature.   4. He considers his problems minor.   5. We find him interesting.

Practice C: 1. Sentence Pattern 5 (N/P LV Adj.)   2. Sentence Pattern 3 (N/P V N/P N)   3. Sentence Pattern 1 (N/P V)   4. Sentence Pattern 1 (N/P V)   5. Sentence Pattern 6 (N/P V N/P N)   6. Sentence Pattern 7 (N/P V N/P Adj.)   7. Sentence Pattern 5 (N/P LV Adj.)   8. Sentence Pattern 6 (N/P V N/P N)   9. Sentence Pattern 6 (N/P V N/P N)   10. Sentence Pattern 5 (N/P LV Adj.)

Word Usage: The Predicate of a Sentence (pp. 41–42)

Practice A: 1. ate   2. rushed   3. is   4. are studying   5. Go.

Practice B: 1. waved, shouted   2. played, swam   3. laughed, cried, babbled   4. shouted, waved   5. was frightened, acted.

Practice C: 1. is the study of the earth's crust   2. is the study of mankind   3. writes the life stories of famous people   4. studied and passed Astronomy 1 in my freshman year   5. explained the work to us.

Practice D: (sample sentences)   1. James and Susan jog and play tennis. 2. Francis and Mary play ball.   3. Jack loves Pat.   4. My pet eats our food and drinks coffee and tea.

Compound Words (pp. 42–46)

Practice A: (sample answers)   bedroom, airport, airline, bedjacket, doorway, lifejacket, lifeboat, floodlight, bedlight, doorman, bookjacket, airman, air pocket, air line*.

Practice B: (sample answers)   go-cart, go around, go-around, go by, soft top, hardtop, afterthought, bypass, softball, runaround, playground, overrun, overturn, pick up, upstream, sit up, sit-up, uplift, page boy, pack rat, rock candy, piece goods, police court, cover charge, ghost story, hot line, hot pepper, nursing home, toothpick, ground ball, home run.

* This word has a meaning different from *air-line*.

Practice C: (sample sentences)   1. In the *holdup* three people were killed. The instructor does not *hold up* anyone's work to ridicule.   2. My *great-niece* is my sister's daughter's child. She is a *great niece.*   3. The police chief gave the reporters the *lowdown.* What he did is really *low-down.*   4. She is treated as a *second-class* citizen. Don't send that *second class.*   5. He is a *live wire.* The *live wire* was dangerous and had to be removed by the telephone company.

Practice D: (sample answers)   1. another   2. bell jar   3. candy striper   4. doormat   5. everyone   6. footrest   7. grab bag   8. hourglass   9. in-group   10. jack-in-the-box

Practice E: 1. eyeglasses   2. headline   3. fingerbowl   4. toothpick   5. football   6. handout   7. chestnut   8. tongue-lash   9. necktie   10. nosegay

Spelling: Contractions (pp. 46–47)

Practice A: 1. I will   2. He is *or* He has   3. I have   4. Who is *or* Who has   5. What is *or* What has   6. Could not   7. Were not   8. Will not   9. Do not   10. Is not   11. Has not   12. Let us   13. I am   14. There is.

Practice B: 1. There's   2. I'll   3. I've   4. She's   5. We'll   6. They've   7. Who's   8. Let's   9. Doesn't   10. I'm   11. You're   12. You've   13. We've   14. Wouldn't   15. It's.

UNIT I REVIEW CROSSWORD PUZZLE

Directions: Your knowledge of the material presented in Lessons 1-4 will help you to solve this crossword puzzle.

Across

1. An expression of approval
6. The ninth letter of the alphabet
7. A_____is not capitalized
11. Used to control an animal
12. Mentions again
14. The opposite of even
16. Color.
18. Abbreviation of for example.
19. An indefinite article
20. The sixteenth letter of the alphabet
21. Jennifer and Carol went for a walk and then for a drive in the park is a(n)_____sentence
23. A period_____a sentence
26._____is the antonym of exit
28. A special hairdo
30. An interjection
31. A simple sentence may be as brief as _____ word.

Down

1._____nouns are capitalized
2. A communist is called this
3. Help
4. A small word used to indicate location
5. Forms the plural of many nouns
6. Abbreviation of that is
7. A trick; something put in the mouth to prevent speech
8. An auxiliary verb
9. Average; to have in mind; stingy
10. Forms the plural of words ending in s, ss, sh, ch, or x
12. Obnoxious
13. For the future tense you_____ an auxiliary
16. One who employs others
17. Used to express hesitation or doubt

Across

32. Abbreviation of gram
33. Destiny
35. The verb in the sentence, <u>Seth kissed Sharon</u> is a(n)_____ verb
39. _____ makes the world go round
42. A musical syllable
43. Another word for you that is used in church or literary writings
45. <u>Become</u> is a_____ verb
48. An often used irregular verb
49. Perform
50. The ending for the past tense of regular verbs
51. Won't is a(n) _____
54. A prefix meaning <u>away</u>, <u>out</u>, <u>forth</u>
55. Same as #54 Across
56. What you can do on the ice

Down

21. <u>When he came</u> is not a(n)_____
22. Trademark for a certain kind of phonograph record
24. Fruit of the palm
25. A word that refers to a female
27. A homonym of <u>two</u>
29. A poetic exclamation
33. A celebration in Spain and Latin America
34. Abbreviation of <u>avenue</u>
36. A(n)_____ skirt.
37. A word that refers to a thing
38. _____ and thin
40. Antonym of <u>young</u>
41. Roman numeral 6
44. Two thousand pounds
46. Knockout
47. Abbreviation of <u>gram</u>
49. Female deer
52. Word that signals a simile
53. Same as #37 Down

Check answers on this page.

UNIT I REVIEW CROSSWORD PUZZLE ANSWER

WORD PUZZLES

Word Puzzle 1

Here are ten sentences. Each sentence has something hidden in it. The word in parentheses will tell you what to look for.

1. He is neither devil nor angel. (a fruit)

2. I saw a car rotate on its wheels. (a vegetable)

3. When we saw him, he seemed all right. (a bird)

4. Zeb ran across the street to meet his friend. (an animal)

5. The school wants to admit more students next year. (a cold-blooded animal)

6. In the story the peasant eloped with the princess. (an animal)

7. Was your nap pleasant? (a fruit)

8. The leaders said that they would ban an amendment to the constitution. (a fruit)

9. Susan's wanton manner will have to stop. (a bird)

10. We bought the acre amidst a forest. (a dairy product)

Answers:

1. orange 2. carrot 3. hen 4. zebra 5. toad 6. antelope 7. apple
8. banana 9. swan 10. cream

Word Puzzle 2

See how many of the word puzzles you can solve.

1. I'm what you do when you're in a hurry; add two letters to me, and I'll fly away.

2. I'm a large water fowl; change one of my letters, and I'll become a member of the deer family.

3. I'm an insect; change one of my letters, and I'll become a member of the rodent family.

4. I'm a farm animal; add one letter to me, and you can walk on me.

Answers:

1. rush—thrush 2. goose—moose 3. louse—mouse 4. ram—ramp

Word Puzzle 3

The answers for the following clues are two rhyming words.

1. a frightening bird

2. a tardy companion

3. dual difficulties

4. large acting crew

5. unhappy wanderer

6. obese rodent

7. weak boy

8. underdone rabbit

9. crazy villain

10. maker of wheel guard indentations

Answers:

1. scary canary 2. late date 3. double trouble 4. vast cast 5. sad nomad 6. fat rat 7. frail male 8. rare hare 9. mad cad 10. fender bender

REVIEW TEST 1

A. Underline all those in the following list that are sentences.

1. Stop that.   2. Please help.

3. Go.   4. I need.

5. When he goes.   6. Peggy and Sally should.

7. Why is that?   8. The plants will become.

9. Not one of them.   10. Rushed into the house.

B. Follow the directions in parentheses for each of the following.

1. (Write a simple sentence.)

_____

2. (Write a simple sentence that has an intransitive verb.)

_____

3. (Write a simple sentence that has a transitive verb.)

_____

4. (Write a sentence that has an object and an indirect object.)

_____

_____

5. (Write a sentence that has a direct object.)

_____

6. (Write a sentence that has a linking verb and a word that describes the subject.)

_____

7. (Write a sentence that has a linking verb and a word that renames the subject.)_____

_____

8. (Write an interrogative sentence.)

_____

9. (Write an exclamatory sentence.)

_____

10. (Write an imperative sentence.)

_____

C. For the following sentences, put one line under the complete subject and two lines under the complete predicate.

1. Sharon, Carol, and Jennifer went to the same school.
2. Traffic on the freeway is bumper to bumper.
3. It is difficult to find a good-paying job today.
4. Sara, Tom, and George decided to rent a house together.

REVIEW TEST 2: A TRUE/FALSE TEST

Directions: This is a true/false test on Lessons 1-4. Read each sentence carefully. Decide whether it is true or false. Put a T for *true* or an F for *false* in the blank.

_____ 1. The sentence *He is happy* contains a linking verb.

_____ 2. In the sentence *I have a daughter in law*, daughter in law can have more than one meaning in this sentence.

_____ 3. In the sentence *I have a grandfather*, grandfather is a compound word.

_____ 4. There are no errors in the sentence *The Rev. Johnson is a learned man.*

_____ 5. The title "Life is too Much With Us" is written correctly.

_____ 6. The abbreviation is used correctly in the sentence, *I am taking very easy courses this semester, i.e., canoeing, tennis, art, sociology, and music.*

_____ 7. The abbreviation is used correctly in the sentence *Socrates lived in the fifth century* B.C.

_____ 8. The ending *ify* signals a noun.

_____ 9. The ending *tion* signals a noun.

_____10. The ending *ize* signals a verb.

_____11. The past tense of regular verbs is *s* or *es.*

_____12. A simple sentence must contain only a single subject and a single verb.

_____13. When *beautiful* is changed to *beauty* it becomes a noun.

_____14. The word *an* signals that a noun follows.

_____15. The sentence *Sharon is happy* has a direct object in it.

_____16. *Running down the street* is a sentence.

_____17. In the nonsense sentence *The bloob bleebed the nibs, bleebed* is a verb.

_____18. Punctuation marks help to convey meaning.

_____19. An interjection is independent of the rest of the sentence.

_____20. Charleses is the plural of Charles.

_____21. *Deers* is the plural of *deer.*

_____22. *Dwarfs* is the plural of *dwarf.*

_____23. *Won't* is the contraction of *would not.*

_____24. *They're* is the contraction of *they are.*

_____25. *Doesn't* is the correct contraction of *does not.*

UNIT II

Compound Sentences
Word Usage: Agreement of Subject and Verb I
Punctuation: The Comma
Spelling: Some Often Misspelled Words I
Answers to Practices

Lesson 5

Compound Sentences

1. A **compound sentence** is made up of two or more simple sentences. *Examples: The rain fell,* and *the wind blew. The music majors attended the concert, and the theater majors went to the dance. Mother is an excellent homemaker,* but *her career is important, too. We played basketball,* and *then we went swimming.*

2. Two simple sentences may be joined by certain linking words called **conjunctions** to form compound sentences. Conjunctions that connect groups of words that have the *same* importance are called **coordinate conjunctions**. The most often used coordinate conjunctions are *and, but,* and *or. Nor, for,* and *yet* are used also as coordinate conjunctions. When the words *and, but, or, for, yet,* and *nor* join two simple sentences, a comma (,) is usually used before the linking word. *Examples of compound sentences with coordinate conjunctions:*

Take care of yourself now, *or* you will suffer the consequences later. I wanted to go away to school, *but* my family needed me at home.

Coordinate conjunctions connect groups of words that have the *same* importance. The linking word *and* is used to add one idea to another. *But* and *yet* are used for contrast, *or* is used to separate ideas that are choices or alternatives, *nor* is used to separate ideas that are negative choices, and *for* is used to show the cause or proof of a statement.

SPECIAL NOTES

a. The coordinate conjunctions *and, but,* and *or* are most commonly used to connect words as well as groups of words. When these linking words are used, they must connect words that are equal in importance.

57

Examples:

1. I like to swim. 2. I like to fish.
1. John is happy. 2. Carol is happy.

Sentences   I like to swim and fish.
A   John and Carol are happy.

The pairs of simple sentences presented as examples can be combined to form longer compound sentences.

Sentences   I like to swim, and I like to fish.
B   John is happy, and Carol is happy.

However, the shortened combined simple sentences (sentences A) are usually preferable to the longer combined compound ones (sentences B), in which the same subjects or predicates are repeated.

b. In the following examples, the pairs of sentences cannot be shortened, but they can be combined to form compound sentences. In these examples, the longer combined sentences are preferable to the individual sentences.

Examples:

1. I like to play the piano. 2. Nobody will listen to me.
1. Dress more quickly. 2. We will be late.
1. The church bell rang. 2. The train whistle blew.

Compound sentences:

I like to play the piano, but nobody will listen to me.
Dress more quickly, or we will be late.
The church bell rang, and the train whistle blew.

3. Sometimes linking words are pairs of words. *Either . . . or* and *neither . . . nor* are two pairs of linking words that are commonly used to connect simple sentences. *Example:* Either we do what they say, or we will be hurt.

4. Other linking words that can be used to connect simple sentences are *also, accordingly, besides, however, moreover, nevertheless, so, still, then, therefore, thus, consequently,* and so on. *Examples:* We waited for them for two hours; then they finally arrived. These persons helped us capture the criminals; therefore we should reward them.

When linking words such as *therefore, so, nevertheless, however, moreover,* and so on are used to join two simple sentences, a semicolon (;) usually is used before the linking word. However, for the linking word *so* either a comma or a semicolon may be used. *Examples:* My friend is running for office; *however,* I do not expect her to win. The players tried their best to win; *nevertheless,* they lost.

5. If simple sentences are closely related, they may be joined by a semicolon without a linking word. *Examples:* My father suffered a heart attack; he almost died. We worked hard; it was worth it.

Practice A. Put a *C* in front of the following that are compound sentences and an *S* in front of those that are simple sentences.

_____ 1. Plants and animals are living things.

_____ 2. The phone rang, and at the same time the door opened.

_____ 3. The instructors and students appeared shocked by the gunman's sudden appearance.

_____ 4. The doctors gave little hope for his survival, but there was still a chance.

_____ 5. Some things cannot be directly observed or directly measured.

_____ 6. The teachers and psychologists consulted about the college's new counseling services.

_____ 7. Learning language is a complex task, yet most persons learn to speak.

_____ 8. Help me unlock my door.

_____ 9. They seemed to laugh and cry at the same time.

_____ 10. High school and college students spend about 90 per cent of their time in school in activities requiring listening, but not much time is spent in school in learning how to listen.

Check answers at the end of Lesson 5.

Practice B. Choose the words that make the sentence a compound one.

_____ 1. Girls will read (*a.* "boy" and "girl" books; *b.* more books than boys; *c.* "boy" books, but boys will not read "girl" books).

_____ 2. The men were (*a.* thirsty and hungry; *b.* thirsty, but the women were hungry; *c.* so thirsty when they arrived home).

_____ 3. The phone rang (*a.* , and everyone ran to answer it; *b.* and rang; *c.* very loudly.

_____ 4. The snow was (*a.* piled very high; *b.* white and clean; *c.* too deep for driving, yet many cars were on the road).

_____ 5. The popular student is (*a.* brilliant, athletic and outgoing; *b.* brilliant, but he is also athletic and outgoing; *c.* a brilliant, athletic, and outgoing person).

_____ 6. The child ran (*a.* into the woods; *b.* , but his mother walked; *c.* when he heard the dog bark).

_____ 7. The burglar stole (*a.* our money, and his dirty shoes damaged our rugs; *b.* my watch and my parents' jewelry; *c.* my watch when he broke into our house).

_____ 8. She was (*a.* beautiful and kind; *b.* a successful woman who had overcome many hardships; *c.* a successful reporter, but her friends resented her).

_____ 9. He is (*a.* happy, but his parents are very poor; *b.* happy and content; *c.* happy when he is making money).

_____10. You could wear (*a.* the red dress, but it is really too dressy; *b.* your green or yellow outfit; *c.* your new spring outfit).

Check answers at the end of Lesson 5.

Practice C. Following are pairs of sentences. **Choose a coordinate conjunction such as** *and, but, or,* **or** *for,* **and combine the two sentences into one compound sentence.**

1. The politician's speech was not received very well by the audience. The audience walked out in the middle of it.

   _____

   _____

   _____

2. Do it now. You will have difficulty later.

   _____

3. The rest went hunting. We went canoeing.

   _____

4. It's very late. I'm still not tired.

   _____

5. He will continue to go to college. He will have a lot of wasted time to make up for.

   _____

   _____

6. I don't like meat. My boyfriend doesn't like vegetables.

   _____

7. In Europe I lost my raincoat. My colleague lost his watch.

   _____

8. You have to maintain a good scholastic average. You will not remain on the team.

   _____

   _____

9. Maria and José overheard the confidential statement. They were sitting nearby.

   _____

   _____

10. The snowstorm was over. The damage still had to be repaired.

_____

Check sample sentences at the end of Lesson 5.

Practice D.   Write five compound sentences.

1. _____

_____

2. _____

_____

3. _____

_____

4. _____

_____

5. _____

_____

Check sample sentences at the end of Lesson 5.

Word Usage: Agreement of Subject and Verb I

1.   The subject of a sentence may be a noun or a pronoun. A **pronoun** is a word that is used in the place of a noun.   *Examples:* I, you, she, he, they, we, this, that, who, which, what, any, anyone, myself, herself, each, other, one, another, it.

2.   A subject and its verb should agree in number.

a.   When the subject in a sentence is a single noun or a single pronoun naming only one thing or person, it is singular.

b.   When the subject in a sentence is a compound subject or otherwise names more than one thing or person, the subject is plural.

c.   A singular subject requires a singular verb.

d.   A plural subject requires a plural verb.

e.   A singular verb is used with a singular pronoun.

f.   A plural verb is used with a plural pronoun.

Examples: Sharon *is* a good pianist. She *plays* very complex musical compositions. Miriam, Vince, and Sally *are* good pianists. They *play* very complex musical compositions. Everyone *is* welcome to come to my house.

SPECIAL NOTE

> When *each* is used with singular nouns connected by *and*, the verb is singular. *Example:* Each man and each woman *is* able to participate in the race.

3. When two or more singular subjects are joined by *or* or *nor*, the verb is usually singular. *Examples: Neither you nor Jim plays* tennis very well. *Either the bank's vault or my home safe is* a good place to store special documents.

4. When two or more subjects are joined by *or* or *nor* and one subject is singular and the other is plural, the verb agrees with the subject closest to it. *Examples: Neither the coat nor my dresses are* clean. *Either you or Fred takes* out the garbage. *Neither my parents nor my brother skates* very well.

SPECIAL NOTES

> a. In the following examples, notice the form of the verb with singular and plural pronouns:
>
> | | |
> |---|---|
> | I jump | we jump |
> | you jump | you jump |
> | he, she jumps | they jump |
> | | |
> | I play | we play |
> | you play | you play |
> | he, she plays | they play |
> | | |
> | I am | we are |
> | you are | you are |
> | he, she, it is | they are |
> | | |
> | I have | we have |
> | you have | you have |
> | he, she, it has | they have |
>
> b. In the following sentences, notice the form of the verb with singular and plural pronouns and nouns. *Examples:* Because she *is* on a diet, she *eats* nothing between meals. They *work* very hard. I *work* every other Saturday. She *plays* tennis very well. He *studies* all the time. I *am* happy to be here. She *is* a premed student. My motorcycle *needs* a new tire. Tuition costs *are* higher each year. The cabin *has* no electricity or plumbing. My dormitory *is* too noisy for me.

Practice A.   Circle the verb that correctly completes the sentence.

1. They (swim/swims) very well.

2. The audience (appear/appears) interested in the play.

3. Artists (is/are) usually temperamental people.

4. A friend of my family (plays/play) the harpsichord.

5. Happiness and good fortune (are/is) hard to attain.

6. Neither my mother nor my aunts (is/are) rich.

7. Either my brother or my father (get/gets) to read the newspaper first.

8. My sisters (read/reads) lots of books.

9. In the winter the robins (fly/flies) to a warmer climate.

10. Neither my friend nor my relative (has/have) been selected to serve on that committee.

Check answers at the end of Lesson 5.

Practice B. Choose the predicate that *best* fits the subject.

Subject	Predicate
1. After the hike, my friend _____	a. is for sale.
2. The artist _____	b. were exhausted from the long climb.
3. Neither the boat nor the tent _____	c. swim undersea.
4. The hikers _____	d. is painting my portrait.
5. An average-sized apple _____	e. was exhausted.
6. Raisins _____	f. have over fifty calories.
7. Aquanauts _____	g. swims undersea.
8. My friend, the aquanaut, _____	h. are dried grapes.
9. Average-sized apples _____	i. is a dried grape.
10. A raisin _____	j. has over fifty calories.

Check answers at the end of Lesson 5.

Practice C. Choose the verb that agrees with its subject. Then construct a sentence using the given subject and the chosen verb.

Subject	Verb
1. Large, expensive automobiles	consumes/consume

_____

_____

| 2. Most actresses and actors | has/have |

_____

_____

3. George   seems/seem

_____

_____

4. Either you or your twin   was/were
   brother

_____

_____

5. Neither Pete nor his parents   knows/know

_____

_____

Check sample sentences at the end of Lesson 5.

Punctuation: The Comma

The **comma** (,) is the most often used punctuation mark. The comma, like other punctuation marks, is a signal that helps readers grasp the writer's meaning. A comma signals a pause. This pause is not as strong as the stop signaled by a period (.) or a semicolon (;).

1. See how the comma helps writers to shorten their sentences. *Examples:*

    a. The girl laughs and the boy laughs and the man laughs.
       The girl, boy, and man laugh.
    b. The children ran and played and screamed.
       The children ran, played, and screamed.
    c. The boy is handsome and kind and smart.
       (1) The boy is handsome, kind, and smart.
       (2) The handsome, kind boy is smart.

In the preceding sentences the comma is used to replace *and* in a **series** (a group of three or more things or events). If you are not sure whether to use a comma in a series of words that describe other words, check to see whether *and* can be used in place of the comma, or whether you can **invert** (reverse the order of) the descriptive words.

2. You do not use a comma before the first or after the last member of a series. *Example (incorrect):* It seemed impossible *that*, three men, three women, four children, a dog, and a *cat*, could all fit in the small car. (Commas after *that* and *cat* are wrong.)

SPECIAL NOTE

In the following examples, notice that no comma is used because *and* cannot be placed between the words. You would not say *green and summer jacket*, or *big and German shepherd*, or *brown and Siamese cat*, or *chrome and storm doors*, and so on.

Examples: green summer jacket; big German shepherd; yellow kitchen oven; brown Siamese cat; chrome storm doors; strong window shutters; sweet little old lady; precious little child. (Usually commas are not placed before descriptive words that refer to size, color, or age.)

Practice A. Shorten the following sentences with the use of commas.

1. The parade was made up of clowns and acrobats and animal trainers.

2. I intend to take geography and history and English and sociology next semester.

3. The factory noise and the traffic noise and the children's yelling helped give me a headache.

4. We are taking canoeing or slimnastics or modern dance next semester.

5. He stood up and braced himself and waited.

6. All my aunts and uncles and cousins visited us last year.

7. The foods I like best are peanut butter and jelly and bacon and eggs and ham and eggs.

8. Last night I read a book and listened to music and talked to my friend.

9. I like fine-quality furniture that is sturdy and attractive and inexpensive.

10. I enjoy tennis and football and swimming.

Check answers at the end of Lesson 5.

Practice B. Insert commas where needed in the following sentences. If a sentence does not require any comma, put a *0* in front of it. *Hint:* If you are unsure about adding a comma in a series of words that describe other words, check to see if *and* could replace the comma.

_____ 1. The little white cat ran away.

_____ 2. The procession halted started again and then halted once more.

_____ 3. She is very old tired and down on her luck.

_____ 4. He is a good kind and faithful husband.

_____ 5. She bought a beautiful red winter coat.

_____ 6. We knew that it would be a long hard year.

_____ 7. Your big black dog bit me.

_____ 8. I love your blue spring hat.

_____ 9. The flag is red white and blue.

_____ 10. We had meat for breakfast meat for lunch and meat for dinner.

Check answers at the end of Lesson 5.

Spelling: Some Often Misspelled Words I

Following, presented in sentences, are forty often misspelled words.

1. His *absence* from classes has been noticed by everyone.
2. I cannot *advise* you.
3. That's good *advice*.
4. What kind of *effect* will that have on you?
5. How will that *affect* my grades?
6. I am feeling *all right*.
7. His *achievement* is very good.
8. My head *aches*.
9. *Although* I like her *a lot*, we always have lots of *arguments*.
10. Are you here *already*?
11. My *annual* wages are not high.
12. What *arrangements* did you make?
13. I am going into *business*.
14. It is *apparent* that you are an *amateur*.
15. At *around* ten o'clock, she made her *appearance*.
16. He is an *excellent athlete*.
17. Start at the *beginning*.
18. Do you have a *calendar*?
19. He *committed* a crime.
20. Do you belong to that *committee*?
21. We visited my father's grave at the *cemetery*.
22. She must have a guilty *conscience*.
23. They are very *conscientious* students.
24. I am very *conscious* of what I do.
25. The noise was *continuous*.
26. There was a lot of *criticism* about the *decision* that we *finally* made.
27. They said that it was not *desirable*.
28. They were *dissatisfied* with our plans to *develop a separate* proposal.
29. We were *definite* about it.
30. We do not want to *disappoint* you.
31. Don't embarrass anyone.

Practice A. Look at each word carefully. Cover the word. Write the covered word in the blank. Check to see if you have spelled it correctly.

1. absence _____

2. advise _____

3. advice _____

4. effect _____

5. affect _____

6. all right _____

7. achievement _____

8. aches _____

9. although _____

10. a lot _____

11. arguments _____

12. already _____

13. annual _____

14. arrangements _____

15. business _____

16. apparent _____

17. amateur _____

18. around _____

19. appearance _____

20. excellent _____

21. athlete _____

22. beginning _____

23. calendar _____

24. committed _____

25. committee _____

26. cemetery _____

27. conscience _____

28. conscientious _____

29. conscious _____

30. continuous _____

31. criticism _____

32. decision _____

33. finally _____

34. dissatisfied _____

35. develop _____

36. separate _____

37. definite _____

38. desirable _____

39. disappoint _____

40. embarrass _____

You should have checked the spelling immediately after writing each word.

Practice B. Look at each word carefully. If the word is spelled correctly, put a *C* in the blank. If the word is not spelled correctly, spell it correctly. (Sentences are given for words that can be confused with others.)

1. absense _____

2. I need *advise.* _____

3. Please *advice* me. _____

4. That will *effect* me. _____

5. What *affect* will that have? _____

6. alright _____

7. achievement _____

8. ackes _____

9. although _____

10. alot _____

11. arguement _____

12. allready _____

13. anual _____

14. arrangments _____

15. bussness _____

16. apparant _____

17. amatur _____

18. around _____

19. apearance _____

20. excelent _____

21. atlete _____

22. begining _____

23. calander _____

24. commited _____

25. comittee _____

26. cemetary _____

27. conscience _____

28. concientious _____

29. consious _____

30. continous _____

31. criticism _____

32. decision _____

33. finaly _____

34. disatisfied _____

35. develope _____

36. seperate _____

37. definate _____

38. desirable _____

39. dissappoint _____

40. embarass _____

Check words at the end of Lesson 5.

LESSON 5 ANSWERS

Compound Sentences (pp. 57–61)

Practice A: 1. S 2. C 3. S 4. C 5. S 6. S 7. C 8. S 9. S 10. C.

Practice B: 1. c 2. b 3. a 4. c 5. b 6. b 7. a 8. c 9. a 10. a.

Practice C: (sample sentences) 1. The politician's speech was not received very well by the audience, for the audience walked out in the middle of it. 2. Do it now, or you will have difficulty later. 3. The rest went hunting, but we went canoeing. 4. It's very late, but I'm still not tired. 5. He will continue to go to college, or he will have a lot of wasted time to make up for. 6. I don't like meat, and my boyfriend doesn't like vegetables. 7. In Europe I lost my raincoat, and my colleague lost his watch. 8. You have to maintain a good scholastic average, or you will not remain on the team. 9. Maria and José overheard the confidential statement, for they were sitting nearby. 10. The snowstorm was over, but the damage still had to be repaired.

Practice D (sample sentences): 1. The car is too big for your garage, yet it fits nicely into mine. 2. I opened the window, and three birds flew into the house. 3. The flood destroyed everything, but the people returned. 4. The ship finally arrived; however, my friends were not on it. 5. Their business does very well in the summer months, but it does very poorly the rest of the year.

Word Usage: Agreement of Subject and Verb I (pp. 61–64)

Practice A: 1. swim 2. appears 3. are 4. plays 5. are 6. are 7. gets 8. read 9. fly 10. has.

Practice B: 1. e 2. d 3. a 4. b 5. j 6. h 7. c 8. g 9. f 10. i.

Practice C (sample sentences): 1. Large, expensive automobiles consume a great quantity of gasoline. 2. Most actresses and actors have a difficult time finding a job. 3. George seems to be having a good time at the party. 4. Either you or your twin brother was at my house yesterday. 5. Neither Pete nor his parents know how to play bridge.

Punctuation: The Comma (pp. 64–65)

Practice A: 1. The parade was made up of clowns, acrobats, and animal trainers. 2. I intend to take geography, history, English, and sociology next semester. 3. The factory noise, the traffic noise, and the children's yelling helped give me a headache. 4. We are taking canoeing, slimnastics, or modern dance next semester. 5. He stood up, braced himself, and waited. 6. All my aunts, uncles, and cousins visited us last year. 7. The foods I like best are peanut butter and jelly, bacon and eggs, and ham and eggs. 8. Last night I read a book, listened to music, and talked to my friend. 9. I like fine-quality furniture that is sturdy, attractive, and inexpensive. 10. I enjoy tennis, football, and swimming.

Practice B: 1. 0   2. halted, started again, and   3. very old, tired, and
4. good, kind, and   5. 0   6. long, hard   7. 0   8. 0   9. red, white, and
10. meat for breakfast, meat for lunch, and.

Spelling: Some Often Misspelled Words I (pp. 66–69)

Practice A: Check words on the page for correct spelling.

Practice B: 1. absence 2. advice 3. advise 4. affect 5. effect 6. all
right 7. C 8. aches 9. C 10. a lot 11. argument 12. already 13. annual
14. arrangements   15. business   16. apparent   17. amateur   18. C   19. appearance   20. excellent   21. athlete   22. beginning   23. calendar   24. committed   25. committee   26. cemetery   27. C   28. conscientious
29. conscious   30. continuous   31. C   32. C   33. finally   34. dissatisfied
35. develop   36. separate   37. definite   38. C   39. disappoint
40. embarrass.

UNIT II

Combining Similar Sentence Patterns to Form Compound Sentences
Word Usage: Agreement of Subject and Verb II
Punctuation: The Semicolon
Spelling: Some Often Misspelled Words II
Answers to Practices

Lesson 6

Combining Similar Sentence Patterns to Form Compound Sentences

1. The sentence patterns presented in Lessons 2–4 in Unit 1 can be combined with a coordinate conjunction such as *and, but, or, yet,* or *for* to form a compound sentence.

Examples of Combining Sentences of Similar Patterns:

Sentence Pattern 1 (N/P V)*
  Bruce jogs in the park, and Ellen hikes in the woods.
  Wounds heal with time, but scars remain for a long time.

Sentence Pattern 2 (N/P V N/P)
  José threw the ball, but Jim didn't catch it.
  At home I eat no fried foods, but at school I eat mostly fried foods in the cafeteria.

Sentence Pattern 3 (N/P V N/P N)
  Jennifer gave Jill the notes from the biology class, and Jill gave Jennifer the math notes.
  Mark bought Amy a present, for Amy had bought him one.

Sentence Pattern 4 (N/P LV N/P)
  Sharon is my best friend, and Seth is her boyfriend.
  He is an astronaut, and his wife is an aquanaut.

Sentence Pattern 5 (N/P LV Adj.)
  My history exam appeared easy, but it was hard.
  That looks good, but it doesn't taste very good.

---

* Remember that N refers to a *noun,* P refers to a *pronoun,* V refers to a *verb,* LV refers to a *linking verb,* Adj. refers to an *adjective,* and N/P means that the word can be either a noun or a pronoun.

Sentence Pattern 6 (N/P V N/P N)

The senior class appointed Herbert their class representative for faculty meetings, but Herbert considered the meetings a bore.

The students consider Dennis a genius, but Dennis considers himself a hard worker.

Sentence Pattern 7 (N/P V N/P Adj.)

Everyone found the exam hard, for the instructor made the questions tricky.

Everyone considers Mary attractive, but Mary considers herself homely.

2. The sentence patterns just presented can also be combined with a linking word such as *therefore, however, besides, moreover, then, still, so, nevertheless,* and so on. When a linking word such as *therefore, however, then, still,* and so on is used, a semicolon (;) usually is used before the linking word.

Examples of Combining Sentences of Similar Patterns:

Mary rides her bike to school; therefore she conserves energy. (Sentence Pattern 2—N/P V N/P)

Mr. Xano, our English instructor, considers his class lectures interesting; however, the students voted his class sleep-inducing. (Sentence Pattern 7—N/P V N/P Adj.)

My criminology professor read the class a fascinating article on crime prevention; then he showed the class a film on it. (Sentence Pattern 3—N/P V N/P N)

Chuck jogs every day; however, he never jogs at night. (Sentence Pattern 1—N/P V)

Anne appears content; however, she is very disturbed. (Sentence Pattern 5—N/P LV Adj.)

Practice A. Choose a sentence pattern from column 1 and combine it with a sentence pattern from column 2. The two sentence patterns should be similar, a coordinate conjunction should be used to combine the sentence, and the combined sentence should make sense. Make eleven compound sentences.

Column 1	*Column 2*
I'm the only unattached male of all my friends.	I avoid attachments.
I have six older sisters.	I'm a loner.
I enjoy my freedom.	I play the field a lot.

I'm a very economical person.	I'm the most solvent person.

I avoid serious commitments.	They smother me.

I date the same girl twice only.	I dislike commitments.

The guys elected me the champion heartbreaker.	I don't care.

I consider girls dangerous traps.	I need my space.

I like girls.	Girls consider me a challenge.

I like my life.	The girls voted me a cheapskate.

Check sample answers at the end of Lesson 6.

Practice B. In the parentheses you are given a simple sentence. Use this sentence to write a compound sentence in which the simple sentences are all of the same pattern.

1. (I'm studying hard this semester.) _____

_____

_____

2. (Jerry is brilliant.) _____

_____

_____

3. (José plays the lead in the play.) _____

_____

_____

4. (The disturbed man attacked the judge.) _____

_____

_____

5. (The jury acquitted the young man.) _____

_____

_____

   6. (No one believed Jim guilty.) _____

_____

_____

   7. (The evidence seemed conclusive.) _____

_____

_____

   8. (My friend considers himself a ladies' man.) _____

_____

_____

   9. (He taught us his technique.) _____

_____

_____

  10. (I kissed a beautiful girl on her cheek.) _____

_____

_____

Check sample answers at the end of Lesson 6.

Practice C. Write three compound sentences using two similar patterns in each sentence.

   1. _____

_____

   2. _____

_____

   3. _____

_____

Check sample sentences at the end of Lesson 6.

Word Usage: Agreement of Subject and Verb II

    1. A collective noun may take either a singular verb or a plural verb. The choice of the verb depends on the meaning you wish to give. *Examples:* The class is sending a get-well card to Susan. The class are receiving letters of commendation for their community help. (If you mean the word *class* as a group or unit, use a singular verb. However, if you mean a class made up of separate individuals, use a plural verb.)

PEANUTS ®   **By Charles M. Schulz**

©1958 United Feature Syndicate, Inc.

2. A noun that is plural in form but singular in meaning usually requires a singular verb. Some plural nouns requiring singular verbs are *mathematics, economics, civics, physics, ethics, measles,* and *mumps.* *Example: Physics deals* with light, sound, heat, electricity, and matter in motion.

3. A noun that is plural in form and plural in meaning usually requires a plural verb. Some plural nouns requiring plural verbs are *pants, athletics, spectacles (glasses), scissors,* and *riches.* *Example: Spectacles are* very expensive today.

SPECIAL NOTE

You should check the dictionary to determine whether a plural noun requires a singular verb or a plural verb.

4. When the subject of the sentence is a group of words describing a quantity or number, and the subject is thought of as a whole, the verb is usually singular. *Examples:* Twenty-five years of marriage is a long time. Five and five makes (or make) ten. Twenty from thirty is ten. One hundred dollars is too much to pay for spectacles.

5. When a sentence has a singular subject with a plural modifier (a word that describes or limits), the verb is singular. *Examples:* The significance of the studies has been shown. The possibility of errors is very high in this type of work. The strength of various irons and steels depends on their different carbon contents. (*Of the studies, of errors,* and *of various irons and steels* are prepositional phrases that describe their singular subjects.)

6. When a subject is joined to other words by *with, together with, including, as well as,* or *no less than,* the verb agrees with the subject. The verb is not influenced by the words joined to the subject. *Examples:* My mother, as well as my father, is a vegetarian. The children, together with their babysitter, were frightened by the loud noise.

SPECIAL NOTES

a. Words such as *about, above, across, against, among, around, at, before, behind below, beside, between, beyond, by, down, during, except, for, from, in, inside, into, like, near, of, off, on, out, over, since, through, to, toward, under, until, up, upon, within,* and *without,* are called **prepositions**.

b. *By the way of, because of, in spite of, on account of, in front of,* and *in place of* are prepositions that contain more than one word.

c. Prepositions show the relation or connection between a noun or pronoun and another word in the sentence. A preposition is followed by a noun or pronoun to form a unit called a **prepositional phrase**. The prepositional phrase consists of the **preposition**, the **noun** or **pronoun**, and **any word or words that describe the noun or pronoun**. The noun or pronoun in the prepositional phrase is the **object** of the preposition. As prepositional phrases modify nouns or verbs, they are used as adjectives or adverbs. An adjective is a word that limits or describes a noun or pronoun. An adverb is a word that limits or describes a verb, an adjective, or another adverb. *Examples:* The crowd jeered *at the speaker.* (adverb) My dormitory is *near the fraternity houses.* (adjective) The students attended a play *with their English professor.* (adverb) The alumni *of the college* spoke *to the freshmen.* (adjective) (adverb) We went *with them.* (adverb) The danger *of the projects* had alarmed many people (adjective) She refused to go *with me.* (adverb) *With whom* are you playing tennis? (adverb). (Notice that the pronouns are in the objective case.)

d. There are times when the preposition may come at the end of the sentence and be separated from its noun or pronoun. This is done to avoid awkward writing. *Examples:* (1) We don't know where she comes *from.* We don't know *from* where she comes. (2) Which house do you live *in?* *In* which house do you live?

Practice A. Circle the verb that correctly completes the sentence.

1. Meat with potatoes (is/are) my brother's favorite dish.

2. The tribe of Indians (was/were) moving across the plains to new lands.

3. The box of crayons (is/are) filled with various colors.

4. The list of items (includes/include) everything I will need at school next year.

5. My brother, as well as his wife and children, (is/are) visiting us this fall.

6. Boxes of fruit (was/were) loaded on the truck for delivery.

7. The cost of repairs for the car (was/were) very high.

8. The nature of the problems (is/are) not known.

9. The percentage of absences in schools across the nation (has/have) been increasing.

10. The captain, together with his men, (was/were) able to fight off the invaders.

11. Civics (is/are) the study of the workings of the national and local government.

12. Three from twenty (leaves/leave) seventeen.

13. Two hundred years (has/have) passed since the signing of the Declaration of Independence.

14. Ninety dollars for a pair of shoes (is/are) ridiculous.

15. Mathematics (is/are) a difficult subject for me.

16. Measles (is/are) very contagious.

17. Mumps (causes/cause) the salivary glands to swell.

18. My scissors (is/are) for a left-handed person.

19. Riches (is/are) not easy to attain.

20. Athletics (is/are) an important part of college life.

Check answers at the end of Lesson 6.

Practice B. Choose the verb that agrees with its subject. Construct a sentence using the given subject and the chosen verb.

Subject	*Verb*
1. Nine from twenty-five	leaves / leave

_____

_____

| 2. Ten years | equals / equal |

_____

_____

| 3. My green pants | is / are |

_____

_____

| 4. The ethics of the situation | is / are |

_____

_____

| 5. Economics | is / are |

_____

_____

| 6. The importance of the discoveries | is / are |

_____

_____

| 7. A parent with newborn twins | needs / need |

_____

_____

8. The college administration, including the deans,

has / have

_____

_____

9. Games of chance

is / are

_____

_____

10. The size of the coats

seems/seem

_____

_____

Check sample answers at the end of Lesson 6.

Punctuation: The Semicolon

1. The **semicolon** (;) is a punctuation signal used to connect two simple sentences to form a compound sentence. However, the semicolon is usually not used when two simple sentences are connected by the **coordinate conjunctions** *and, or, but, for, yet,* or *nor.* A **comma** is usually used when simple sentences are linked together with *and, or, but, for, yet* or *nor.* *Examples:* The men stopped work, but they didn't go home. The men stopped work; they took their lunch pails and left.

2. A semicolon or a period is used because the stop or break between the two simple sentences is too important to be marked by a comma if a conjunction such as *and, or, but, for,* or *nor* is missing. If the simple sentences are closely related, a semicolon without a linking word usually is used. If the simple sentences are not closely related, a period usually is used. *Examples:* a. The men stopped work. On the way home they stopped for a beer. b. The men stopped work; they needed a rest.

3. When the linking words *hence, so, however, also, then, nevertheless, in fact, therefore, accordingly, besides, moreover, thus, still, otherwise,* and so on join two simple sentences to form a compound sentence, a semicolon usually is used before the linking word.   *Examples:* a. School closed at 1:00 P.M. on Wednesday; then the children went home. b. As a freshman at college, she was very popular; however, as a senior, she was not.

SPECIAL NOTES

a. Either a comma or a semicolon may be used with the linking word *so.*
b. A semicolon signals a stronger pause than a comma.

4. A period may be used in place of the semicolon. However, as already stated, a period is usually used if the two simple sentences are not closely related to one another, and a semicolon without a linking word is used if the two simple sentences are closely related. *Examples:* a. As a freshman at college, she was unhappy; as a senior, she was not. b. As a freshman at college, she was very popular. As a senior, however, she became a recluse. c. School closed at 1:00 P.M. on Wednesday. The children went home. d. School closed at 1:00 P.M. on Wednesday; the furnace broke down.

5. In special cases when a sentence has a long involved series that contains commas, a semicolon is used to separate the larger units of the sentence. *Examples:* The board of trustees at our college includes such persons as Dr. D. L. Smith, president of Reese Corporation; Mr. P. Baker, attorney-at-law; Dr. J. Brown, president of Morgan College; and Dr. Mary Jones, superintendent of schools. Last summer my buddies and I traveled to Hartford, Connecticut; New York City, New York; Chicago, Illinois; and San Francisco, California.

Practice A. Insert a comma or a semicolon in each of the following sentences.

1. They felt good for they had gotten everything correct.
2. The sun was hot and shining brightly therefore we went swimming.
3. John has his tennis Carol has her photography.
4. The group stopped in the middle of their tour they were too tired to continue.
5. Interviews can be very tiring sleep the night before is essential.
6. The waitress came to wait on us but she forgot to bring the menus.
7. I find studying exhausting therefore I take lots of vitamins in the days before exams.
8. We were tired so we stopped to rest.
9. I put Sharon through college and she supported me through medical school.
10. I like to go for long walks in the park but my boyfriend doesn't.

Check answers at the end of Lesson 6.

Practice B. Combine the following pairs of sentences into one sentence using a semicolon without a linking word.

1. The day was a nightmare. We couldn't believe what had happened.

_____

_____

2. I was tired. We decided to stay home.

_____

_____

3. Help is on the way. Try not to move the victim.

_____

_____

Check sample sentences at the end of Lesson 6.

Practice C. Finish writing each of the following sentences.

1. We heard _____ ; then we _____ .

2. It's fun _____ ; however, you _____ .

3. That's a good _____ ; besides, _____ .

4. It sounds _____ ; nevertheless, _____ .

5. We will _____ ; therefore _____ .

Check sample answers at the end of Lesson 6.

Spelling: Some Often Misspelled Words II

Following, presented in sentences, are forty often misspelled words.

1. He is *especially* nice to everyone.
2. She likes to *exaggerate*.
3. Do *exercise* nine in the book.
4. That has been in *existence* for a long time.
5. What was his *explanation*?
6. That was an *expensive experience* that you had.
7. What were the effects of the *experiment*?
8. That is *fascinating*.
9. I am going to a *foreign* country on the *fourth* of *February*.
10. My mother is past *forty* years of age.
11. These are *fundamental* truths.
12. The *government* is *generally* not trusted by many people.
13. What *guarantee* do you have for it?
14. My *height* is not a problem.
15. The *heroes* and *heroines* in films are usually good looking.
16. What a *humorous* story!
17. That is an *imaginary* story.
18. Some people need more *guidance* than others.
19. The people wanted *independence immediately*.
20. *Incidentally*, we can't go with you.

21. He is a very *influential* person.
22. She doesn't have too much *intelligence*.
23. I don't *interfere* in other people's business.
24. That is *irrelevant* to the issue at hand.
25. Do you have any *knowledge* about the *fictitious* story that was told?
26. She is *jealous* when anyone talks to her boyfriend.
27. I don't have much *leisure* time.
28. What is the *length* of that object?
29. He works in a *laboratory*.
30. I go to the *library* every week.
31. Do you have a driver's *license*?
32. That is a *likely* story!
33. Many old people suffer from *loneliness*.

Practice A. Look at each word carefully. Cover the word. Write the covered word in the blank. Check to see if you have spelled it correctly.

1. especially _____
2. exaggerate _____
3. exercise _____
4. existence _____
5. explanation _____
6. expensive _____
7. experience _____
8. experiment _____
9. fascinating _____
10. foreign _____
11. fourth _____
12. February _____
13. forty _____
14. fundamental _____
15. government _____
16. generally _____
17. guarantee _____
18. height _____
19. heroes _____
20. heroines _____
21. humorous _____
22. imaginary _____

23. guidance _____

24. independence _____

25. immediately _____

26. incidentally _____

27. influential _____

28. intelligence _____

29. interfere _____

30. irrelevant _____

31. knowledge _____

32. fictitious _____

33. jealous _____

34. leisure _____

35. length _____

36. laboratory _____

37. library _____

38. license _____

39. likely _____

40. loneliness _____

You should have checked the spelling immediately after writing each word.

Practice B. Look at each word carefully. If the word is spelled correctly, put a *C* in the blank. If the word is not spelled correctly, spell it correctly. (Sentences are given for words that can be confused with others.)

1. especally _____

2. exagerate _____

3. exersise _____

4. existance _____

5. explanation _____

6. expensive _____

7. experence _____

8. experiment _____

9. fasinating _____

10. foregn _____

11. Today is the *forth.* _____

12. Febuary _____

13. fourty _____

14. fundamental _____

15. goverment _____

16. generaly _____

17. guarrante _____

18. hieght _____

19. heores _____

20. herines _____

21. humoures _____

22. imaginery _____

23. guidence _____

24. independence _____

25. imediately _____

26. incidently _____

27. influentul _____

28. inteligence _____

29. interfere _____

30. irelevent _____

31. nowledge _____

32. ficticious _____

33. jealus _____

34. liesure _____

35. length _____

36. labratory _____

37. library _____

38. lisence _____

39. likly _____

40. lonliness _____

Check answers at the end of Lesson 6.

LESSON 6 ANSWERS

Combining Similar Sentence Patterns to
Form Compound Sentences (pp. 73–76)

Practice A: (sample answers)   1. I'm the only unattached male of all my friends, for I'm a loner.   2. I'm the only unattached male of all my friends, and I'm the most solvent person.   3. I have six older sisters, and they smother me.   4. I enjoy my freedom, and I need my space.   5. I enjoy my freedom, and I dislike commitments.   6. I'm a very economical person, and I'm a loner.   7. I avoid serious commitments, and I avoid attachments.   8. I date the same girl twice only, for I play the field a lot.   9. The guys elected me the champion heartbreaker, and the girls voted me a cheapskate.   10. I like girls, but they smother me.   11. I consider girls dangerous traps, and girls consider me a challenge.

Practice B: (sample answers)   1. I'm studying hard this semester, and I'm working too.   2. Jerry is brilliant, but he's unmotivated.   3. José plays the lead in the play, and his girlfriend watches every performance.   4. The disturbed man attacked the judge, for the judge had sentenced him to life imprisonment.   5. The jury acquited the young man; the young man thanked them.   6. No one believed Jim guilty; everyone considered him innocent.   7. The evidence seemed conclusive, and his situation appeared hopeless.   8. My friend considers himself a ladies' man, but the ladies consider him a bore.   9. He taught us his technique, so we showed him our secret formula.   10. I kissed a beautiful girl on her cheek; she kissed me back.

Practice C: (sample sentences)   1. I considered Jim my best friend, but now I consider him my worst enemy.   2. I gave Jennifer a cookie, and then I read her a story.   3. Debra is a reporter, and her brother is a ballet dancer.

Word Usage: Agreement of Subject and Verb II (pp. 76–80)

Practice A: 1. is   2. was   3. is   4. includes   5. is   6. were   7. was   8. is   9. has   10. was   11. is   12. leaves   13. have   14. is   15. is   16. is   17. causes   18. are   19. are   20. are.

Practice B (sample answers):   1. Nine from twenty-five leaves sixteen.   2. Ten years equals a decade.   3. My green pants are too big for me.   4. The ethics of the situation is not very clear.   5. Economics is a social science concerning the production, distribution, and consumption of goods.   6. The importance of the discoveries is not obvious yet.   7. A parent with newborn twins needs a great amount of help.   8. The college administration, including the deans, has requested a special meeting of the faculty.   9. Games of chance are a poor source of income.   10. The size of the coats seems to vary too much.

Punctuation: The Semicolon (pp. 80–82)

Practice A: 1. They felt good, 2. The sun was hot and shining brightly; therefore 3. John has his tennis; 4. The group stopped in the middle of their tour; 5. Interviews can be very tiring; 6. The waitress came to wait on us, 7. I find studying very exhausting; therefore 8. We were tired, 9. I put Sharon through college, 10. I like to go for long walks in the park, .

Practice B: (sample sentences) 1. The day was a nightmare; we couldn't believe what had happened. 2. I was tired; we decided to stay home. 3. Help is on the way; try not to move the victim.

Practice C (sample answers): 1. We heard the bell ring; then we rushed to class. 2. It's fun to play and do nothing; however, you don't accomplish much that way. 3. That's a good idea about more relaxation; besides, we need more free time. 4. It sounds good to me; nevertheless, you must get the whole group's opinion about it. 5. We will be going away for a long trip; therefore we have a lot of work to do to prepare for it.

Spelling: Some Often Misspelled Words II (pp. 82–85)

Practice A: Check words on the page for correct spelling.

Practice B: 1. especially 2. exaggerate 3. exercise 4. existence 5. C 6. C 7. experience 8. C 9. fascinating 10. foreign 11. fourth 12. February 13. forty 14. C 15. government 16. generally 17. guarantee 18. height 19. heroes 20. heroines 21. humorous 22. imaginary 23. guidance 24. C 25. immediately 26. incidentally 27. influential 28. intelligence 29. C 30. irrelevant 31. knowledge 32. fictitious 33. jealous 34. leisure 35. C 36. laboratory 37. C 38. license 39. likely 40. loneliness.

Lesson 7

Combining Different Sentence Patterns to Form Compound Sentences

In Lesson 6 you combined similar sentence patterns to form compound sentences. In this lesson you will be combining different sentence patterns to form compound sentences. Here are examples of a number of different sentence patterns that have been combined to form a compound sentence using coordinate conjunctions such as *and, but, or, for, yet,* and so on or a linking word such as *therefore, however, then, nevertheless,* and so on.

Examples of Combining Sentences of Different Patterns:

1. The rain fell heavily, but we continued the game anyway. (Sentence Patterns 1 and 2 — N/P V and N/P V N/P)*

2. Jill is an excellent student, but her boyfriend hates school. (Sentence Patterns 4 and 2 — N/P LV N/P and N/P V N/P)

3. The instructor gave the students a very hard exam, and they failed it. (Sentence Pattern 3 and 2 — N/P V N/P N and N/P V N/P)

4. Jim gave the coach his uniform; then he slowly walked away. (Sentence Patterns 3 and 1 — N/P V N/P N and N/P V)

5. Everyone considers Marsha a secret alcoholic; however, Marsha ignores everyone. (Sentence Patterns 6 and 2 — N/P V N/P N and N/P V N/P)

6. Marsha needs help; however, she doesn't consider herself an alcoholic. (Sentence Patterns 2 and 6 — N/P V N/P and N/P V N/P N)

---

* Remember that N refers to a *noun,* P refers to a *pronoun,* V refers to a *verb,* LV refers to a *linking verb,* Adj. refers to an *adjective,* and N/P means that the word can be either a noun or a pronoun.

Practice A. Choose a sentence pattern from column 1 and combine it with a sentence pattern from column 2. The two sentence patterns should be different, a coordinate conjunction should be used to combine the sentence, and the combined sentence should make sense. Construct fifteen compound sentences.

Column 1	*Column 2*
My best friend is a jock.	Girls avoid me.
I'm a heavy-weight thinker.	He doesn't take himself seriously.
At times I envy him.	The girls love him.
He gets me dates.	He is a good friend.
The girls don't like me.	My muscles are ping pong balls.
I'm trying to build muscles.	No one wants a muscle-bound brain.
Nothing helps.	I have a charley horse.
I ache all over.	We've been friends since elementary school.
The college voted him chief jock.	He'd rather be a heavy thinker.

Check sample answers at the end of Lesson 7.

Practice B. In the parentheses you are given a simple sentence. Use this sentence to write a compound sentence in which the simple sentences are of different patterns.

1. (I drive a school bus during the day.) _____

_____

2. (I can't make expenses meet.) _____

_____

3. (I fall asleep in class.) _____

_____

4. (My classes aren't boring.) _____

_____

5. (I need a rest.) _____

_____

6. (I'm moving to less expensive quarters.) _____

_____

7. (I consider steak a rare luxury.) _____

_____

8. (I'm a vegetarian.)   _____

_____

9. (My girlfriend is an understanding person.) _____

_____

10. (My goal is survival.) _____

_____

Check sample sentences at the end of Lesson 7.

Practice C. Write three compound sentences using two different patterns in each sentence.

1. _____

_____

2. _____

_____

3. _____

_____

Check sample sentences at the end of Lesson 7.

Word Usage: Agreement of Subject and Verb III

1. The verb agrees with the subject of the sentence and not with the noun in the complete predicate of the sentence. *Examples:* Apples *are* a delicious fruit to eat. Our political discussion usually *ends* in terrible arguments. (In the first example, the verb agrees with *apples*, the subject of the sentence rather than with *fruit*, the noun in the complete predicate of the sentence. In the second example, the verb agrees with *discussion* rather than with *arguments*.)

2. The words *there is* should be followed by a singular noun. The words *there are* should be followed by a plural noun. *Examples: There are* a great number of people at this concert. *There is* no one here that I want to meet.

3. A singular verb is used with such words as *neither, either, nobody, anybody, somebody, everybody, anyone, someone, one, not one,* and *no one. Examples:* Not one of my friends *has* dropped out of school. Nobody I know *is* failing English this year.

4. The word *none* may either be singular or plural, but the plural meaning is more commonly used. When the writer wishes to express a meaning that is definitely singular, the words *nobody, no one,* or *not one* usually are used in place of *none. Examples:* None of my friends *are* going to the dance. Not one of my friends *is* going to the dance.

5. The word *all* may be either singular or plural. *All* is singular when it means the whole amount of something. *Examples:* All of us are going. All is forgiven.

6. When the subject of the sentence is the name of a television show, a book, a poem, a newspaper, a film, a play, and so on, a singular verb is used. *Examples: Gone with the Wind* is a classic. The *Daily News* has one of the largest circulations of any newspaper in the country. *Roots* is a book by Alex Haley that was adapted for television. "Fog" is a poem by Carl Sandburg. *The Waste Land* is a poem by T. S. Eliot.

7. The word *it* requires a singular verb. *Example:* It is raining today.

8. When a sentence has both a negative and a positive subject, the verb agrees with the subject in the positive. *Example:* You, not I, are going to wash the dishes.

Practice A. Circle the verb that correctly completes the sentence.

1. Anybody (is/are) welcome to come to the party.

2. None of them (is/are) welcome to come to the party.

3. Not one of the couples I know (skis/ski).

4. There (was/were) no one present.

5. Each of the children (seems/seem) to be a good dancer.

6. There (is/are) a great amount of money to be made on the stock market.

7. The strongest part of the foundation (is/are) the large boulders.

8. Neither of the dishes (is/are) very appetizing.

9. *War and Peace* (is/are) a famous novel about Russia.

10. It (is/are) not ready yet.

11. Jim and George, not Mary, (is/are) going.

12. Many newspapers (is/are) closed because of the strike.

13. Most poems (needs/need) to be heard to be enjoyed.

14. The Smiths' relative, not the Smiths, (owns/own) the diner.

15. *Green Mansions* (is/are) a good book to read.

16. The *Daily Record* (carries/carry) many advertisements.

17. "The Death of the Hired Man" (is/are) a poem by Robert Frost.

18. The reference section, not the encyclopedias, (is/are) being moved to another room.

Check answers at the end of Lesson 7.

Practice B. Circle the verb that *best* fits the subject.

Subject	*Predicate*
1. None	(seems/seem) good to eat.
2. Not everybody	(writes/write) clearly.
3. Not one of the cakes	(is/are) special.
4. The causes of crime	(is/are) many.
5. There	(is/are) too many to count.
6. There	(is/are) no one available.
7. The smallest particles of an element	(is/are) atoms.
8. The major supplier of blood from the heart to the lungs and other parts of the body	(is/are) the arteries.
9. Not one of my relatives	(plays/play) a musical instrument.
10. Every one of my friends	(has/have) varsity letters.

Check answers at the end of Lesson 7.

Practice C. Choose the predicate that agrees with the subject. Construct a sentence using the given subject and the chosen predicate.

Subject	*Predicate*
1. None	is/are
2. No one	has/have
3. Everybody	likes/like
4. There	is too many people/are too many people

5. Nobody   has/have

Check sample answers at the end of Lesson 7.

Practice D. Choose the verb that agrees with its subject. Construct a sentence using the given subject and the chosen verb.

Subject	*Verb*
1. It	helps/help

---

2. Your younger sister, not your older ones,	is/are

---

3. The *New York Times*	has/have

---

4. *Alice in Wonderland*	is/are

---

5. My stock, not my bonds,	is/are

Check sample answers at the end of Lesson 7.

Punctuation: The Colon

A **colon** (:) is used in a formal sense to show that something is to follow. Following are some examples of when a colon is used:

1. To introduce a list.   *Examples:* The following are examples of conjunctions: *and, or,* and *but.* The marketing list includes these items: fruit, vegetables, meat, and dairy products. We supply necessary linen to our guests: towels, sheets, and blankets.

2. After a formal heading.   *Examples:* Dear Miss Jones: Dear Sir: Gentlemen: Dear Mr. Smith:

3. In writing time.   *Examples:* 12:15 P.M., 9:30 A.M., 1:40 P.M.

4. To introduce a long quotation.   *Example:*

"There Was an Old Party of Lyme" is an amusing limerick written by an anonymous author:

> There was an old party of Lyme
> Who married three wives at one time.
>   When asked: "Why the third?"
>   He replied: "One's absurd,
> And bigamy, sir, is a crime."

5. In a title to separate parts of the title.   *Examples:* "Looking Beyond: A Study of Divergent Thinking"; "Robert Frost: An Analysis of His Works."

SPECIAL NOTE

When a colon is used to introduce a list, the statement that comes before the colon should be able to stand alone as a sentence. If the statement cannot stand alone as a sentence, a colon is *not* used. The lists or enumerations that follow a colon should be **appositives** (nouns or pronouns that follow a noun and give additional information about the noun).   *Examples:* 1. I took geography, history, English, and French last semester. 2. I took the following subjects last year: geography, history, English, and French. 1. I love beagles, dachshunds, great Danes, and schnauzers. 2. Following are examples of dogs I love: beagles, dachshunds, great danes, and schnauzers.

Practice A. Read each of the following. If the punctuation marks are correct, put a *C* in the blank. If the punctuation marks are incorrect, underline what is incorrect and put in the correct punctuation mark(s).

_____ 1. 12;00 P.M.

_____ 2. Dear Sir, (formal letter)

_____ 3. Dear Aunt Jane,

_____ 4. I like: apples, oranges, and bananas.

_____ 5. *Art History: Another Look*

_____ 6. We played many games: tennis, soccer, dodge ball, and basketball.

_____ 7. 9:20 A:M.

_____ 8. He said: Let's go.

_____ 9. Gentlemen:

_____ 10. The textbook list has the following books: *Gaining Word Power, English Composition, United States History.*

Check answers at the end of Lesson 7.

Spelling: Some Often Misspelled Words III

Following, presented in sentences, are forty often misspelled words.

1. I read many *magazines.*
2. Some *bachelors* do not believe in *marriage.*

3. *Mathematics* is one of my favorite courses.
4. I enjoy playing *miniature* golf.
5. Is that *necessary*?
6. I have some very nice *neighbors*.
7. My great grandmother is *ninety* years old.
8. It's my *niece's ninth* birthday.
9. What is the *occasion*?
10. In my *opinion,* he is telling the truth.
11. He has many *pastimes.*
12. He is a *peculiar* person, but *peaceable.*
13. Do you have a *permanent* job yet?
14. Is that *practical*?
15. He *preferred* dating my sister to dating me.
16. I think that he is *prejudiced.*
17. My *science instructor* is a good lecturer.
18. I *realize* that I am late.
19. My childhood friend did not *recognize* me.
20. That is a *ridiculous* story.
21. Is that on your *schedule*?
22. The study had *significant* results.
23. I am a *sophomore* at college.
24. Please show me your *specimen* for the microscope.
25. I do lots of *studying.*
26. I would like to *succeed.*
27. What is the *temperature* outside?
28. He did a *thorough* job of cleaning the attic.
29. The accident was a terrible *tragedy.*
30. I enjoy eating *vegetables.*
31. On *Wednesday,* if the *weather* is hot, we're going to the beach.
32. *Whether* I go or not depends on a number of things.
33. That is not *wholly* true.
34. Have you *written* to your family yet?
35. Who is that *woman*?

Practice A. Look at each word carefully. Cover the word. Write the covered word in the blank. Check to see if you have spelled it correctly.

1. magazines _____

2. bachelors _____

3. marriage _____

4. mathematics _____

5. miniature _____

6. necessary _____

7. neighbors _____

8. ninety _____

9. ninth _____

10. occasion _____

11. opinion _____

12. pastimes _____

13. peculiar _____

14. peaceable _____

15. permanent _____

16. practical _____

17. preferred _____

18. prejudiced _____

19. science _____

20. instructor _____

21. realize _____

22. recognize _____

23. ridiculous _____

24. schedule _____

25. niece _____

26. significant _____

27. sophomore _____

28. specimen _____

29. studying _____

30. succeed _____

31. temperature _____

32. thorough _____

33. tragedy _____

34. vegetables _____

35. Wednesday _____

36. weather _____

37. whether _____

38. wholly _____

39. written _____

40. woman _____

You should have checked the spelling immediately after writing each word.

Practice B. **Look at each word carefully. If the word is spelled correctly, put a *C* in the blank. If the word is not spelled correctly, spell it correctly. (Sentences are given for words that can be confused with others.)**

1. magzines _____

2. bachalors _____

3. mathmatics _____

4. minature _____

5. necesary _____

6. nieghbors _____

7. ninty _____

8. niece _____

9. nineth _____

10. ocassion _____

11. opinion _____

12. pasttimes _____

13. peculiar _____

14. peacable _____

15. permanent _____

16. practical _____

17. prefered _____

18. prejudiced _____

19. science _____

20. instructer _____

21. realize _____

22. recognize _____

23. ridicalous _____

24. skedule _____

25. marrage _____

26. signfcant _____

27. sophmore _____

28. specman _____

29. studing _____

30. suceed _____

31. temperature _____

32. thorogh _____

33. trajedy _____

34. vegtables _____

35. Wedesday _____

36. The *wether* is clear today. _____

37. *Wether* I go or not is no one's business. _____

38. wholly _____

39. writen _____

40. woman _____

Check answers at the end of Lesson 7.

LESSON 7 ANSWERS

Combining Different Sentence Pattern to
Form Compound Sentences (pp. 89–91)

Practice A: (sample answers)   1. My best friend is a jock, and the girls love him.   2. My best friend is a jock, but he doesn't take himself seriously. 3. I'm a heavy-weight thinker, but no one wants a muscle-bound brain.   4. I'm a heavy-weight thinker, and girls avoid me.   5. At times I envy him, but he is a good friend.   6. At times I envy him, but we've been friends since elementary school.   7. He gets me dates, but the girls love him.   8. He gets me dates, for he is a good friend.   9. He gets me dates, but no one wants a muscle-bound brain.   10. The girls don't like me, for my muscles are ping pong balls.   11. Nothing helps, for girls avoid me.   12. I ache all over, and I have a charley horse.   13. I ache all over, and my muscles are ping pong balls. 14. The college voted him chief jock, but he'd rather be a heavy thinker. 15. The college voted him chief jock, but he doesn't take himself seriously. 16. The college voted him chief jock, and the girls love him.

Practice B: (sample sentences)   1. I drive a school bus during the day, and I go to school at night.   2. I can't make expenses meet, but I try.   3. I fall asleep in class, for I am tired.   4. My classes aren't boring, but I need sleep.   5. I need a rest, for I am always tired.   6. I'm moving to less expensive quarters, and I'm eating less food.   7. I consider steak a rare luxury, for I can't afford it.   8. I'm a vegetarian, but I love meat.   9. My girlfriend is an understanding person, so I love her.   10. My goal is survival, and I'll make it.

Practice C: (sample sentences)   1. My girlfriend left me, so I'm depressed. 2. My friends consider me a fool, for I still love her.   3. I considered her a very special person, but she's dating someone else now.

Word Usage: Agreement of Subject and Verb III (pp. 91–94)

Practice A: 1. is   2. are   3. skis   4. was   5. seems   6. is   7. is   8. is 9. is   10. is   11. are   12. are   13. need   14. owns   15. is   16. carries   17. is 18. is.

Practice B: 1. seem   2. writes   3. is   4. are   5. are   6. is   7. are   8. is 9. plays   10. has.

Practice C (sample answers):   1. None are available for sale.   2. No one has seen my missing dog.   3. Everybody likes to receive an *A* in a course. 4. There are too many people at this gathering.   5. Nobody has chosen a topic for his or her term paper yet.

Practice D (sample answers):   1. It helps to be a member in good standing.   2. Your younger sister, not your older ones, is my girlfriend.   3. The *New York Times* has excellent articles.   4. *Alice in Wonderland* is read and loved by many children.   5. My stock, not my bonds, is rising in value.

Punctuation: The Colon (pp. 94–95)

Practice A: 1. 12:00 P.M.   2. Dear Sir: 3. C   4. I like apples, oranges, and bananas.   5. C   6. C   7. 9:20 A.M.   8. He said, "Let's go." (quotation too short to use a colon)   9. C   10. C.

Spelling: Some Often Misspelled Words III (pp. 95–99)

Practice A: Check words on the page for correct spelling.

Practice B: 1. magazines   2. bachelors   3. mathematics   4. miniature 5. necessary   6. neighbors   7. ninety   8. C   9. ninth   10. occasion   11. C 12. pastimes   13. C   14. peaceable   15. C   16. C   17. preferred   18. C 19. C   20. instructor   21. C   22. C   23. ridiculous   24. schedule   25. marriage   26. significant   27. sophomore   28. specimen   29. studying   30. succeed   31. C   32. thorough   33. tragedy   34. vegetables   35. Wednesday 36. weather   37. whether   38. C   39. written   40. C.

UNIT II

Lesson 8

Combining Sentence Patterns to Form Compound Sentences

In this lesson you will be combining similar and different sentence patterns to form compound sentences. In Lesson 5 and in the punctuation section of Lesson 6 in this unit, you learned that a semicolon (;) is a punctuation mark that may be used to connect two simple sentences to form a compound sentence. The semicolon (;) may be used alone without any linking word to connect two simple sentences if the simple sentences are closely related.

Examples of Combining Sentence Patterns Using a Semicolon Without a Linking Word to Form a Compound Sentence:

The circus lady is obese; she devours all food in sight. (Sentence Patterns 5 and 2 — N/P LV Adj. and N/P V N/P)*

I needed help; I didn't get it. (Sentence Pattern 2 — N/P V N/P and N/P V N/P)

Tony receives the highest grades in English; he is a genius. (Sentence Patterns 2 and 4 — N/P V N/P and N/P LV N/P)

Help is coming; stay put. [Sentence Patterns 5 and 1 — N/P LV Adj. and N/P (you is understood in this sentence) V]

---

* Remember that N refers to a *noun,* P refers to a *pronoun,* V refers to a *verb,* LV refers to a *linking verb,* Adj. refers to an *adjective,* and N/P means that the word can be either a noun or a pronoun.

103

Practice A. Here are two columns of simple sentences. See how many compound sentences you can make by combining the simple sentences. You may use a coordinate conjunction such as *and, or, but, for,* and so on; a linking word such as *therefore, however, then, besides, nevertheless,* and so on; or a semicolon without a linking word if the two simple sentences are closely related. You may combine any sentence from column 1 with any sentence from column 2.

Column 1	*Column 2*
At the circus the clown stood on his head.	It was a funny sight to see.
My friend tried to sit on the fat lady's lap.	We felt good.
We stuffed ourselves with peanuts and popcorn.	It's cheaper than a psychiatrist.
The elephant squirted water on us.	None of us wanted to go home.
One of the horses jumped out of the ring.	It was fun being a child again.
The price of admission has certainly risen.	We were startled.
At the end of the day we were exhausted.	We were not too full for dinner.

Check sample answers at the end of Lesson 8.

Practice B. In the parentheses you are given a sentence. Use this sentence to write a compound sentence in which the simple sentences are of a similar or different pattern. Use a semicolon without a linking word, a coordinate conjunction, or a linking word such as *however, nevertheless, then, therefore, besides,* and so on to join the simple sentences.

1. (Fuel prices are rising.) _____

_____

2. (Inflation has decreased the value of the dollar.) _____

_____

3. (I work twice as much.) _____

_____

4. (We consider the fuel prices a holdup.) _____

_____

5. (Everyone is complaining about high prices.) _____

_____

6. (My whole family works.) _____

_____

7. (A single wage-earner has a difficult time.) _____

_____

_____

_____

8. (Wages keep going up.) _____

_____

9. (Tuition costs increase each year.) _____

_____

10. (I am an optimist.) _____

_____

Check sample answers at the end of Lesson 8.

Practice C. Write three compound sentences using similar or dissimilar sentence patterns.

1. _____

_____

2. _____

_____

3. _____

_____

Check sample sentences at the end of Lesson 8.

Word Usage:
Pronouns and Their Antecedents

1. A **pronoun** is a word used in place of a noun.   *Examples:* Mary is sleeping. *She* is sleeping.   The idea is a good one. *It* is a good idea.
2. The word for which a pronoun stands is called its **antecedent.**   *Examples: Mary* is sleeping. She is sleeping. The *idea* is a good one. It is a good idea. My *brother* showed his stamp collection to the interested guest.

(*Mary* is the antecedent of *she*, *idea* is the antecedent of *it*, and *brother* is the antecedent of *his*. The pronouns *she*, *it*, and *his* all refer to nouns that come before the pronouns. The pronouns *she*, *it*, and *his* are used in place of the nouns.)

Agreement of Pronouns with Their Antecedents

1. A singular antecedent requires a singular pronoun. *Examples:* The book is too long. It is difficult to read. The chair is very uncomfortable. It is also too low.

2. Such words as *each, any, every, man, person, either, neither, anybody, everybody, anyone, everyone, nobody, no one, somebody,* and *someone* require a singular pronoun. *Examples: Nobody* knows what his or her potential is. *Each* one must make his or her own decision about what to do. Is *everybody* ready to give his or her talk?

3. A plural antecedent requires a plural pronoun. *Examples:* The judges based their decision on a number of factors. The defeated athletes returned to their lockers with heavy hearts.

4. If a pronoun has two or more antecedents connected by *and*, the pronoun referring to them is plural. *Examples:* My cat and her kittens are eating their dinner. My jacket and coat need their linings fixed.

SPECIAL NOTE

When *each* is used with singular nouns connected by *and*, the pronoun referring to the two antecedents is singular. *Example:* Each man and each woman must do what he or she thinks is best.

5. If a pronoun has two or more singular antecedents connected by *or* or *nor*, the pronoun is singular. *Examples:* Either Herb or Jack must give up his place. Neither Aunt Ada nor Cousin Lisa had brought her slides of the Grand Canyon.

6. When *or* or *nor* connects two or more nouns of different number or of different gender (male or female), the nouns usually cannot be referred to by one common pronoun. *Examples:* Neither the Smiths nor Colonel Black received the credit they or he deserved. If either Carl or Yolanda turns up with his or her confounded ukelele, I'm walking out.

Such sentences can usually be rewritten to avoid the awkward pronoun reference. *Examples:* Neither the Smiths nor Colonel Black received proper credit. If Carl brings his confounded ukelele, or if Yolanda turns up with hers, I'm walking out.

7. If the antecedent of a pronoun is a collective noun, the pronoun is singular or plural depending on the meaning of the collective noun in the sentence. *Examples:* The class roared at the proofs of their pictures. The audience gave their approval by clapping their hands. At the bullfight, the crowd shouted its approval of the matador.

8. An **appositive** (a noun or pronoun or a noun or pronoun with its own descriptive words that follows a noun and gives additional information about the noun) is in the same case as its antecedent. *Examples:* The men, *John, Jim, and I,* are going. He told us, *John and me,* to stay. (*I* is in the subjective case because *men,* its antecedent, is in the subjective case. *Me* is in the objective case because *us,* its antecedent, is in the objective case.)

SPECIAL NOTES

a. In the past, the pronouns *he, his,* and *him* were used to stand for nouns that could apply to either a man or a woman. Although this is still done, there is a growing preference for using both the male and female **pronouns** *he or she, his or her,* and *him or her* if the usage occurs once or twice. If it is necessary to repeat the pronouns a number of times, many writers turn to the plural to avoid a specific sexual designation. *Examples:* If a *person* has high blood pressure, *he or she* may be under unusual stress. A *lawyer* must store a great deal of legal precedent in *his or her* memory. *Lawyers* must store a great deal of legal precedent in *their* memories.

b. Following are some ways that a pronoun can be used in a sentence.

Subjective case:	*I* am happy.	*I* is what the sentence is about.
Objective case:	He loves *her.*	*Her* is the object of loves. *Her* is receiving the action. *He* is the subject doing the action.
Possessive case:	The house is *mine.* This is *my* house.	*Mine* and *my* are pronouns showing ownership or possession. Another way to show this would be to say: *The house belongs to me.*
Subjective case — comparison:		Carmen can sing louder than *I.* The subjective case, *I,* is correct because the comparison is between the way Carmen sings and the way I sing. In such a comparison the words *than I can sing* are to be understood.
		Carman loves her family more than *I.* The words *than I do* or *than I love her family* are understood.
Objective case — comparison:		Carmen loves her family more than *me.* The objective case, *me,* is correct if the meaning intended is *Carmen loves her family more than she loves me.*

Case refers to the relationship between a noun or pronoun and the other words in the sentence. Case is shown by a **change in the form of the word** or by the **position of the word in a sentence.** *Examples:* (1) the football *team's* biggest problem is the star quarterback. (*Team* changes its form to *team's* to show possession. *Team's* is in the **possessive case.**) (2) The *dog* bit the *child.* (The position of *dog* in the sentence shows that it is the subject of the sentence. *Dog* is in the **subjective case.** The position of *child* in the sentence shows that *child* is the object of the verb *bit.* *Child* is receiving the action. *Child* is in the **objective case.** When we change the positions of *dog* and *child* in the sentence, we change the meaning of the sentence.) (3) The *child* bit the *dog.* (*Child* is the subject. *Dog* is the object. *Dog* is receiving the action. *Child* is in the **subjective case.** *Dog* is in the **objective case.**)

c. There are different kinds of pronouns. Following are some of them:

Personal pronouns:

These pronouns indicate the person speaking, the person spoken to, or the person or thing spoken about. *I, you, he, she, we, you, they, it.* (Personal pronouns change their form to show a change in person. See list at the end of Special Notes.) *Example: You* must leave.

Demonstrative pronouns:

(These pronouns point out the specific person or thing that is referred to.) *this, that, these, those.* Examples: *This* is what I want. *These* are enough.

Interrogative pronouns:

(These pronouns are used in asking questions.) *who, which, what.* Examples: *What* is that? *Who* are you?

Relative pronouns:

(These pronouns introduce a clause modifying [describing or limiting] an antecedent.) *who, which, that.* Examples: The man *who spoke* was in charge. John, *who is a valuable employee,* should get a raise. (*Who spoke* identifies *man* and *who is a valuable employee* describes *John.*)

Indefinite pronouns:

(These pronouns refer to persons or things not easily identifiable). *any, anyone, some, someone, no one, nobody, somebody, anybody,* and so on. Examples: *Anyone* could have done it. *No one* saw the accident.

Reflexive pronouns:

(These pronouns are used as the object of a sentence. They point out or refer to the same person as the subject. Like personal pronouns, they change form with person.) *myself, yourself, oneself, himself, herself, itself,* and so on. Examples: He hurt *himself.* (*Himself* refers to he. *Himself* is what was hurt.) I helped *myself.* (*Myself* refers to *I.* *Myself* is what was helped.)

Intensive pronouns:

(These pronouns are identical to the reflexive pronouns but intensify or emphasize the noun that they are used with.) *myself, yourself, oneself, himself, herself, itself,* and so on. Examples: You, *yourselves,* are the thieves. Jane, *herself,* told the manager about the problem. (*Yourselves* is in apposition to the pronoun *you* to which it is attached. *Herself* is in apposition to the proper noun *Jane* to which it is attached. When a word is in apposition to another, it tends to emphasize it.)

d. Following is a list of personal pronouns. These pronouns are used very often. However, they frequently are used incorrectly because many change their form to show the different cases.

PERSONAL PRONOUNS

	Singular	Plural
First person		
Subjective	I	we
Possessive	my, mine	our, ours
Objective	me	us
Second person		
Subjective	you	your
Possessive	your, yours	your, yours
Objective	you	you
Third person (masculine)		
Subjective	he	they
Possessive	his	their, theirs
Objective	him	them
(feminine)		
Subjective	she	they
Possessive	her, hers	their, theirs
Objective	her	them
(neuter — no gender [neither masculine nor feminine]).		
Subjective	it	they
Possessive	its	their, theirs
Objective	it	them

Pronouns such as *I, me,* and *our* refer to the first person and point out the person speaking.

Pronouns such as *you* and *your* refer to the second person or the person spoken to.

Pronouns such as *he, she, it, they,* and *them* refer to the third person or thing or the person or thing spoken about.

e. The relative pronoun *who* is the only one of the relative pronouns (*who, which, that, what*) that changes its form based on how it is used in a sentence.

RELATIVE PRONOUNS

	Singular	Plural
Subjective	who	who
Possessive	whose	whose
Objective	whom	whom

Practice A. Circle the correct pronoun for each sentence.

1. Although the apartment is lovely, (it/their) is too small for my family.

2. Neither Frank nor Seth had received (his/their) grades yet.

3. My uncle and my father finished (his/their) work.

4. Everybody is working on (his/their) English theme.

5. The children asked (his/their) mother if (he/they) could go to the movies.

6. Neither Carol nor Sharon had eaten (her/their) dinner.

7. Each person must decide for (himself/theirselves) what (he/they) wishes to do with (his/their) life.

8. The two girls told (her/their) teacher that (she/they) couldn't go on the class trip.

9. Nobody is able to predict what (his/their) life has in store for (him/them).

10. The crowd as one cheered on (its/their) favorite opponent.

Check answers at the end of Lesson 8.

Practice B. Complete each sentence by inserting the correct pronoun in each blank.

1. All of my friends obtained _____ driving licenses.

2. Not one person I know had _____ own car.

3. Neither of our friends owned _____ own home.

4. Some wild animals will breed only in _____ natural environment.

5. The hunters lost _____ way.

6. Pie and ice cream made _____ own special place in my heart.

7. Jennifer asked _____ mother if _____ could spend the night at _____ friend's house.

8. Not everyone takes such good care of _____ plants and pets.

9. Not one person in our driver education class failed _____ driving test.

10. The students said that _____ needed more time to finish _____ class project.

Check answers at the end of Lesson 8.

Practice C. In the following sentences, if the sentence is correct, put a *C* in the blank. If the sentence is not correct, rewrite it correctly. (Check verbs as well as pronouns.)

1. Not one of us are going to change their mind concerning that.

_____

2. Everybody knew what they was supposed to say.

_____

3. Although Mary worked her way through school, she was not prepared for the hard life that awaited her.

_____

4. If you see anybody whom I know, tell them "hello" for me.

_____

5. Neither Jim nor Carlos are doing what they are expected to do.

_____

6. Each of the studies is evaluated on their own merits.

_____

7. Everyone must determine their own career goals.

_____

8. Every day has its own special excitement.

_____

9. In the fall the trees are decked out in their finest colors.

_____

10. My plants do poorly here because the summers are too hot for it.

_____

Check answers at the end of Lesson 8.

Punctuation: Quotation Marks

1. A direct quotation is always enclosed in **quotation marks** (" "); there is a comma after *said*, and the first word of the quotation is capitalized. (A **direct quotation** gives a statement in the exact words that come, or would come, from a speaker. An **indirect quotation** merely gives the gist of what was, or might have been said. An *indirect* quotation is *not* enclosed in quotation marks.)   *Examples:* a) He said, "This is the best course that I've ever taken." b) She said, "I will take a course in botany next semester." (Indirect quotation: She said that she would take a course in botany next semester.)

SPECIAL NOTE

> Because an indirect quotation is not enclosed in quotation marks, it includes no internal marks of punctuation other than those required by the sentence of which it is a part. *Examples:* a) He asked who that person was. (a statement, not a question) b) Does she say that she can come with us? (a question, not a statement). c) They state in their defense, with some justice, that they were given poor instructions.

2. Separate sentences that follow one another and are part of the same speech should be enclosed in the same pair of quotation marks. *Example:* She replied, "I am having trouble with a course this semester. If I don't get help soon, I'll have to drop it."

3. Sentences that follow one another but are not part of the same speech should be enclosed in separate quotation marks. *Example:* The following statements were made at the meeting: "I wouldn't vote for her because she's too political." "I wouldn't vote for him because he's hypocritical." "I'm not voting for either one."

4. If the quotation comes before *he said* or *she said*, a comma usually separates the quotation from *he said* or *she said*, unless the quotation is a question or exclamation. *Examples:* a) "My God!" he exclaimed. b) "Who is that person?" she asked. c) "No, I can't go with you," he said.

5. If the words *she said* or *he said* occur in the middle of a quotation, *she said* or *he said* should not be included within the quotation marks. *Examples:* a) "If that's right," she said, "you can go." b) "If that is true," he said, "we are in trouble." (Notice that a comma usually follows *he said* or *she said*, and the rest of the sentence following *he said* or *she said* is enclosed in separate quotation marks and does not begin with a capital letter.)

6. If the quotation coming before *she said* or *he said* forms a complete sentence, a period should come after *she said* or *he said*. *Examples:* a) "I can't go with you," she said. "Go without me." b) "Who are you?" he asked. "I don't know you." (Notice that the sentence following *he said* or *she said* is enclosed in separate quotation marks and begins with a capital letter.)

7. If the expression *she said* or *he said* comes in the middle of a question or exclamation, the exclamation mark or question mark is placed at the end of the quotation. *Examples:* a) "How much will you make," he asked, "on your new job?" b) "That is so extraordinary," she exclaimed, "that I don't believe it!"

8. If omitted material designated by ellipsis (. . .) is part of the quotation, the ellipsis should be included within the quotation marks. *Example:* Abraham Lincoln said, "Fourscore and seven years ago our fathers . . ."

9. A quotation within a quotation is designated by single quotation marks. *Example:* The storyteller said, "The frightened man asked, 'Who are you?' However, there was no answer . . ."

10. When you use an author's exact words in your writing, the author's words should be enclosed in quotation marks. If the quote is a sentence that comes in the middle of your sentence and it fits into what you are writing,

the quote does not need a capital or a period. (Obviously, a period would be necessary if the quoted material came at the end of the sentence.)   *Examples:* a) The writer says that "in education we tend to turn out conformists," but he doesn't tell us how to change. b) Mark Twain writes with biting satire about politicians. My instructor agrees with Mark Twain that "a jay hasn't got any more principles than a Congressman."

11.   Titles of poems (except long poems such as epics), stories, articles, and chapters are put in quotation marks.   *Examples:* "The Colonel's Lady"; "Gerontion"; "Listening Skills."   Exception: *Paradise Lost.*

12.   Quotation marks are used when defining a word.   *Example:* *Pseudoscience* means "false science."

SPECIAL NOTES

a.   Periods and commas always should be placed within the quotation marks. *Examples:* a) "I can't last any longer," said Jack. "Please get help." b) The word *apodal* means "having no feet."

b.   Semicolons and colons always should be placed outside the quotation marks. *Example:* Ms. Smith said, "Never mind, I'll stay"; however, her boss didn't hear her.

c.   Question marks and exclamation marks may be placed inside or outside the quotation marks depending on whether they refer to the whole sentence or merely the quotation. *Examples:* a) John asked, "What do you want?" b) Did Hilda scream, "I need help"? (The question mark belongs to the whole sentence.)

Practice A. Insert quotation marks where they are needed. Put a *0* in front of those sentences that do not require quotation marks.

_____   1. He said that he was happy.

_____   2. How could you do that to me? he asked.

_____   3. The following remarks were overheard at an art show: I don't get it! Who are they kidding? Is that art?

_____   4. Classes begin early this semester, said Fran, but they end early too.

_____   5. She said, I'm taking difficult courses this year.

_____   6. We read Walt Whitman's poems O Captain! My Captain! and When Lilacs Last in the Dooryard Bloom'd.

_____   7. Are you sure, she asked, that you will drop out of the swimming team?

_____   8. Did you get the job you wanted? she asked.

_____   9. What did you say that was so important?

_____ 10. No, I'm not going with you, she said.

Check answers at the end of Lesson 8.

Practice B. Put in the correct punctuation and capitalization in the following sentences.

1. don't go said my brother because I am afraid

2. she asked how can that be

3. william blake's poem the tyger starts with very strong imagery said our professor

4. the line my heart leaps up when I behold . . . comes from william wordsworth's poem my heart leaps up

5. the man phoned and told me I am going to rob the bank next to your business said Mr. Thompson

6. Why have you decided to change your major asked my advisor

Check answers at the end of Lesson 8.

Spelling: Some Often Misspelled Words IV

Following, presented in sentences, are forty often misspelled words.

1. That is an *altogether* different problem.
2. They tried to do a thorough *analysis* of the problem.
3. Some persons have great *anxiety* before an exam.
4. The scientific *apparatus* that we have is very costly.
5. My *appetite* is a little too good.
6. *Arithmetic* is not difficult if you like to work with numbers.
7. Ms. Brown accepted the *apology* on behalf of the students.
8. My *bureau* drawer always seems to get stuck.
9. I don't like to listen to *coarse* language.
10. My uncle is a *colonel* in the army.
11. I write a *column* for the school paper.
12. Thank you for the *compliment.*
13. I try hard not to *criticize* anyone.
14. What kind of *device* is that?
15. He said that he was going to *devise* a plan that would solve a lot of our problems.
16. I *doubt* if that is going to work.
17. That cost is *exorbitant.*
18. Please *excuse* his behavior.
19. A person in the audience tried to *harass* the speaker.
20. Ms. Johnson is one of our *indispensible* people.
21. We feel that their behavior was *outrageous.*
22. The *maintenance* on my car is too costly.
23. I earn my *livelihood* from selling.

24. The *professor*'s best seller gained him a lot of unwanted *notoriety* because of some very *explicit* sex scenes that he described in his book.
25. Some *pollutants accidentally* got into the *reservoir*.
26. I like balance or *symmetry* in paintings.
27. *Tuesday* is always my hardest day.
28. The *villain* in the movie was *severely* punished.
29. I use personalized *stationery* when I write a friendly letter.
30. The soliders were *stationary* for a long time.
31. When *lightning* struck, we were by a tree.
32. I believe that the statement you made is *irrelevant* to the argument.
33. Although the suspect had the *opportunity* to commit the crime, she did not have a motive.
34. That is an *ingenious* plan.
35. Some persons have to *sacrifice* many things to go to college.

Practice A. Look at each word carefully. Cover the word. Write the covered word in the blank. Check to see if you have spelled it correctly.

1. altogether _____

2. analysis _____

3. anxiety _____

4. apparatus _____

5. appetite _____

6. arithmetic _____

7. apology _____

8. bureau _____

9. coarse _____

10. colonel _____

11. column _____

12. compliment _____

13. criticize _____

14. device _____

15. devise _____

16. doubt _____

17. exorbitant _____

18. excuse _____

19. harass _____

20. indispensible _____

21. outrageous _____

22. maintenance _____

23. livelihood _____

24. professor _____

25. notoriety _____

26. explicit _____

27. pollutants _____

28. accidentally _____

29. reservoir _____

30. symmetry _____

31. Tuesday _____

32. villain _____

33. severely _____

34. stationery _____

35. stationary _____

36. lightning _____

37. irrelevant _____

38. opportunity _____

39. ingenious _____

40. sacrifice _____

You should have checked the spelling immediately after writing each word.

Practice B. Look at each word carefully. If the word is spelled correctly, put a *C* in the blank. If the word is not spelled correctly, spell it correctly. (Sentences are given for words that can be confused with others.)

1. alltogether _____

2. analyzis _____

3. anxiety _____

4. aparatus _____

5. apettite _____

6. arithmatic _____

7. apology _____

8. bureau _____

9. coarse _____

10. colnel _____

11. column _____

12. compliment _____

13. criticise _____

14. The *device* he used to fool us was very clever. _____

15. I will try to *device* a formula that will help us. _____

16. doubt _____

17. exoribitant _____

18. excuse _____

19. harrass _____

20. indispencible _____

21. outragous _____

22. maintenance _____

23. livlihood _____

24. profesor _____

25. notority _____

26. explisit _____

27. polutants _____

28. acidently _____

29. resevoir _____

30. symmetry _____

31. Tuesday _____

32. villain _____

33. severly _____

34. I have personalized *stationary*. _____

35. I can't remain *stationery* for too long. _____

36. lightening _____

37. irevelant _____

38. opportunity _____

39. ingenious _____

40. sacrafice _____

Check answers at the end of Lesson 8.

LESSON 8 ANSWERS

Combining Sentence Patterns to Form
Compound Sentences (pp. 103–105)

Practice A: (sample answers)   1. At the circus the clown stood on his head; it was a funny sight to see.   2. My friend tried to sit on the fat lady's lap; it was a funny sight to see.   3. We stuffed ourselves with peanuts and popcorn, but we felt good.   4. We stuffed ourselves with peanuts and popcorn, but we were not too full for dinner.   5. We stuffed ourselves with peanuts and popcorn; it was fun being a child again.   6. The elephant squirted water on us; we were startled.   7. One of the horses jumped out of the ring; we were startled.   8. One of the horses jumped out of the ring; it was a funny sight to see.   9. The price of admission has certainly risen, but it's cheaper than a psychiatrist.   10. The price of admission has certainly risen, but it was fun being a child again.   11. At the end of the day we were exhausted, but we felt good.   12. At the end of the day we were exhausted, yet none of us wanted to go home.

Practice B: (sample answers)   1. Fuel prices are rising, and we are paying them.   2. Inflation has decreased the value of the dollar, and it has increased the value of gold.   3. I work twice as much; but I get half as much for my money.   4. We consider the fuel prices a holdup, but we can't do anything about it.   5. Everyone is complaining about high prices, but no one is doing anything about them.   6. My whole family works; however, we can't save any money.   7. A single wage-earner has a difficult time, but I'm not getting married.   8. Wages keep going up, and prices keep going up.   9. Tuition costs increase each year, and all other costs increase also.   10. I am an optimist; however, it's not easy to be one today.

Practice C: (sample sentences)   1. Money is necessary to live, but other things are more important for me.   2. My friends want wealth; however, I want other things.   3. My friends are materialistic; I'm a dreamer.

Word Usage: Pronouns and Their Antecedents (pp. 105–111)

Practice A: 1. it   2. his   3. their   4. his   5. their, they   6. her   7. himself, he, his   8. their, they   9. his, him   10. its.

Practice B: 1. their   2. his or her   3. his or her   4. their   5. their   6. their   7. her, she, her   8. his or her   9. his or her   10. they, their.

Practice C: 1. Not one of us is going to change his mind concerning that.   2. Everybody knew what he was supposed to say.   3. C   4. If you see anybody whom I know, tell him "hello" for me.   5. Neither Jim nor Carlos is doing what he is expected to do.   6. Each of the studies is evaluated on its own merits.   7. Everyone must determine his or her own career goals.   8. C   9. C   10. My plants do poorly here because the summers are too hot for them.

Punctuation: Quotation Marks (pp. 111–114)

Practice A: 1. 0 2. "How could you do that to me?" he asked. 3. "I don't get it!" "Who are they kidding?" "Is that art?" 4. "Classes begin early this semester," said Fran, "but they end early, too." 5. She said, "I'm taking difficult courses this year." 6. "O Captain! My Captain!" and "When Lilacs Last in the Dooryard Bloom'd." 7. "Are you sure," she asked, "that you will drop out of the swimming team?" 8. "Did you get the job you wanted?" she asked. 9. 0 10. "No, I'm not going with you," she said.

Practice B: 1. "Don't go," said my brother, "because I am afraid." 2. She asked, "How can that be?" 3. "William Blake's poem 'The Tyger' starts with very strong imagery," said our professor. 4. The line "My heart leaps up when I behold . . ." comes from William Wordsworth's poem "My Heart Leaps Up." 5. "The man phoned and told me, 'I am going to rob the bank next to your business,'" said Mr. Thompson. 6. "Why have you decided to change your major?" asked my advisor.

Spelling: Some Often Misspelled Words IV (pp. 114–117)

Practice A: Check words on the page for correct spelling.

Practice B: 1. altogether 2. analysis 3. C 4. apparatus 5. appetite 6. arithmetic 7. C 8. C 9. C 10. colonel 11. C 12. C 13. criticize 14. C 15. devise 16. C 17. exorbitant 18. C 19. harass 20. indispensible 21. outrageous 22. C 23. livelihood 24. professor 25. notoriety 26. explicit 27. pollutants 28. accidentally 29. reservoir 30. C 31. C 32. C 33. severely 34. stationery 35. stationary 36. lightning 37. irrelevant 38. C 39. C 40. sacrifice

UNIT II REVIEW CROSSWORD PUZZLE

Directions: Your knowledge of the material presented in Lessons 4–8 will help you solve this crossword puzzle.

Across:

1. Past tense of <u>is</u>
4. Abbreviation of <u>South Carolina</u>
6. A neuter pronoun
8. An infant wears this
10. A poetic exclamation
11. Punctuation mark used to replace *and* in a series.
12. Signals a noun
13. Same as #10 Across
14. More than one
16. Units equal to 5280 feet
18. A boy's nickname
20. Make believe
22. Personal pronoun

Down:

1. Very small
2. Signals a noun
3. <u>Yes</u> in Spanish
4. <u>Jack and Herb rushed to their farm in the middle of the night</u> is a(n)_____ sentence.
5. A European fabric of silk and wool
7. Two thousand pounds
8. Perform
9. A comma or period signals a(n) _____
11. A(n)_____ sentence contains two or more simple sentences

23. A conjunction often used to connect simple sentences to form a compound sentence.
24. The objective case of a personal pronoun
25. Brought an action against
27. Abbreviation of humidity
28. A conjunction often used to connect two simple sentences to form a compound sentence
29. Clever
32. Double
33. A dangerous insecticide
34. Used with an apostrophe to form the contraction of will
35. A linking word
36. An exclamation
38. A punctuation mark
42. A subject must agree with its _____
43. This is found on a subjective test
44. A prefix meaning back, again

Check answers on this page.

12. A beverage
15. A conjunction often used to connect simple sentences to form a compound sentence
17. Go, is, and run are _____ verbs
19. This helps you lose weight
21. A homonym of know
24. Be urged to
25. Same as #3 Down
26. You do this to cards
27. A greeting
28. An incompletely opened flower
30. An abbreviation of National League
31. Scents
35. Homonym of sea
36. Abbreviation of audiovisual
37. Masculine pronoun
39. A linking verb
40. Used to row a boat
41. To impart new color to

UNIT II CROSSWORD PUZZLE ANSWERS

WORD PUZZLES

Word Puzzle 1

Here are clues to seven words. Each new word adds one letter and uses all the letters of the word preceding it. To form the new word you may rearrange the letters in any way.

1. a pronoun (one letter)

2. extremely fashionable (two letters)

3. to commit an offense (three letters)

4. a mathematical function of an angle in a right triangle (four letters)

5. a river in France (five letters)

6. relatives (six letters)

7. knowledge attained through study (seven letters)

Answers:

1. I 2. in 3. sin 4. sine 5. Seine 6. nieces 7. science

Word Puzzle 2

See how many of the riddles you can solve.

1. I'm a domesticated animal; take away one of my letters, and I'll have something to eat.

2. I mean "anger"; add one letter to me, and I'll become deep mud or sludge.

3. I mean "incline"; take away one of my letters, and I'll have the natural gait of a horse.

4. I mean "a mountain pass" or "a break in a barrier"; add one letter to me, and I'll yawn or gaze stupidly at you.

5. I get this when I'm cold; take away two letters, and I'll be sick.

Answers:

1. goat—oat 2. ire—mire 3. slope—lope 4. gap—gape 5. chill—ill

Word Puzzle 3

The answers for the following clues are two rhyming words.

1. stingy royalty

2. tardy companion

3. delicate twisted string

4. best hour

5. fragile bird

6. false friend

7. head crook

8. counterfeit cash

9. good-looking horse

10. corpulent feline

Answers:

1. mean queen   2. late mate   3. fine twine   4. prime time   5. frail quail
6. phony crony   7. chief thief   8. funny money   9. fair mare   10. fat cat

REVIEW TEST 1

A. Underline all those in the following list that are simple sentences.

1. After ten years, I'm returning to school.

2. My best friend and my sister are getting married and moving to another state.

3. Some of my friends have left school to go to work.

4. My brother gets high grades without studying; I get poor grades, but I study a lot.

5. My brother and I have been on our own for a long time.

6. I live on campus, but my brother doesn't.

7. Stay where you are; help is on the way.

8. Falling in love is an occupational hazard for me.

9. Falling out of love is very painful, but I do it quite frequently.

10. My best friends, Mary and Beth, consider me a hopeless case, but I don't think so.

B. Follow the directions in parentheses for each of the following.

1. (Write a compound sentence using the coordinate conjunction *but*.)

_____

_____

2. (Write a compound sentence using the coordinate conjunction *and*.)

_____

3. (Write a compound sentence using the coordinate conjunction *or*.)

_____

4. (Write a compound sentence using the coordinate conjunction *for*.)

_____

5. (Write a compound sentence using the linking word *therefore*.)

_____

6. (Write a compound sentence using the linking word *however*.)

_____

7. (Write a compound sentence in which the simple sentences are connected by a semicolon without a linking word.)

_____

8. (Write a compound sentence which consists of two *different* sentence patterns.)

_____

9. (Write a compound sentence which consists of two sentence patterns that are similar.)

_____

10. (Write a compound sentence that consists of any two sentence patterns.)

_____

C. Here are ten sentences. Read each sentence carefully. If the sentence is correct, put a C in the blank. If the sentence is not correct, rewrite it correctly.

1. My parents have been married for twenty-seven years, they just got a divorce. _____

2. Not one of my friends has divorced parents, I'll be the first in my group.

_____

3. My parents were not happily married; but I didn't know it.

_____

4. My mother is going back to school, it'll be hard for her. _____

_____

5. My mother has been out of school for over twenty-seven years, but she's determined, so I think she'll make it. _____

_____

6. My mother is a hard-working, determined, and intelligent lady. _____

_____

7. My father is confused, for he lived with her for so long, yet he didn't understand her. _____

_____

8. My father doesn't understand himself either, he wants to relive his youth.

_____

_____

9. I always wanted to be older; my father always wanted to be younger.

_____

10. Our parents' divorce made us feel sad, we didn't want our comfortable world shattered. _____

_____

REVIEW TEST 2: A TRUE/FALSE TEST

Directions: This is a true/false test on Lessons 5–8. Read each sentence carefully. Decide whether it is true or false. Put a T for true or an F for false in the blank.

_____ 1. *Absense* is spelled correctly.

_____ 2. When the conjunctions *and, or, but,* or *for* join simple sentences, no punctuation mark is ever needed.

_____ 3. A comma is the least often used punctuation mark.

_____ 4. A colon is used after a formal heading.

_____ 5. *But* and *yet* are used for contrast.

_____ 6. *Alot* is one word.

_____ 7. All collective nouns take plural verbs.

_____ 8. *Economics* is a word that requires a singular verb.

_____ 9. *Scissors* is a word that requires a plural verb.

_____ 10. A singular subject with a plural modifier requires a plural verb.

_____ 11. A nonrestrictive phrase is set off with commas.

_____ 12. Restrictive modifiers give additional information.

_____ 13. In the sentence *My sister Jane is pretty*, Jane is not the only sister.

_____ 14. A comma should be used to separate the compound predicate of a simple sentence.

_____ 15. Prepositions are words that show a connection between a noun or pronoun and another word in the sentence.

_____ 16. A prepositional phrase is usually composed of a preposition and a verb.

_____ 17. *Around the corner* is a prepositional phrase.

_____ 18. Prepositional phrases are only used as adjectives because they can only modify nouns.

_____ 19. *Exagerate* is spelled correctly.

_____ 20. The word *none* can only be singular.

_____ 21. A sentence with both a negative and a positive subject always has a plural verb.

_____ 22. The name of a play used as the subject of a sentence requires a singular verb.

_____ 23. The subject *War and Peace* requires a plural verb.

_____ 24. A pronoun connected with *and* and another pronoun requires a singular verb.

_____ 25. A pronoun with two or more singular antecedents connected by *or* or *nor* is singular.

Complex Sentences
Word Usage: Adjectives
Punctuation: More Uses of the Comma
Spelling: Positive and Comparative Degrees of Adjectives
Answers to Practices

Lesson 9

Complex Sentences

1. A **complex sentence** is made up of one simple sentence and one or more groups of words that cannot stand alone as sentences.

2. In order to understand a complex sentence you must be familiar with the terms **independent clause** and **dependent clause**. A **clause** is a group of words that contains both a subject and a predicate.

a. A clause that makes an independent statement is called an independent clause. An independent clause may also be referred to as a **main** or **principal clause**. An independent clause can stand alone as a simple sentence because it expresses a complete thought. *Example:* The guest speaker arrived late, but we greeted him warmly. (*The guest speaker arrived late* is an independent clause, *we greeted him warmly* is also an independent clause.)

b. A clause that is not by itself complete in meaning is called a **dependent clause**. A dependent clause may also be referred to as a **subordinate clause**. A dependent clause cannot stand alone as a sentence because it does not express a complete thought. *Example:* Since there isn't much time left, I need to spend the rest of the week working on my psychology paper. (*Since there isn't much time left* is a dependent clause; *I need to spend the rest of the week working on my psychology paper* is an independent clause.) *More Examples of Complex Sentences:* (a) Although John is a good athlete, he does not spend too much time in sports. (b) Since that happened a long time ago, when she was very young, I wouldn't hold it against her. (c) When the conductor appeared on the stage, the audience applauded loudly. *Analysis of examples:* (a) Independent clause—*he does not spend too much time in sports*; dependent clause—*Although John is a good athlete.* (b) Independent clause—*I wouldn't hold it against her*; dependent clauses—*Since that happened a long time ago; when she was very young.* (c) Independent clause—*the audience applauded loudly*; dependent clause—*When the conductor appeared on the stage.*

3. Linking words that connect **dependent clauses** (groups of words that cannot stand alone as sentences) with their **independent clauses** (groups of words that can stand alone as sentences) to form complex sentences are called **subordinate** (dependent) **conjunctions**. The most often used subordinate conjunctions are as follows: *although, as, because, before, if, since, that, unless, until, after, as if, as though, as soon as, in order that, even if,* and *so that.* *Examples:* Although he said that he was not angry, he left immediately. Jane will not walk again unless the operation is a success.

Subordinate conjunctions are used to show more involved relations than coordinate conjunctions. Coordinate conjunctions such as *and, but, or,* and *for* are used to connect two independent clauses to form a compound sentence.

4. Other words such as *where, when,* and *while* often function as subordinate conjunctions. *Examples:* They didn't say *where they were going. When you see Joe,* tell him I can't attend the meeting. *While I am in charge,* no one will be treated badly.

5. Pronouns such as *who, which, that,* and *what* also function as subordinate conjunctions to relate a dependent or subordinate clause to its main or principal clause. *Examples:* I don't understand the problem *that we did in class.* The students *who are in my philosophy class* are all majoring in it.

SPECIAL NOTES

a. Subordinate conjunctions introduce dependent clauses. The dependent clauses that are introduced by a subordinate conjunction cannot stand alone as sentences even though they contain a subject and a verb. They are only sentence fragments, because they do not express complete thoughts. *Examples:* When he arrived; Although I may go; Before I speak; Because the dance was fun; Since the hour is near.

b. The words *when* and *where* are not always subordinate conjunctions used to introduce a dependent clause. These words can begin a question sentence when they are at the beginning of the sentence. *Examples:* When are you going? Where are you going?

Practice A. Put an *S* in front of the following that are simple sentences, a *C* in front of those that are compound sentences, an *X* in front of those that are complex sentences, and a *0* in front of those that are not sentences.

_____ 1. Help me!

_____ 2. The moon seemed to be beaming at me.

_____ 3. Although Joan and Laura are my best friends, they sometimes get on my nerves.

_____ 4. I think that John should be commended because he works so hard to support his family.

_____ 5. Let's go.

_____ 6. The rain has stopped, and we are ready to go now.

_____ 7. Adults spend the most time in listening and speaking.

_____ 8. Elementary school children spend about 58 per cent of their time in listening while high school students spend about 90 per cent of their time in listening.

_____ 9. The telephone rang for an extremely long time, but no one answered it.

_____10. They completed the work on time, but they did not get any recognition for it.

Check answers at the end of Lesson 9.

Practice B.   Choose the phrase that makes the sentence a complex one.

_____ 1. Sharon went (*a.* to the football game, and then she went to the party; *b.* to the party as soon as she left the football game; *c.* to the football game and to the party).

_____ 2. The twins found the windows open (*a.* when they came home; *b.* and the door open; *c.* , and they found the door open, too).

_____ 3. The bell was (*a.* ringing; *b.* ringing, and in a moment everyone left the building; *c.* the signal that alerted everyone).

_____ 4. We often get (*a.* up early; *b.* up early when we are on a trip; *c.* up early and eat breakfast early).

_____ 5. It's (*a.* fun to play and do nothing all day; *b.* fun to play when you want to; *c.* fun to play, but it's not fun to play all the time).

Check answers at the end of Lesson 9.

Practice C.   Following are groups of sentences. Choose a subordinate conjunction from the list that follows and combine the sentences in each group into a single complex sentence (a sentence having one independent clause and one or more dependent clauses). Subordinate conjunctions: *although, as, because, before, if, since, that, unless, as if, as though, as soon as, in order that, even if, so that, while, after.*

1. The man uses a cane. The man walks slowly.

_____

_____

2. The policeman stopped the car. It was going too fast.

_____

_____

3. The children are poor. They are hungry. They have no parents.

_____

_____

4. Children were playing in the park. They saw a large eagle.

_____

_____

5. The thief ran very fast. He was captured.

_____

_____

6. The wild dogs are hunted. They are killing sheep.

_____

_____

7. She screamed for help. The woman had been robbed.

_____

_____

8. Return on time. We have to attend a meeting.

_____

_____

9. You can do it. I will not go.

_____

_____

10. The plane crash was reported. The rescue teams departed immediately.

_____

_____

Check sample sentences at the end of Lesson 9.

Practice D. Write three complex sentences.

1._____

_____

2. _____

_____

3. _____

_____

Check sample sentences at the end of Lesson 9.

Word Usage: Adjectives

It is helpful to know something about **adjectives** and their forms so that you can use them correctly in writing.

1. An adjective describes or limits a noun or a pronoun. The more adjectives you use, the more specific you make the noun or pronoun you are describing. *Examples of adjectives that describe or limit: a good* friend; *the healthy* child; *an old* lady; *a big white* cat; *a funny old* hat; *two* students; *the first* game.

2. Sometimes a noun may have a group or pair of adjectives that follow it rather than come before it. *Examples:* The man, *limping and old,* looked in vain for a seat on the bus. My father, *loving, kind, and hardworking,* never missed a day of work in his life. The children, *frightened, hungry, and tired,* started to cry for their mother. My wool sweater, *itchy and rough,* irritated my delicate skin. The subway travelers, *rushing and harassed,* squeezed through the barely opened train doors.

3. The sentences presented as examples in paragraph 2 can be written with the group or pair of adjectives starting the sentence. If the group or pair of adjectives begins a sentence, the noun that it describes must immediately follow the descriptive words. *Examples: Limping and old,* the man looked in vain for a seat on the bus. *Loving, kind, and hardworking,* my father never missed a day of work in his life. *Frightened, hungry, and tired,* the children started to cry for their mother. *Itchy and rough,* my wool sweater irritated my delicate skin. *Rushing and harassed,* the subway travelers squeezed through the barely opened train doors.

SPECIAL NOTE

Adjectives arranged in a group or a pair are not broken up. They are presented as a unit and set off by commas.

4. Certain **suffixes** (endings added to words) signal that the word is an adjective. By adding these suffixes to nouns or verbs, you can change the words into adjectives. *Examples of some suffixes that signal an adjective:* -less, -ful, -ic, -y, -ous, -able, -ible, -al, -ive. *Examples of nouns and verbs changed into adjectives:*

truth — truthful	terror — terrible	beauty — beautiful
vision — visible	train — trainable	courage — courageous
sale — salable	fame — famous	communicate — communicative
ice — icy	frost — frosty	apprehension — apprehensive
dirt — dirty	athlete — athletic	music — musical
fear — fearless	sleep — sleepless	

SPECIAL NOTE

Endings such as *-ing* and *-ed* also may signal an adjective.

Practice A. Change the following words into adjectives. Some of the words can change into more than one adjective.

1. fear _____
2. home _____
3. help _____
4. rest _____
5. fright _____
6. pity _____
7. shame _____
8. tear _____
9. beauty _____
10. joy _____
11. cheer _____
12. itch _____
13. rose _____
14. fault _____
15. sleep _____
16. salt _____
17. hero _____
18. acid _____
19. patriot _____
20. courage _____
21. outrage _____
22. nerve _____
23. mystery _____
24. space _____
25. force _____
26. laugh _____
27. enjoy _____
28. agree _____
29. comfort _____
30. accept _____

Check answers at the end of Lesson 9.

Practice B. Change the following five words into adjectives using one of the suffixes given in this lesson. Then put each into a compound or complex sentence. State what the sentence is.

1. excite _____

_____

2. care _____

_____

3. option _____

_____

4. cat _____

_____

5. craft _____

_____

Check sample answers at the end of Lesson 9.

Practice C.   Write two sentences with a pair or group of adjectives following the noun.

1. _____

_____

2. _____

_____

Check sample sentences at the end of Lesson 9.

Practice D.   Write two sentences with a pair or group of adjectives coming before the noun.

1. _____

_____

2. _____

_____

Check sample sentences at the end of Lesson 9.

Punctuation: More Uses of the Comma

1.   A comma (,) is usually used before a coordinate conjunction (linking word) such as *and, for, or,* and *nor* when the coordinate conjunction joins independent clauses to form a compound sentence   *Examples:* My parents spend a lot of their hard-earned money on me, and now I want to make it up to them.   The dinner bell kept ringing, but no one responded to it.   We went to see our advisor, but he had left town for a week.   I like him but he doesn't like me.   (The comma may be omitted when the coordinate conjunction connects short independent clauses.)

SPECIAL NOTE

A comma is *not* used in a simple sentence to separate the compound predicate. *Examples:* They robbed their investors and then left the country.   It's difficult to set up a good schedule and still include all the courses you need.   The campus athletes jog and swim every day.

2. Commas are usually used to set off such words and phrases as *also, moreover, perhaps, therefore, besides, of course, nevertheless, likewise, however, I believe, I am sure, I think, for example,* and *to tell the truth.*   *Examples:* Nevertheless, it's a good idea. Of course, I think we should see more of the proposal before we decide. Also, take your books with you. However, I may decide to do it alone. Think, for example, what you can do with your experiences. She said, moreover, that she never wanted to see him again. We tried, nevertheless, to bring them together again. We felt, of course, that it was a waste of time.

SPECIAL NOTE

When such linking words as *perhaps, therefore, moreover, nevertheless, consequently,* and *however* are used to join independent clauses, a semicolon rather than a comma is used before the linking word.

3. Commas are used to set off modifiers that give *additional* information in a sentence or such information that is not necessary to the thought of the sentence. In other words, if the *additional* information were omitted from the sentence, the omission would not change the meaning of the sentence or deprive the sentence of sense. Modifiers that give additional information that is not required, are called **nonrestrictive modifiers**.   *Examples:* We visited England, my parents' birthplace, to learn more about our heritage. My old hat, which is faded and frayed, is my favorite. The long, tiring train ride, which seemed never to end, terminated in disaster for three people aboard it. Maria, my best friend, is my maid of honor. (*My parents' birthplace; which is faded and frayed; which seemed never to end;* and *my best friend* are not necessary information for the sentences. These groups of words can be omitted because they are merely giving additional information. As a result, the groups of words should be set off by commas.)

4. Commas are *not* used to set off modifiers that give essential information that is necessary for the thought of the sentence. If the essential information were omitted, the meaning or sense of the sentence would be changed. Modifiers that give necessary information are called **restrictive modifiers**.   *Examples:* Persons who are secret agents must be especially trained for their jobs. The man who looks a little sheepish is the one who threw the lighted cigarette in the wastebasket. The author Samual Clemens wrote many books under the pseudonym of Mark Twain. (*Who are secret agents; who looks a little sheepish;* and *Samual Clemens* are necessary for the meanings of the sentences. If these groups of words were omitted, the meanings of the sentences would change. In the first example, *who are secret agents* identifies those persons to be especially trained. *Who are secret agents* limits persons to a specific group. In the second example, *who looks a little sheepish* identifies the man who threw the lighted cigarette in the wastebasket. *Who looks a little sheepish* limits *man* to a specific person. In the third example, because *Samuel Clemens* limits the author to a specific one, it is essential information and requires no commas.)

SPECIAL NOTE

In the sentence *Jane, my friend, is very pretty*, the phrase *my friend* is set off with commas because it is additional information. However, in the sentence *My friend Jane is very pretty*, the word *Jane* is not set off with commas because *Jane* limits or restricts the noun *friend*. *Jane* tells you which friend is very pretty.

5. A comma is usually used after a dependent clause (a group of words that cannot stand alone as a sentence) when it comes before an independent clause in a complex sentence. *Examples:* When they arrived, we were prepared for them. Although she is good in sports, she does not like to practice too much. If she wants to marry him, we will not stand in her way.

6. A comma is used when a dependent clause follows an independent clause if the dependent clause is nonrestrictive (provides additional rather than essential information). *Examples:* She likes parties, while I prefer solitary walks. (*While I prefer* . . . cannot stand alone and is therefore a dependent clause. However, it does not add information that limits the statement *She likes parties.*) You ought to visit Stone Mountain, although it is a little out of your way. (Clauses introduced by *though* or *although* are always nonrestrictive.)

SPECIAL NOTE

A comma is not used between an independent clause and a following dependent one if the dependent clause is restrictive (provides information essential to the meaning of the independent clause). *Examples:* He should not go on hay rides if he's allergic to hay. (Clauses introduced by *if* are always restrictive. *If he's allergic to hay* restricts to a single reason why he should not go on hay rides.) Don't fan the fire while the meat is broiling over it. (*While* restricts the time of the main verb, *do not fan.*) Sally will not come unless the sun shines. (*Unless* . . . is a condition restricting the main clause.) Loosen the nuts so that the wheel turns freely. (*So that* . . . is a clause restricting the main clause to a specific purpose.) The wheel will spin freely on its axle, so that any misalignment will show clearly as a pronounced wobble. (In this example, the words *so that* introduce a dependent clause that describes a result of what is stated in the main clause. The result, however, imposes no restriction on the main clause — the wheel will spin freely, no matter what happens. The clause is therefore nonrestrictive and takes a comma.)

Practice A. Insert commas where needed in each sentence below. Put a *0* in front of those sentences that do not require a comma.

_____ 1. The work is hard and boring.

_____ 2. After the woman arrived the party became more lively.

_____ 3. Although I try not to spend a lot of money I always seem to spend too much.

_____ 4. Sharon went to college and then went to graduate school.

_____ 5. The work in graduate school was very demanding but I would not allow it to get the better of me.

_____ 6. Moreover I have a lot of will power and stamina.

_____ 7. Laura and Donna went to Europe and a month later toured the United States.

_____ 8. Indeed that is a splendid idea.

_____ 9. When some of the employees did not go out on strike there was tension between the striking and nonstriking workers.

_____ 10. When the fire alarm rang the firemen reached for their gear jumped on their trucks and rushed to the fire.

_____ 11. She dressed very quickly because she couldn't wait to get to the party.

_____ 12. The workers remained until they had completed the job.

_____ 13. She said however that she would remain at school another semester.

_____ 14. If I live at home this semester I can save enough money to go to Europe next summer.

_____ 15. The person who said that was very brave.

_____ 16. Furthermore any student who has no outstanding debts can receive a low-interest loan at our school.

_____ 17. We felt moreover that we could make a great amount of money on that deal.

_____ 18. Instructors who speak in a monotone put me to sleep.

_____ 19. Of course we will attend the party in honor of our well-liked and famous colleague.

_____ 20. Chairman Burns who is well known made a powerful speech opposing the other board members' positions.

_____ 21. All students who wish to take more than eighteen credits must obtain permission from their advisors.

_____ 22. Air travel which is fast and convenient is necessary to our way of life.

_____ 23. A person who always tells the truth is hard to find.

_____ 24. Our teacher who looked a little sheepish suddenly blew a large bubble of gum in front of the class.

_____ 25. My brother the big spender is always throwing his hard-earned money away.

_____ 26. We decided to enter the talent show although we had no chance of winning.

Check answers at the end of Lesson 9.

Spelling: Positive and Comparative Degrees of Adjectives

Many one- and two-syllable **adjectives** (words that describe or limit a noun or pronoun) change their spelling to show degree. **Degree** is a measure of how much. There are three degrees of adjectives. The first is called the **positive** degree, the second is called the **comparative** degree, and the third is called the **superlative** degree.

Positive Degree

The positive degree is the simplest and most commonly used form of an adjective. It does not involve any comparison. *Examples:* John is a *tall* man. The *frightened* women called the police. The *large* rock tumbled off the cliff.

Comparative Degree

1. The comparative degree of an adjective is used to show a difference of quantity, quality, or manner between two and only two persons, animals, places, ideas, or things. *Examples:* John is *taller* than Jim. This rock is *larger* than the other one. Helen is *older* than Susan.

2. To show that something is more than something or someone else, *-er* is usually added to the end of most one- and many two-syllable adjectives. *Examples:* nicer, taller, shorter, larger, bigger.

3. Longer adjectives (adjectives of more than two syllables) and many adjectives ending in *-ive, -ful,* and *-ish* usually do not add *-er* to show degree. They show degree by placing the word *more* or *less* in front of the adjective. *Examples:* He is *more popular* than his brother. She is *more beautiful* than Mary. The crop is *more plentiful* this year than last year. The weather is *more delightful* today than it was yesterday. This problem is *less difficult* than the other one that I did. Our house is *more expensive* than the Brown's house. Jane is *more prudish* than Joyce.

4. A few adjectives change their spelling to form the comparatives. *Examples:*

Positive	*Comparative*
bad	worse
good	better
many	more
much	more
far	farther or further
little	less or littler
old	older or elder

SPECIAL NOTE

Adjectives ending in -*y* preceded by a consonant change the *y* to *i* before adding the ending -*er*.   *Examples:* early — earlier; busy — busier; sorry — sorrier.

Practice A.   Give the comparative for the following adjectives.

1. bad_____

2. good_____

3. pretty_____

4. much_____

5. small_____

6. little_____

7. difficult_____

8. expensive_____

9. thick_____

10. strong_____

11. many_____

12. happy_____

13. early_____

14. cheerful_____

15. important_____

16. funny_____

17. tiny_____

18. light_____

19. bright_____

20. heavy_____

Check answers at the end of Lesson 9.

Practice B. Put each of the following adjectives in a comparative form, and then use each in a complex sentence.

1. serious _____

_____

2. important _____

_____

3. intelligent _____

_____

4. ignorant _____

_____

5. playful _____

_____

Check sample answers at the end of Lesson 9.

LESSON 9 ANSWERS

Complex Sentences (pp. 129–132)

Practice A: 1. S 2. S 3. X 4. X 5. S 6. C 7. S 8. X 9. C 10. C

Practice B: 1. b 2. a 3. c 4. b 5. b

Practice C (sample sentences): 1. Because the man uses a cane, he walks slowly. 2. The policeman stopped the car because it was going too fast. 3. Because the children have no parents, they are poor and hungry. 4. While the children were playing in the park, they saw a large eagle. 5. Although the thief ran very fast, he was captured. 6. The wild dogs are hunted because they are killing sheep. 7. After the woman had been robbed, she screamed for help. 8. Return on time because we have to attend a meeting. 9. Unless you can do it, I will not go. 10. After the plane crash was reported, the rescue teams departed immediately.

Practice D (sample sentences): 1. I can't go with you because I have a lot of work to do. 2. When my parents found out about my situation, they tried to help me. 3. Although he has a lot of money, he is not very happy.

Word Usage: Adjectives (pp. 133–135)

Practice A: 1. fearful, fearless 2. homeless 3. helpless, helpful 4. restful, restless 5. frightful 6. pitiless, pitiful 7. shameless, shameful 8. tearless, tearful 9. beautiful 10. joyless, joyful 11. cheerful, cheerless 12. itchy 13. rosy 14. faultless, faulty 15. sleepy, sleepless 16. salty 17. heroic 18. acidic 19. patriotic 20. courageous 21. outrageous 22. nervous 23. mysterious 24. spacious 25. forcible, forceful 26. laughable 27. enjoyable 28. agreeable 29. comfortable 30. acceptable.

Practice B (sample answers): 1. (excitable) Because my mother is a very excitable woman, we try very hard not to excite her. (complex sentence) 2. (careless) Careless smokers have caused forest fires that have destroyed many lovely forests. (complex sentence) 3. (optional) Although the plan is an optional one, most persons seem to take it. (complex sentence) 4. (catty) I do not like catty people, for they are always saying things about other people behind their backs. (compound sentence) 5. (crafty) The crafty salesman was able to convince my friend to buy a new car, even though my friend did not need one. (complex sentence)

Practice C (sample sentences): 1. The young children, hopeful, eager, and curious, began their school careers. 2. The loser, tired and defeated, walked away.

Practice D (sample sentences): 1. Unhappy, broke, and disillusioned, the young actress decided to go home. 2. Deserted and dark, the street took on a menacing look.

Punctuation: More Uses of the Comma (pp. 135–139)

Practice A: 1. 0   2. After the women arrived,   3. Although I try not to spend a lot of money,   4. 0   5. The work in graduate school was very demanding,   6. Moreover,   7. 0   8. Indeed,   9. When some of the employees did not go out on strike,   10. When the fire alarm rang, the firemen reached for their gear, jumped on their trucks,   11. 0 12. 0 13. She said, however,   14. If I live at home this semester,   15. 0   16. Furthermore, 17. We felt, moreover,   18. 0   19. Of course,   20. Chairman Burns, who is well known,   21. 0   22. Air travel, which is fast and convenient,   23. 0 24. Our teacher, who looked a little sheepish,   25. My brother, the big spender,   26. We decided to enter the talent show, .

Spelling: Positive and Comparative Degrees of Adjectives (pp. 139–141)

Practice A: 1. worse   2. better   3. prettier   4. more   5. smaller 6. littler or less   7. more difficult, less difficult   8. more expensive, less expensive   9. thicker   10. stronger   11. more   12. happier   13. earlier 14. more cheerful, less cheerful   15. more important, less important 16. funnier   17. tinier   18. lighter   19. brighter   20. heavier.

Practice B (sample answers):   1. (more serious) Although he is more serious about his studies than I am, my grades are better than his.   2. (more important) Mr. Smith's job is more important than mine because he is responsible for more things than I am.   3. (more intelligent) As you are more intelligent than the other supervisor, the employees enjoy working with you. 4. (more ignorant) Because he is more ignorant than anyone I know, I ignore him.   5. (more playful) My dog is more playful than my cat because my dog is much younger than my cat.

Compound–Complex Sentences
Word Usage: Using Nouns, Pronouns, and Verbs As Adjectives
Punctuation: Comma Errors
Spelling: Superlative Degree of Adjectives
Answers to Practices

Lesson 10

Compound-Complex Sentences

A **compound-complex sentence** is made up of two or more independent clauses (groups of words that can stand alone as simple sentences) and one or more dependent clauses (groups of words that cannot stand alone as sentences). *Examples:* (*a*) When the train stopped abruptly, some people fell on other people, and some people landed on the floor. (*b*) The announcement was made, and, as the President entered, there was a great cheer.

Analysis of examples: (*a*) Independent clauses (those that can stand alone as simple sentences) — *some people fell on other people; some people landed on the floor*; dependent clause (cannot stand alone as a sentence) — *When the train stopped abruptly.* (*b*) Independent clauses — *the announcement was made; there was a great cheer*; dependent clause — *as the President entered.*

Practice A. Put an *S* in front of the following that are simple sentences, a *C* in front of those that are compound sentences, an *X* in front of those that are complex sentences, and a *CC* in front of those that are compound-complex sentences.

_____ 1. My mother bakes delicious apple pies and nut cakes.

_____ 2. Although Janet's parents are divorced, they are still friends.

_____ 3. Good readers are usually able to concentrate, but poor readers usually have difficulty in fixing their attention for long.

_____ 4. I made a lot of new friends while I was at college.

_____ 5. I usually eat a snack at 3:00 P.M.

_____ 6. After everyone had left, I sat down, and then the phone and the doorbell rang.

_____ 7. Whenever I feel sad, I choose a humorous book to read, but it never cheers me up.

_____ 8. Persons who have a good vocabulary and read a lot usually do well in school.

_____ 9. The Great Lakes, which are made up of five lakes, are at the north central border of the United States, and they look like an outline of a hand.

_____10. Whenever I go shopping for clothes, I like to take my brother with me because he knows so much about styles and fabrics.

Check answers at the end of Lesson 10.

Practice B. For each compound, complex, or compound-complex sentence in Practice A, state which clause is independent and which clause is dependent.

Check answers at the end of Lesson 10.

Practice C. Combine the following groups of sentences to make compound-complex sentences that make sense. You may change or add words in combining your sentences.

1. I enjoy English courses. I failed English 102.
   I received an *A* in all my math courses.

   _____

   _____

   _____

2. The workers went on strike. The factory owner refused to close the plant. The police tried to keep order.

   _____

   _____

   _____

3. He had to pay the fine. He would go to jail.
   He claimed that he was innocent.

   _____

   _____

   _____

4. Jennifer is the best actress. She has the lead in the play. Nobody resents it.

   _____

   _____

   _____

5. Many people wrote to their congressman to vote for a certain bill. The congressman did not vote for the bill. The bill passed anyway.

_____

_____

_____

6. The bank's burglar alarm went off. It alerted many people. The burglar was unaware that it had gone off.

_____

_____

_____

7. Vocabulary knowledge is necessary to be a good reader. Students should spend time in vocabulary development. Teachers should provide help in this area.

_____

_____

_____

8. The car went through a stop sign. The policeman flagged down the driver of the car. The driver refused to stop.

_____

_____

_____

9. Jim became ill at the party. We called a doctor. He is a good friend of the family. The doctor rushed Jim to the hospital.

_____

_____

_____

10. I have to work to pay for my college tuition. I don't have time for many social events. My friends make me go to the special activities.

_____

_____

_____

Check sample sentences at the end of Lesson 10.

Practice D. Write three compound-complex sentences.

1. _____

_____

2. _____

_____

3. _____

_____

Check sample sentences at the end of Lesson 10.

Practice E.   Read carefully the following synopsis of "The Lady Or The Tiger?" by Frank R. Stockton. Before each sentence is a number which refers to that sentence. In the space provided put an S if the sentence is a simple one, a C if the sentence is a compound one, an X if the sentence is a complex one, and a CC if the sentence is a compound-complex one.

Synopsis of "The Lady or the Tiger?" by Frank R. Stockton

[1] Many years ago a semi-barbaric king punished crime or meted out rewards by decrees of impartial chance. [2] When a subject was accused of a crime of sufficient importance to warrant the notice of the king, notice was given, and a day was appointed on which the fate of the accused would be determined. [3] All persons would gather on that day and assemble in the galleries, while the accused would be below in the king's amphitheater. [4] In front of the accused were two doors exactly alike and side by side. [5] The person on trial had to choose one. [6] Behind one door was a ferocious, hungry tiger who would spring on its victim and immediately devour him. [7] Behind the other door was a fair and beautiful maiden, who would then become the accused person's bride. [8] The king's daughter, unknown to the king, was in love with one of his courtiers. [9] When the king discovered this romance, he threw the handsome young man into prison, because no subject was allowed to love the princess. [10] The appointed day for the youth's trial came. [11] The princess, known also for her barbaric nature, sat next to her father. [12] She had learned the secret of the doors and knew that her father had chosen one of the fairest and loveliest of all maidens to wed the accused youth if he chose her door. [13] Her lover knew that she would learn the secret of the doors, and from the arena he looked at her. [14] The princess unnoticed by anyone but the youth raised her right hand. [15] The youth without hesitation opened the right-hand door.

Now the question is this: Did the tiger come out of that door, or did the lady?

1. _____   2. _____

3. _____   4. _____

5. _____   6. _____

7. _____   8. _____

9. _____   10. _____

11. _____   12. _____

13. _____   14. _____

15. _____

Check answers at the end of Lesson 10.

Word Usage: Using Nouns, Pronouns, and Verbs As Adjectives

1.   Sometimes nouns and pronouns are used to describe or limit a noun. *Examples of nouns describing or limiting other nouns: peach* tree; *maple* tree; *tea* kettle; *rose* garden; *study* hall; *wine* cellar; *typewriter* ribbon.   *Examples of pronouns describing or limiting other nouns: my* house; *his* brother; *our* friend; *this* skirt; *each* mother; *some* students; *these* teachers; *which* boys; *what* girls.

SPECIAL NOTES

a.   In *a pretty rose garden, a large peach tree, a copper tea kettle,* and *a black typewriter ribbon,* there is no comma after *pretty, large, copper,* or *black.* No comma is used because the adjectives *pretty, large, copper,* and *black* modify both nouns as a unit. *Rose garden, peach tree, tea kettle,* and *typewriter ribbon* are each a unit of a whole.

b.   A comma is used to separate the adjectives if the adjectives modifying the same noun are coordinate (equal). Coordinate adjectives can be separated by *and;* that is, the comma can be replaced by *and.*   *Examples:* a friendly, charming person — a friendly and charming person; a white, sturdy kitchen sink — a white and sturdy kitchen sink. Notice that you cannot say *a sturdy and kitchen sink* because *sturdy* modifies *kitchen sink* as a unit or whole. Also, you cannot say *kitchen and sink.* It would have an entirely different meaning.

c.   Nouns that act as adjectives do not have comparative and superlative degrees. That is, you cannot say *more* or *most* peach tree or *more* or *most* tea kettle.

2.   If *-ing* is added to a verb, it can act as an adjective.   *Examples:* the *running* man; the *crying* baby; the *talking* doll; the *sleeping* child; a *folding* chair; a *singing* kettle.

3.   If *-d, -n, -ed* or *-en* is added to some verbs, they can act as adjectives. *Examples:*   the *balanced* books; *pleased* persons; *satisfied* customers; *fallen* snow; *damaged* goods; *troubled* areas.

SPECIAL NOTES

a.   The present participle of regular and irregular verbs is formed by adding *-ing* to the verb.   *Examples:* running, walking, crying.

b.   The past participle of regular verbs is formed by adding *-d* or *-ed* to the verb. *Examples:* pleased, cleaned. The past participle of irregular verbs does not follow a regular pattern. *Examples:* sunk, swung, risen, set, seen.

c.   A participle may be used as a modifier as well as a verb. When a participle is used as an adjective, it modifies a noun.   *Examples:* broken toy, torn shirt, squeezed oranges, stopped clock, swinging gate, growing child.

Practice A.   Change the words in parentheses into adjectives.

1. the (break) chair _____

2. the (color) shirt _____

3. the (rust) beam _____

4. the (cry) child _____

5. the (run) dog _____

6. the (ache) arm _____

7. the (damage) goods _____

8. the (starve) children _____

9. the (tear) curtains _____

10. the (ring) bell _____

11. the (crack) lips _____

12. the (hide) money _____

13. the (clear) land _____

14. the (sing) bird _____

15. the (train) animals _____

Check answers at the end of Lesson 10.

Practice B.   Write a noun to act as an adjective for the given nouns.

1. _____ bracelet   2. _____ dish

3. _____ tree   4. _____ soup

5. _____ wagon   6. _____ music

7. _____ sink   8. _____ boiler

9. _____ stove   10. _____ cooler

11. _____ cocktail   12. _____ leaves

13. _____ house   14. _____ certificate

15. _____ hunt   16. _____ clock

17. _____ test   18. _____ teacher

19. _____ class   20. _____ player

Check sample answers at the end of Lesson 10.

Practice C.   Construct a sentence according to the directions in parentheses.

1. (Construct a compound-complex sentence using at least one verb and one pronoun as adjectives.)

_____

_____

2. (Construct a complex sentence using a noun and pronoun as adjectives.)

_____

_____

3. (Construct a simple sentence using a verb and noun as adjectives.)

_____

_____

4. (Construct a compound sentence using a verb and noun as adjectives.)

_____

_____

Check sample sentences at the end of Lesson 10.

Punctuation: Comma Errors

Although it is important to know when to use a comma, it is also important to know when *not* to use a comma. Following are examples of when *not* to use a comma.

1. Do not put a comma after *said* if there is no direct quotation. *Examples:* He said that she is very pretty. (indirect quotation) He said, "She is very pretty." (direct quotation)

2. Do not put a comma between a subject and verb. *Examples:* His great skill helped save the child's life. Her way of doing things is different.

3. Do not put a comma before the first item in a series or after the last member in a series. *Examples:* I love oranges, apples, and bananas. The courses that I like the best are geography, English, Spanish, and history. The roses, daffodils, tulips, and irises were wilted from lack of water.

The Run-On Sentence: A Comma Error

Some writers combine two sentences with only a comma and without a linking word to form one sentence. When this is done, the writers are making a run-on sentence error. *Examples:* The cab driver stopped, we all got into his cab. The Dean was disturbed about the incidence of vandalism, all the instructors and students were called together for a special meeting. Our football team is the best in the state, it wins all the games.

The preceding sentences can be corrected in the following ways:

a. Make them into two separate sentences ending with a period. *Examples:* The cab driver stopped. We all got into his cab. The Dean was disturbed about the incidence of vandalism. All the instructors and students were called together for a special meeting. Our football team is the best in the state. It wins all the games.

b. Connect them with a coordinate conjunction (linking word) such as *and, but, or* or *for* to make them compound sentences (combining independent clauses).   *Examples:* The cab driver stopped, and we all got into his cab. All the instructors and students were called together for a special meeting, for the Dean was disturbed about the incidence of vandalism. Our football team is the best in the state, for it wins all the games.

    c. Connect them with a subordinate conjunction (linking word) such as *because, although, since, that,* and so on to make them complex sentences (combining one independent clause and one or more dependent clauses). *Examples:* When the cab driver stopped, we all got into his cab. All the instructors and students were called together for a special meeting because the Dean was disturbed about the incidence of vandalism. Our football team is the best in the state because it wins all the games.

    d. Connect them with a linking word such as *therefore, however,* or *nevertheless* to make them compound sentences (combining independent clauses).   *Examples:* The cab driver stopped; then we all got into his cab. The Dean was disturbed about the incidence of vandalism; therefore all the instructors and students were called together for a special meeting. Our football team is the best in the state; therefore it wins all the games.

    e. Connect them with a semicolon without a linking word to make them compound sentences (combining independent clauses).   *Examples:* The cab driver stopped; we all got into his cab. The Dean was disturbed about the incidence of vandalism; all the instructors and students were called together for a special meeting. Our football team is the best in the state; it wins all the games.

Practice A.   Following are ten run-on sentences. The letter in parentheses at the end of the sentence refers to one of the five methods given earlier for correcting run-on sentences. Correct the sentence according to the method represented by this letter (see paragraphs *a–e* above).

1. Afini did not want to remain, she took her hat and coat and left. (*e*)

_____

_____

2. Arthur is very clever with numbers, he makes a lot of money on the stock market. (*c*)

_____

_____

3. Florence is an excellent hostess, people enjoy going to her parties. (*d*)

_____

_____

4. Terry is the best player on our team, our team is lucky to have him. (*a*)

_____

_____

5. The train jumped the track, a lot of people were hurt. (c)

_____

_____

6. I am determined to lose ten pounds on this diet, the diet is not very appetizing. (a)

_____

_____

7. I was asked to the semiformal by Frank, I did not want to go with him. (b)

_____

_____

8. School was out, we all went for a snack. (e)

_____

_____

9. The house was recently painted, it needs a new paint job. (c)

_____

_____

10. The twins own a discotheque, it is a huge success. (b)

_____

_____

Check sample answers at the end of Lesson 10.

Practice B. In the following sentences, put a *C* in front of those that have no comma errors. Correct the comma errors in the other sentences.

_____ 1. She loves to, bake, cook, and sew.

_____ 2. He said that, they would go to the party.

_____ 3. "I can't go," said my friend.

_____ 4. The boys and girls, are very friendly.

_____ 5. She said that she would not go with us.

_____ 6. The child, was, tired, bored, and hungry.

_____ 7. Her apple pie, always wins a prize at the fair.

_____ 8. I enjoy walking, skiing, and swimming.

_____ 9. The semester break is almost over.

_____ 10. We said that we would have a party soon.

Check answers at the end of Lesson 10.

Spelling: Superlative Degree of Adjectives

1. The superlative degree is used only when making a comparison involving more than two people or things. The superlative degree shows that the adjective used to describe quality, quantity, or manner is at its extreme. *Examples:* She is the *tallest* girl in our class. He is the *best* student in our class. That is the *oldest* house in our neighborhood. Which is the *least attractive* picture here? She is the *most attractive* woman I have ever seen.

2. To show that something is the "most," *-est* is usually added to almost all one-syllable and many two-syllable adjectives. *Examples:* biggest, smallest, highest, brightest, prettiest, greatest, nicest, proudest.

3. Longer adjectives (adjectives of more than two syllables) and many adjectives ending in *-ive, -ful,* and *-ish* usually do not add *-est* to show the superlative degree. They show the superlative degree by placing the word *most* or *least* in front of the adjective. *Examples:* This sofa is the *least expensive* one here. She is the *least helpful* salesperson that I have ever met. He is the *most foolish* person that I know. My dog is the *most playful* animal that I have ever seen. That person must be the *most selfish* person in this city. He is the *most productive* person that I've ever met.

4. A few adjectives change their spelling to form the superlatives. *Examples:* bad — worst; good — best; many — most; much — most; far — farthest or furthest; little — least or littlest; old — oldest or eldest.

SPECIAL NOTES

a. Adjectives ending in *-y* preceded by a consonant change the *y* to *i* before adding the ending *-est*. *Examples:* early — earliest; pretty — prettiest; sorry — sorriest; busy — busiest; nosy — nosiest.

b. The comparative and superlative degrees cannot be used with adjectives that have **absolute meanings**. *Examples:* circular, round, square, dead, true, entire, equal, false, factual, immortal, unique, perfect, equal. For example, it wouldn't make sense to say that something is more round, or more square, or most true, or most dead. However, you could say that something is almost true, almost square, or nearly dead.

Practice A. Give the superlative for the following adjectives.

1. short _____

2. funny_____

3. bright _____

4. bad _____

5. little _____

6. humorous _____

7. expensive _____

8. difficult _____

9. terrible _____

10. straight _____

11. great _____

12. many _____

13. marvelous _____

14. tasteful _____

15. gorgeous _____

16. truthful _____

17. sinful _____

18. thin _____

19. tall _____

20. happy _____

Check answers at the end of Lesson 10.

Practice B. Put each of the following adjectives in a superlative form, and then use each in a compound or complex sentence.

1. good _____

_____

2. difficult _____

_____

3. intelligent _____

_____

4. happy _____

_____

5. terrible _____

_____

Check sample answers at the end of Lesson 10.

LESSON 10 ANSWERS

Compound-Complex Sentences (pp. 145–148)

Practice A: 1. S   2. X   3. C   4. X   5. S   6. CC   7. CC   8. X   9. CC   10. X.

Practice B: 2. complex sentence; independent clause—*they are still friends*; dependent clause—*Although Janet's parents are divorced*   3. compound sentence; independent clauses—*Good readers are usually able to concentrate; poor readers have difficulty fixing their attention for long*   4. complex sentence; independent clause—*I made a lot of new friends*; dependent clause—*while I was at college*   6. compound-complex sentence; independent clauses—*I sat down; then the phone and the doorbell rang*; dependent clause—*After everyone had left*   7. compound-complex sentence; independent clause—*I choose a humorous book to read; it never cheers me up*; dependent clause—*Whenever I feel sad*   8. complex sentence; independent clause—*Persons usually do well in school*; dependent clause—*who have a good vocabulary and read a lot*   9. compound-complex sentence; independent clauses—*The Great Lakes are at the north central border of the United States; they look like an outline of a hand*; dependent clause—*which are made up of five lakes*   10. Complex sentence; independent clause—*I like to take my brother with me*; dependent clauses—*Whenever I go shopping for clothes; because he knows so much about styles and fabrics.*

Practice C: (sample sentences)   1. Although I enjoy English courses, I failed English 102, but I received an *A* in all my math courses.   2. When the workers went on strike, the factory owner refused to close the plant, and the police tried to keep order.   3. Although he claimed that he was innocent, he had to pay the fine, or he would go to jail.   4. Because Jennifer is the best actress, she has the lead in the play, and nobody resents it.   5. Although many people wrote to their congressman to vote for a certain bill, he did not vote for it, but the bill passed anyway.   6. When the bank's burglar alarm went off, it alerted many people, but the burglar was unaware that it had gone off.   7. Because vocabulary knowledge is necessary to be a good reader, students should spend time in vocabulary development, and teachers should provide help in this area.   8. When the car went through a stop sign, the policeman flagged down the driver of the car, but the driver refused to stop.   9. When Jim became ill at the party, we called a doctor who is a good friend of the family, and the doctor rushed Jim to the hospital.   10. Because I have to work to pay for my college tuition, I don't have time for many social events, but my friends make me go to the special activities.

Practice D (sample sentences):   1. It was a beautiful summer day, and the flowers were all in bloom, when tragedy struck.   2. The school bell rang, and there was a deafening roar as the school children departed for their summer vacation.   3. Although he had made a bad mistake, which was very costly to the company, we forgave him, and the company did not fire him.

Practice E:

Synopsis of "The Lady or the Tiger?" by Frank R. Stockton

[1] Many years ago a semi-barbaric king punished crime or meted out rewards by decrees of impartial chance. [2] When a subject was accused of a crime of sufficient importance to warrant the notice of the king, notice was given, and a day was appointed on which the fate of the accused would be determined. [3] All persons would gather on that day and assemble in the galleries, while the accused would be below in the king's amphitheater. [4] In front of the accused were two doors exactly alike and side by side. [5] The person on trial had to choose one. [6] Behind one door was a ferocious, hungry tiger who would spring on its victim and immediately devour him. [7] Behind the other door was a fair and beautiful maiden, who would then become the accused person's bride. [8] The king's daughter, unknown to the king, was in love with one of his courtiers. [9] When the king discovered this romance, he threw the handsome young man into prison, because no subject was allowed to love the princess. [10] The appointed day for the youth's trial came. [11] The princess, known also for her barbaric nature, sat next to her father. [12] She had learned the secret of the doors and knew that her father had chosen one of the fairest and loveliest of all maidens to wed the accused youth if he chose her door. [13] Her lover knew that she would learn the secret of the doors, and from the arena he looked at her. [14] The princess unnoticed by anyone but the youth raised her right hand. [15] The youth without hesitation opened the right-hand door.

Now the question is this: Did the tiger come out of that door, or did the lady?

1. S   2. CC   3. X   4. S   5. S   6. X   7. X   8. S   9. X   10. S   11. S
12. X   13. CC   14. S   15. S

Word Usage: Using Nouns, Pronouns, and Verbs as Adjectives (pp. 149–151)

Practice A: 1. broken   2. colored   3. rusted   4. crying   5. running   6. aching   7. damaged   8. starved, starving   9. torn,   10. ringing   11. cracked   12. hidden   13. cleared   14. singing   15. trained.

Practice B: (sample answers):   1. charm   2. candy   3. oak, apple, pear, etc.   4. beef   5. station   6. chamber, rock   7. kitchen, bathroom   8. water   9. gas, kitchen   10. water   11. fruit, champagne   12. tea, oak, maple, etc.   13. tree, ranch   14. treasury   15. treasure, egg   16. grandfather   17. arithmetic   18. gym   19. history   20. tennis.

Practice C (sample sentences):   1. My cracked and hurting lips were swollen, and my tongue was dry and filled with blisters when I was ill.   2. Although our ranch house is not new, it is in excellent condition.   3. We will have to throw this broken tea bag away.   4. The leading test question was not difficult, but all the other questions were very hard.

Punctuation: Comma Errors (pp. 151–153)

Practice A (sample answers):   1. Afini did not want to remain; she took her hat and coat and left.   2. Because Arthur is very clever with numbers, he makes a lot of money on the stockmarket.   3. Florence is an excellent hostess; therefore people enjoy going to her parties.   4. Terry is the best player on our team. Our team is lucky to have him.   5. A lot of people were hurt when the train jumped the track.   6. I am determined to lose ten pounds on this diet. The diet is not very appetizing.   7. I was asked to the semiformal by Frank, but I did not want to go with him.   8. School was out; we all went for a snack. 9. Although the house was recently painted, it needs a new paint job.   10. The twins own a discotheque, and it is a huge success.

Practice B: 1. She loves to bake, cook, and sew.   2. He said that they would go to the party.   3. C   4. The boys and girls are very friendly.   5. C 6. The child was tired, bored, and hungry.   7. Her apple pie always wins a prize at the fair. 8. C 9. C 10. C.

Spelling: Superlative Degree of Adjectives (pp. 154–155)

Practice A: 1. shortest   2. funniest   3. brightest   4. worst   5. least, littlest,   6. most humorous, least humorous   7. most expensive, least expensive   8. most difficult, least difficult   9. most terrible, least terrible 10. straightest   11. greatest   12. most   13. most marvelous, least marvelous 14. most tasteful, least tasteful   15. most gorgeous, least gorgeous   16. most truthful, least truthful   17. most sinful, least sinful   18. thinnest   19. tallest 20. happiest

Practice B (sample answers):   1. (best) Last May was the best month of my life because I met my fiance then.   2. (most difficult) Although I find math courses the most difficult of all my courses, I enjoy the challenge that they give me.   3. (most intelligent) He is the most intelligent person I have ever met, but he is not very friendly or cheerful.   4. (happiest) This is one of the happiest days of my life because I am graduating today.   5. (most terrible) That was the most terrible accident that I have ever seen.

Sentence Combining and Parallel Construction
Word Usage: Adverbs
Punctuation: The Dash
Spelling: Possessives I
Answers to Practices

Lesson 11

Sentence Combining and Parallel Construction

Good writers often balance their simple sentences with longer and more involved ones. You have been learning to combine sentences throughout this book. This lesson will give you more practice in sentence combining.

1. In writing sentences, you must decide which ideas are the more important ones and which are the less important ones. The less important ideas are subordinate to (dependent on) the more important ones. Your more important ideas are presented in your independent or principal clause, and your less important ideas are presented in your subordinate or dependent clause. Subordinate ideas are often introduced by such words as *although, as, because, if, since, until,* and *after.*

2. If the ideas that you wish to present are of equal importance, then you will have two or more independent clauses, using coordinate (equal) conjunctions such as *and, but, or,* or *for* to link your clauses.

3. There are many ways to express the same or nearly the same idea. Only you can determine the exact meaning that you want. However, you should try to present ideas as clearly as possible. Knowledge of parallel construction helps you do this. Let's combine the following three sentences:

Students enjoy dances.
Students enjoy parties.
Students enjoy concerts.
Students enjoy dances, parties, and concerts.

The combined sentence is a parallel one. By this, we mean that the elements that have been combined are all identical in importance; nouns should be joined only with nouns, adjectives only with adjectives, and adverbs only

159

with adverbs. In the example, the nouns *dances, parties,* and *concerts* are linked together with the coordinate conjunction *and.* (You learned in Lesson 5 that coordinate conjunctions combine sentence elements that are equal or have the same importance.)

4. Parallel construction may involve a series of words, such as nouns, verbs, adjectives, or adverbs, or a series of clauses or phrases.

5. The coordinate conjunctions (linking words that show an equal relation between or among things) such as *and, but,* and *or,* as well as the correlative conjunctions (linking words that show a one-to-one necessary relation between two sets of things) such as *either . . . or, neither . . . nor, not only . . . but also, on the one hand . . . on the other hand,* and *the one . . . the other,* are used in constructing parallel sentences.

Following are examples of sentences with parallel construction. Notice how you can show differences and similarities with such sentences: The men *worked hard, drank hard, and played hard.* I can eat neither *fatty foods* nor *sweets.* I feel *that college is worthwhile, that it helps you meet many people, that it prepares you for a profession,* and *that it helps you gain a broader education.* She said that she would go to either *France* or *Spain* this summer. Scuba diving is *dangerous* and *costly* but *thrilling.* The police looked for the criminal *in the vacant house, in the swampland,* and *in the woods beyond the swampland.* He said *that he would help me with my problem* but *that he would not tell me what to do.*

SPECIAL NOTE

Any sentence that uses coordinate conjunctions is a parallel sentence. However, the most common parallel sentences consist of a *series* (a group of three or more things or events) of nouns, verbs, adjectives, adverbs, phrases, or clauses.

6. The following are examples of various ways that sentences can be combined or joined together. *Examples:* (a) Carlos is athletic. Carlos is intelligent. *Carlos is athletic and intelligent.* (simple sentence) (b) Juanita likes rock music. Juanita likes classical music. *Juanita likes rock music and classical music.* (simple sentence) *Although Juanita likes rock music, she also likes classical music.* (complex sentence) (c) I studied astronomy. I studied physiology. I studied geology. *I studied astronomy, physiology, and geology.* (simple sentence) (d) The deer fled from the hunters. The hunters continued to pursue them. *The deer fled from the hunters, but the hunters continued to pursue them.* (compound sentence) (e) The finals were very difficult. We passed all of them. *Although the finals were very difficult, we passed all of them.* (complex sentence) *The finals were very difficult, but we passed all of them.* (compound sentence) *Although we passed all of them, the finals were very difficult.* (complex sentence) *The finals were very difficult; nevertheless, we passed all of them.* (compound sentence) (f) Jim came to school on crutches. He had a broken leg. *Jim came to school on crutches because he had a broken leg.* (complex sentence) *Although he had a broken leg, Jim came to school on crutches.* (complex sentence) *Jim came to school*

on crutches when he had a broken leg. (complex sentence) (g) Anthony developed laryngitis on the night of the big debate. Anthony is our best debater. *Anthony, our best debater, developed laryngitis on the night of the big debate.* (simple sentence) *Anthony, who is our best debater, developed laryngitis on the night of the big debate.* (complex sentence) (h) Jack is a hunter. His brother, Herb, is a trapper. They both went to pursue the elusive Big Foot. *Jack, a hunter, and his brother, Herb, a trapper, went to pursue the elusive Big Foot.* (simple sentence) *Jack, who is a hunter, and his brother Herb, who is a trapper, went to pursue the elusive Big Foot.* (complex sentence) (i) We went shopping. We went to a movie. We went out to supper. *We went shopping, to a movie, and out to supper.* (simple sentence) *First we went shopping and to a movie, and then we went out to supper.* (compound sentence) *After we went shopping and to a movie, we went out to supper.* (complex sentence) (j) The man is sitting over there. He is unhappy. He is depressed. He is looking for a job. He can't find one. *The unhappy, depressed man who is sitting over there is looking for a job, but he can't find one.* (compound-complex sentence) *The man sitting over there is unhappy and depressed because he is looking for a job, but he can't find one.* (compound-complex sentence)

Practice A. Combine each set of sentences so that the combination fits one of the examples given in paragraph 6. You may change or add words in combining your sentences to fit a given example. Some of the sentences can be combined in more than one way.

1. The man was sad. The man was limping. The man was robbed.

_____

_____

2. They went swimming. They went hiking. They went picnicking.

_____

_____

3. The dog barks. The dog bites. The dog is vicious.

_____

_____

4. The sailor is tall. The sailor is thin. The sailor has a red beard.

_____

_____

5. Parties are fun. Dances are fun. Picnics are fun.

_____

_____

6. Mary Johnson is a good singer. She has had difficulty finding a job.

_____

_____

7. They were accepted as counselors at the summer camp. They are very young.

_____

_____

8. The sun was shining. It was raining.

_____

_____

9. I prefer warm climates. My boyfriend prefers cold climates.

_____

_____

10. The sailor was short and stocky. He had a wooden leg. He became involved in a fight with some men.

_____

_____

_____

11. Sharon is going away to school. Terry is going away to school. Donna is going away to school.

_____

_____

_____

12. The Smiths are married. They have a daughter. Her name is Jennifer. Jennifer is very pretty.

_____

_____

_____

13. The pioneers were told that the journey would be dangerous. They decided to go. They worked hard to prepare for their trip. The trip would be long. The trip would claim many lives.

_____

_____

_____

14. Robert is a basketball player. He is seven feet tall. His height is an asset to him rather than a liability.

_____

_____

_____

15. The man was mean. He was angry. He wore shabby clothes. He had a patch over one eye. He was an escaped murderer. He was dangerous.

_____

_____

_____

_____

Check sample answers at the end of Lesson 11.

Practice B. Write five sentences that have parallel construction. The phrase in parentheses after each number tells you what kind of series the sentence should have.

1. (noun series)

_____

_____

2. (verb series)

_____

_____

3. (clause series)

_____

_____

_____

4. (phrase series)

_____

_____

5. (clause series)

_____

_____

_____

Check sample answers at the end of Lesson 11.

Word Usage: Adverbs

Adverbs generally tell *how, when, where,* and *how much.*   *Examples:* The boats sailed *slowly.* (how) The race started *immediately.* (when) We stood *there.* (where) She typed the paper *very* carefully. (how much)

1. Adverbs usually describe or limit verbs.   *Examples:* The man ran swiftly.   She dances gracefully.

2. Adverbs can describe or limit an adjective (words that describe or limit nouns or pronouns) or another adverb.   *Examples:* She is a *very* pretty girl. (*Very* describes the adjective *pretty.*) He works *very* hard. (*Very* describes the adverb *hard.*) We looked at her *carefully* manicured hands. (*Carefully* describes the adjective *manicured.*) She has *softly* appealing eyes. (*Softly* describes the adjective *appealing.*) He is a *really* clever person. (*Really* describes the adjective *clever.* Note that the adverb is *really,* not *real.*)

SPECIAL NOTE

The adverbs *very, rather, quite, too,* and *somewhat* are used to describe other adverbs or adjectives. They qualify the intensity (strength or force) of the adverb or adjective.   *Examples:* He worked *rather* hard. He worked *quite* hard. He worked *very* hard. She is *rather* nice. She is *quite* nice. She is *very* nice.

3. A number of adverbs end in *-ly.*   *Examples:* He left *quietly.* She spoke *softly.* The children shouted *noisily.* The girl spoke *happily.* The dog growled *fiercely.*

SPECIAL NOTES

a. You must be careful because some adjectives also end in *-ly.*   *Examples:* friendly dog, stately mansion, kindly person.

b. There are some adverbs with both *-ly* and non *-ly* endings: slow — slowly; high — highly; deep — deeply; loud — loudly; cheap — cheaply.   *Examples:* He studied his subject *deeply.* She dove *deep* into the pool.

4. Following are some adverbs that do not end in *-ly: then, soon, often, later, afterward, just, below, now, sometimes, always, never, seldom, still, today, yesterday, tomorrow, here, there, well, almost, not, so, ever, somewhat, rather, quite, very, too.*   *Examples:* I will see you *tomorrow.* He is *always* late. She is *never* on time. He is *too* tired. We *almost* made it. The sun is shining *below.* It started to storm *quite* suddenly.

5. Adverbs, like adjectives, have degrees of comparison. The comparison of adverbs is formed in the same way that comparisons of adjectives are formed.

Examples:

Positive	Comparative	Superlative
hard	harder	hardest
early	earlier	earliest
well	better	best
proudly	more proudly, less proudly	most proudly, least proudly
often	oftener	oftenest

SPECIAL NOTE

6. Conjunctive adverbs are used both as modifiers and linking words. They function as both adverbs and conjunctions.   *Examples of conjunctive adverbs: accordingly, consequently, however, therefore, furthermore, so, then, nevertheless, besides, moreover.* Conjunctive adverbs are used to connect two independent clauses and thus to form compound sentences. The conjunctive adverb that connects two independent clauses modifies the second clause as a whole and connects it with the preceding one.   *Example:* We went to so much trouble to obtain this position for your brother; nevertheless, he is not happy.

SPECIAL NOTES

a. The conjunctive adverb is usually preceded by a semicolon and sometimes followed by a comma.

b. The conjunctive adverb is generally placed at the beginning of the second clause, but it sometimes may be located further on in the clause. In that case the two clauses are connected with a semicolon, and the conjunctive adverb is usually set off with commas. *Example:* We went to so much trouble to obtain this position for your brother; he is, nevertheless, not happy.

7. Words such as *also, indeed, however, nevertheless, therefore, consequently, then, so, moreover,* and so on are usually called adverbs rather than conjunctive adverbs when they do not link two independent clauses to form a compound sentence. The adverbs such as *also, however, therefore,* and so on, are used as transition words to connect the ideas of one sentence to those of another. They are usually set off by commas. However, if words such as *also, however, therefore,* and so on do not require a pause in reading, commas are omitted.   *Examples:* She will, *however,* go. She will go, *however. However,* she will go. *Also,* they can go. They can *also* go. (The placement of the adverb in the sentence is determined by the meaning that you wish to convey.)

SPECIAL NOTE

If an adverb such as *consequently, however, also,* or *therefore* is placed at the beginning of the sentence, it modifies the sentence as a whole and gives special emphasis to it.

Practice A.   Change each of the following adjectives into adverbs.

1. sure _____   2. real _____

3. good _____   4. noisy _____

5. rude _____   6. cheerful _____

7. angry _____   8. easy _____

9. critical _____   10. beautiful _____

11. quiet _____   12. clear _____

13. happy _____   14. swift _____

15. steady _____

Check answers at the end of Lesson 11.

Practice B.   Fill in each blank with an adverb.

1. She is a(n) _____ charming lady.

2. He performed _____ .

3. This is the _____ difficult task of all.

4. She is arriving _____ .

5. I've eaten the _____ that I ever have.

6. He ran _____ .

7. That is a(n) _____ good show.

8. She dances very _____ .

9. Speak _____ because the baby is asleep.

10. She sings the _____ .

11. She speaks _____ than her brother.

12. The men worked _____ .

13. He drives _____ fast.

14. Drink more _____ .

15. Her _____ quiet manner frightened us.

Check sample answers at the end of Lesson 11.

Practice C.   Write a sentence using an adverb according to the directions in parentheses.

1. (Construct a sentence with an adverb describing a verb.)

_____

_____

2. (Construct a sentence with an adverb describing another adverb.)

_____

_____

3. (Construct a sentence with an adverb describing an adjective.)

_____

_____

4. (Construct a sentence with a conjunctive adverb.)

_____

_____

Check sample answers at the end of Lesson 11.

Practice D.   Fill in each blank with *well* or *good.*

1. I am not feeling _____ .

2. That sounds _____ .

3. He rides _____ .

4. She looks _____ .

5. That feels _____ .

Check answers at the end of Lesson 11.

Practice E.   Write the comparative and superlative for each of the given adverbs.

1. surely_____   _____

2. friendly_____   _____

3. carefully_____   _____

4. much _____   _____

5. long_____   _____

6. well _____   _____

7. happily_____   _____

8. quietly_____   _____

9. beautifully_____   _____

10. gladly_____   _____

Check answers at the end of Lesson 11.

Punctuation: The Dash

The **dash** (–) is used to indicate some kind of break. If the dash is not overused, it is effective in writing. Following are some uses of the dash:

1. Used to show an abrupt shift in thought.   *Examples:* Oh, yes, let's go—but wait, what did you say? Did I tell you about Jane—well, let's not discuss that now.

2. Used for suspense or emphasis.   *Examples:* All was quiet—too quiet. They heard a sound—a slight sound.

3. Used to summarize or rephrase part of a sentence that came before. *Examples:* She had good looks, charm, intelligence, and money—everything that one could ask for, but she was not happy. The room was filled with cobwebs, the furniture was rat-infested, and dirt covered the floor like a blanket—it was a gruesome sight.

4. Used in place of parentheses where parentheses would separate the information too much from the sense of the surrounding words.   *Examples:* The adjective—it describes or limits a noun or pronoun—can be used to expand sentences. The old houses—they were built during the 1700's—were in danger of being destroyed.

5. Used to show that a sentence is not finished.   *Examples:* It doesn't sound right, but if you think—   I don't know—

SPECIAL NOTES

a. The dash (—) is longer than a hyphen (-). Do not confuse the two. The hyphen is used between the syllables of a divided word or between the parts of some words. (In typing, the dash consists of two hyphens with no space between them and usually no spaces between the dash and the word on either side.)

b. The period is omitted when a sentence ends with a dash.

Practice A. Construct five sentences using the dash in five different ways.

1. _____

_____

2. _____

_____

3. _____

_____

4. _____

_____

5. _____

_____

Check sample sentences at the end of Lesson 11.

Spelling: Possessives I

1. When singular nouns or proper nouns show ownership, an apostrophe (') and *-s* are usually added to the nouns.   *Examples:* Sharon's hair is brown. The dog's tail started to wag when he saw his master. Mr. Brown's family is

away for the summer.   Mr. James's mother is my grandmother's friend. Charles's house is next to mine.   Mr. Jones's yard is filled with leaves.   The school press's editor is resigning.

SPECIAL NOTE

If a word ends in -s, do not cut off the s before adding the apostrophe and -s. Jame's and Charle's are incorrect forms of the possessive.   The correct forms to show ownership are James's and Charles's.

2. Most biblical and classical names form the singular possessive by adding the apostrophe and -s.   Examples: Mars's warning; Zeus's son. Exceptions: Jesus' followers; Moses' followers.

3.   To show ownership for plural nouns ending in -s or -es, an apostrophe is added after the -s.   Examples: our grandparents' house (the house of our grandparents); the curtains' texture (the texture of the curtains); the teachers' room (the room of the teachers); the books' pages (the pages of the books); the girls' clothing (the clothing of the girls); the pirates' treasure (the treasure of the pirates); the daisies' fragrance (the fragrance of the daisies); the Joneses' lawn (the lawn of the Joneses); the Burnses' party (the party of the Burnses); the geese's feathers (the feathers of the geese).

4.   To show ownership for plural nouns not ending in -s or -es, an apostrophe and -s are added.   Examples: the men's room (the room of the men); the children's toys (the toys of the children); the oxen's burden (the burden of the oxen); the women's club (the club of the women); the sheep's wool (the wool of the sheep); the firemen's equipment (the equipment of the firemen).

Practice A.   Form the singular possessive for the following words.

1. coat_____   2. man _____

3. baby_____   4. razor _____

5. chimney_____   6. candy_____

7. Mr. Martin _____   8. Mrs. Ross _____

9. prize_____   10. class _____

Check answers at the end of Lesson 11.

Practice B.   Form the plural possessive for the following words.

1. lady_____   2. child _____

3. man _____   4. candy_____

5. fox _____   6. friend_____

7. Ross _____   8. class _____

9. mouse _____   10. fly_____

11. cargo _____   12. hero_____

13. tomato _____   14. piano_____

15. knife _____   16. box_____

17. glass _____   18. chief_____

19. ox _____   20. sheep_____

Check answers at the end of Lesson 11.

Practice C. Read each sentence carefully. If the sentence is written correctly, put a *C* in the blank. If the sentence is not written correctly, correct any possessive form errors in the sentence.

1. Ms.' Perry wanted to borrow Ms.' Porters' typewriter.

_____

2. My roommates' mother is not feeling well.

_____

3. The foxes tail was caught in a trap.

_____

4. The hostess's dress was a pale blue.

_____

5. Jone's lawn always looks green.

_____

6. "That's an old wives' tale," said Mrs. Charles.

_____

7. Mrs. Charles' daughter refused to attend our meeting.

_____

8. The piano's tone did not sound very true.

_____

9. Because the potato's color looked peculiar, we didn't eat them.

_____

10. The Davises house is decorated beautifully.

_____

Check answers at the end of Lesson 11.

LESSON 11 ANSWERS

Sentence Combining and Parallel Construction (pp. 159–163)

Practice A (sample answers):   1. The man, sad and limping, was robbed. The sad, limping man was robbed.   2. They went swimming, hiking, and picnicking.   First they went swimming and hiking, and then they went picnicking.   3. The vicious dog barks and bites. The dog, which is vicious, barks and bites.   4. The tall thin sailor has a red beard. The sailor, who has a red beard, is tall and thin.   5. Parties, dances, and picnics are fun.   6. Mary Johnson, a good singer, has had difficulty finding a job.   7. Although they are very young, they were accepted as counselors at the summer camp.   8. Although the sun was shining, it was raining. The sun was shining, but it was raining. It was raining while the sun was shining.   9. I prefer warm climates, but my boyfriend prefers cold climates.   10. The short stocky sailor, who had a wooden leg, became involved in a fight with some men.   11. Sharon, Terry, and Donna are going away to school.   12. The Smiths, who are married, have a daughter named Jennifer, who is very pretty.   13. Although the pioneers were told that the journey would be dangerous, they decided to go; so they worked hard to prepare for their long trip, which would claim many lives.   14. Because Robert, who is seven feet tall, is a basketball player, his height is an asset to him rather than a liability. Robert, a basketball player, is seven feet tall, and his height is an asset to him rather than a liability.   15. The mean, angry man in shabby clothes, who had a patch over one eye, was dangerous because he was an escaped murderer. Because the mean, angry man, who had a patch over one eye and was in shabby clothes, was an escaped murderer, he was dangerous. The escaped murderer, who had a patch over one eye, was a mean, angry, dangerous man in shabby clothes.

Practice B (sample answers):   1. Weeds, trees, grass, and moss are all plants.   2. Every morning we jog, walk, or bicycle to class.   3. The minister said in his sermon that man tries, that man is optimistic, and that man is basically good, but that sometimes man needs help.   4. Lincoln believed in government of the people, for the people, and by the people.   5. The police were told that a dangerous animal had escaped from the zoo, that it had frightened a number of people, and that it had attacked a number of others.

Word Usage: Adverbs (pp. 163–167)

Practice A: 1. surely   2. really   3. well   4. noisily   5. rudely   6. cheerfully   7. angrily   8. easily   9. critically   10. beautifully   11. quietly   12. clearly   13. happily   14. swiftly   15. steadily.

Practice B (sample answers):   1. very   2. well, nicely, excellently, and so on   3. most   4. late, early, tomorrow, tonight, and so on   5. most   6. swiftly, quickly, slowly, peculiarly, and so on   7. very, astoundingly, unusually, and so on   8. well, nicely, professionally, and so on   9. quietly, softly   10. nicest, loudest, best, and so on   11. better, more, clearer, and so on   12. hard, slowly, fast   13. very, quite   14. quietly, slowly, quickly   15. very, unusually, suddenly.

Practice C (sample answers):   1. The children played *nicely* together. I eat *slowly*.   2. The students studied *exceedingly* hard for their biology test. The basketball player jumped *exceptionally* high.   3. After the show was over, we had a *very* delicious snack at a nearby restaurant. The *astonishingly* good snack was *most* inexpensive.   4. I knew that the operation was dangerous; *nevertheless,* I decided to go ahead with it.

Practice D: 1. well 2. good 3. well 4. good 5. good.

Practice E: 1. more surely, less surely; most surely, least surely 2. more friendly, less friendly; most friendly, least friendly 3. more carefully, less carefully; most carefully, least carefully 4. more, most 5. longer, longest 6. better, best   7. more happily, less happily; most happily, least happily 8. more quietly, less quietly; most quietly, least quietly 9. more beautifully, less beautifully; most beautifully, least beautifully   10. more gladly, less gladly; most gladly, least gladly.

Punctuation: The Dash (pp. 167–168)

Practice A (sample sentences):   1. "My God, how could you—" (unfinished sentence) 2. The quarterback—an unusually domineering and aggressive fellow—called the signals and directed the offensive play. (used in place of parentheses) 3. The footsteps kept coming closer—still closer. (suspense) 4. Her beauty, sensitivity, and charm—all were captured in the portrait. (a summarizing)   5. I'd love to go with you—but let's not talk about that now. (abrupt shift in thought)

Spelling: Possessives I (pp. 168–170)

Practice A: 1. coat's 2. man's 3. baby's 4. razor's 5. chimney's 6. candy's 7. Mr. Martin's 8. Mrs. Ross's 9. prize's 10. class's.

Practice B: 1. ladies' 2. children's 3. men's 4. candies' 5. foxes' 6. friends'   7. Rosses'   8. classes' 9. mice's 10. flies' 11. cargoes' 12. heroes' 13. tomatoes' 14. pianos' 15. knives' 16. boxes' 17. glasses' 18. chiefs' 19. oxen's 20. sheep's.

Practice C: 1. *Ms.* Perry wanted to borrow *Ms. Porter's* typewriter. 2. My *roommate's* mother is not feeling well.   3. The *fox's* tail was caught in a trap.   4. C 5. *Jones's* lawn always looks green. 6. C 7. Mrs. *Charles's* daughter refused to attend our meeting.   8. C   9. Because the *potatoes'* color looked peculiar, we didn't eat them. 10. The *Davises'* house is decorated beautifully.

UNIT III

Lesson 12

Sentence Variety

Variety in sentence structure usually helps to make writing more interesting. Good writers generally use a mixture of simple, compound, complex, and compound-complex sentences; they usually vary their sentence patterns; they use short as well as long sentences; and they use different types of sentences; that is, they use question sentences, statement sentences, command sentences, as well as exclamatory sentences.

SPECIAL NOTE

Some writers may purposefully use the same sentence structure to achieve a certain effect, balance, or parallelism.

Here are some suggestions that should help give variety to your sentences.

1. Try to use a mixture of simple, compound, complex, and compound-complex sentences rather than all of the same type.
2. Try to vary the beginning of each of your sentences.
3. Try to avoid beginning each sentence with the subject.
4. Try to avoid the overuse of linking words.
5. Try to avoid the use of the same linking words.

6. Try to put your most important point at the end of the sentence.

7. Try to vary your sentence length.

8. Try to vary your sentence patterns.

9. Try to use a mixture of question, statement, exclamatory, and command sentences.

Compare the following two paragraphs which are written about the same thing. Which do you find more interesting to read? In the space provided state which one you feel is better written, and give reasons for your choice. Check your answers with those provided.

a. I was confined in the Birmingham city jail. There, I came across your recent statement calling my present activities "unwise and untimely." I do not have the time to answer all the criticisms that cross my desk. However, I do want to answer your statement patiently and reasonably.

b. While confined here in the Birmingham city jail, I came across your recent statement calling my activities "unwise and untimely." Seldom do I pause to answer criticism of my work and ideas. If I sought to answer all the criticisms that cross my desk, my secretaries would have little time for anything other than such correspondence in the course of the day, and I would have no time for constructive work. But since I feel that you are men of genuine good will and that your criticisms are sincerely put forth, I want to try to answer your statement in what I hope will be patient and reasonable terms.*

Answers:

1. Paragraph b is more interesting to read for the following reasons:
   a. There is more variety in sentence introductions.
   b. The subject is not used at the beginning of each sentence.
   c. There is a variety of sentence patterns.
   d. There is a greater variety of sentence types.
   e. There is a variety of sentence lengths.

* From *Why We Can't Wait* by Martin Luther King, Jr. New York: The New American Library, Inc., 1963.

Practice A. Read each of the following paragraphs. Notice the sentence lengths, the sentence patterns, the sentence types, and so on. Rewrite the sentences in each paragraph so that they are more interesting to read. (Sentences may be combined.)

1. My brother is the oldest sibling in my family. He is continuously in trouble with the law. He has always been in some sort of trouble or another. My parents have never been able to control him. I'm afraid of him. My brothers and sisters are afraid of him. I think that my parents are afraid of him also.

2. School was out of the question. His father had just died. His mother was continuously complaining about money. She was continuously complaining about how hard she worked. She was bitter about the small amount of insurance she collected. Never once did she mourn for his father. He just wanted to pack up and get out.

3. My biology instructor is a hypochondriac. He comes to class late every class meeting. He does this on purpose. He doesn't want to mingle with any of the students. He uses a handkerchief to wipe the door knob before he opens it. He never walks around the room. If anyone coughs or sneezes, he avoids that person. He doesn't allow anyone to come up to talk to him. He makes us write any special or personal questions we may have. These questions are given to him at the end of the class period. He also replies in writing. He doesn't leave the classroom until after everyone has left. While we leave, he waits in a far corner of the room.

4. My friends and I just found out that our biology instructor is married. We can't believe it. We cannot imagine Mr. Hypochondriac with a wife. We feel she too must be a hypochondriac. We can just picture them living together. We see them eating at opposite ends of a twenty-foot table. We see them sleeping in separate beds that are rooms apart. We see them making love ten feet apart. We also see them writing notes to each other whenever they have colds.

Check sample paragraphs at the end of Lesson 12.

Practice B. Read this concluding paragraph from W. W. Jacobs's story "The Monkey's Paw." State how Jacobs achieves variety in his writing.

The knocking ceased suddenly, although the echoes of it were still in the house. He heard the chair drawn back and the door opened. A cold wind rushed up the staircase, and a loud wail of disappointment and misery from his wife gave him courage to run down to her side, and then to the gate beyond. The street lamp flickering opposite shone on a quiet and deserted road.

Check answers at the end of Lesson 12.

Practice C. Read this introductory sentence from Edgar Allan Poe's story "The Fall of the House of Usher." Explain why this sentence is so effective and the purpose it plays in the story.

> During the whole of a dull, dark, and soundless day in the autumn of the year, when the clouds hung oppressively low in the heavens, I had been passing alone, on horseback, through a singularly dreary tract of country; and at length found myself, as the shades of the evening drew on, within view of the melancholy House of Usher.

Check answers at the end of Lesson 12.

Word Usage: Troublesome Prepositions and Idioms

In the "Special Notes of Lesson 6, you learned about prepositions. You learned that prepositions are words such as *about, above, across, against, among, around, at, before, behind, below, beside, between, beyond, by, down, during, except, for, from, in, inside, into, like, near, of, off, on, out, over, since, through, to, reward, under, until, up, upon, within,* and *without.* You learned that some phrases such as *by the way of, because of, in spite of, on account of, in front of,* and *in place of* are also prepositions. You learned that a preposition shows the relation or connection between a noun or pronoun and another word in the sentence. A preposition is followed by a noun or pronoun to form a unit called a *prepositional phrase.* The prepositional phrase consists of the preposition, the noun or pronoun, and any word or words that describe the noun or pronoun. The noun or pronoun in the prepositional phrase is the object of the preposition. You also learned that prepositional phrases are used either as adjectives or adverbs, depending on whether they modify a noun or a verb.

In this lesson you will be concerned with the misuse of prepositions with idioms.

An **idiom** is defined as an expression peculiar to a people or to a district, community, or class. An idiom may not make sense if it is translated word for word, and it may also have a peculiar grammatical construction; however, idioms are expressions that have been long-established by usage or custom. Every language has its idioms, and English is no exception.

Many of the problems that persons have with idioms concern prepositions. The incorrect preposition with an idiom would change the meaning of the idiomatic expression. For example, *dying for* love is certainly different from *dying from* love, *sitting by* the couch is different from *sitting on* the couch, and *waiting for* a person is different from *waiting on* a person.

Many idioms require that certain prepositions follow. Here is a list of idiomatic phrases. Notice the preposition that follows each word. Notice also that the preposition combined with the word makes the idiom. In other words, the word without the preposition would not be an idiom. Here is a list of some commonly used idioms:

accompanied by	correspond to (a thing)
agree to (a proposal)	correspond with (a person)
agree in (principle)	compare to
agree on (a price)	compare with
agree with (a person)	different from
anxious for	identical with
anxious about	interested in
annoyed at	know that
accepted by	know whether
angry at (a thing)	listen to
angry about (a thing)	oblivious of
angry with (a person)	reverse of
argue for or against (something)	wait on
argue with (a person)	wait for
blame for	wait at
blame on	independent of
buy for	possessed by
buy from	superior to

SPECIAL NOTE

Do *not* use unnecessary prepositions. For example:

Correct	*Incorrect*
inside the house	inside of the house
off the road	off of the road
cannot help seeing	cannot help but see

Practice A. Read each of the following sentences carefully. Fill in the blank with the preposition that would correctly complete each of the following sentences.

1. As a salesperson, I have to wait _____ a great number of customers.

2. Please don't wait _____ me if I'm late.

3. If I'm late, wait _____ the same place we always do.

4. We were all very annoyed _____ what had taken place.

5. I am surprised to see that he is different _____ what I expected.

6. I've made a vow to be independent _____ everyone.

7. I can't agree _____ you.

8. I am very angry_____ what happened yesterday.

9. None of my friends will agree_____ that proposal.

10. Her ideas are identical _____ mine.

Check answers at the end of Lesson 12.

Practice B. Here are twenty words. Write a preposition in the blank to form an idiomatic expression.

1. interested_____   2. different_____

3. suitable_____   4. desirous_____

5. love_____   6. deserving_____

7. resentment_____   8. careful_____

9. able_____   10. disgusted_____

11. tired_____   12. hatred_____

13. borrow_____   14. afflicted_____

15. friendly_____   16. concentrate _____

17. pleased_____   18. relate _____

19. relevant_____   20. expected_____

Check answers at the end of Lesson 12.

Practice C. Write a sentence for each of the idiomatic expressions in parentheses.

1. (blame for) _____

_____

2. (free from) _____

_____

3. (adapt to) _____

_____

4. (argue against) _____

_____

5. (sympathize with) _____

_____

Check sample answers at the end of Lesson 12.

Practice D. Here are five sentences. Determine whether each of the sentences is correct. If the sentence is correct, write C in the blank. If the sentence is not correct, correct the sentence in the space provided.

1. Please get your dirty shoes off of the table. _____

_____

2. Among you and me, I believe that he will get what is coming to him.

_____

3. After waiting for more than a half of an hour outside of my advisor's office, I left. _____

_____

4. My parents live in Connecticut in Park Street. _____

_____

5. He is chairman for the Board of Trustees. _____

_____

Check answers at the end of Lesson 12.

Punctuation: Parentheses

1. Parentheses are generally used to enclose added material such as an explanation, a comment, or an elaboration of something in an already complete sentence. *Examples:* The battle decimated (destroyed a large part of) the troops. His boss (a typical Scrooge) is not known for his generosity to his fellow men.

2. Parentheses are used to enclose numbers, symbols, or sums that are repeated in the sentence.   *Examples:* Enclosed you will find the sum of five dollars ($5.00).   One hundred (100) people will attend the reception.   The dash (—) is used to show an abrupt change in the thought of a sentence.

3. Parentheses are used for reference purposes.   *Examples:* When you studied about the uses of the comma (see Unit II), you learned about their misuses also.   Review uses of the colon. (See Lesson 7.)

4. Parentheses are used when the writer inserts some loosely related material in the sentence.   *Example:* After raking leaves for hours (there must have been millions of leaves on my lawn), I was exhausted.

SPECIAL NOTES

a. Brackets [   ] are used to enclose your comments, explanations, word or words in material that is being reported or edited.   *Example:* The man [a poet] was more concerned with his spiritual being than with his bodily needs.

b. Sic (meaning *thus*) is inserted in brackets after a misspelled word in a quotation to show that the misspelled word has been noted by you, but the misspelled word is being left in because it belongs to the original quote.   *Example:* "The car swered [*sic*] and hit a tree."

Practice A. Here are five sentences. Determine whether brackets, parentheses, or the term *sic* should be used with the words in italics. Write your answer in the space provided.

1. The writer's exact words are: "My job is to report the truth, the *hole* truth, and nothing but the truth." _____

2. The reporter wrote about the life of Rev. Dr. Brown *a circus performer as well as a man of the cloth* and how he single-handedly captured five escaped criminals, using circus guile. _____

3. Enclosed you will find a check for twenty-five dollars *$25* to pay for my room reservation. _____

4. Last week, in our local newspaper, it was reported that Jim Brown *our local historian* had uncovered some important information about our town. _____

5. In the report John stated that "studies show that *infidelty* among married men and women is on the rise. _____

Check answers at the end of Lesson 12.

Practice B. Construct three sentences using parentheses in three different ways.

1._____

_____

_____

2._____

_____

_____

3._____

_____

_____

Check sample sentences at the end of Lesson 12.

Practice C. Construct one sentence using brackets and one sentence using the term *sic*.

1. _____

_____

2. _____

_____

Check sample sentences at the end of Lesson 12.

Spelling: Possessives II

1. The possessive form is usually added to the last word of a hyphenated compound word. *Examples:* mother-in-law's party; father-in-law's business; attorney-general's opinion; attorney-at-law's practice.

2. To show ownership by two or more persons, as a group, the last proper noun is put in the possessive. *Examples:* Carol and John's job; Sharon and Seth's house; Pueblo and Tonia's party; Jack and Herb's proceeds.

3. To show individual ownership, not group ownership, each proper noun is put in the possessive. *Examples:* Carol's and John's jobs are very important. (the possessing of separate jobs) Sharon's and Seth's houses are unique. (ownership of separate houses) Pueblo's and Tonia's parties are always fun. (separate parties) Jack's and Herb's proceeds from their businesses are very large every week. (Each person receives separate proceeds.)

4. Indefinite pronouns (pronouns that do not refer to anything definite and may not have a definite antecedent, for example, *any, each, all, some,* and so on), when combined with *body, one, other,* or *else,* add *-s* to form the possessive to show ownership. *Examples:* somebody's; anyone's; one's; no one's; each other's; nobody's; another's.

5. The pronouns *his, her, hers, yours, my, mine, our, ours, their, theirs, its,* and *whose* do not need an apostrophe to form the possessive to show ownership because they are in the possessive form already. *Examples:*

This is his coat. (This coat belongs to him.) Whose dresses are those? (To whom do those dresses belong?) They are ours. (They belong to us.) Has anyone seen our books? (Has anyone seen the books that belong to us?) She doesn't know whose pen that is. (She doesn't know to whom that pen belongs.) What is its name? (What name belongs to it? or What is the name of it?) Is it in its cage? (Is it in the cage that belongs to it?)

SPECIAL NOTE

Do not confuse the contractions *it's* (it is) and *who's* (who is or who has) with the possessive pronouns *its* and *whose*.   *Examples:* It's a lovely day. (It is a lovely day.) Who's in charge here? (Who is in charge here?) Who's been up to mischief? (Who has been up to mischief?) The insect is in its pupa stage. (The insect is in the pupa stage that is part of the natural course of insect development.) Whose uniforms are those? (To whom do those uniforms belong?)

Practice A. Put the following words into their possessive forms.

1. somebody _____

2. no one _____

3. one _____

4. brother-in-law _____

5. attorney-general _____

6. jack-o-lantern _____

7. anybody _____

8. each one _____

9. who _____

10. it _____

Check answers at the end of Lesson 12.

Practice B. Read each sentence carefully. If the sentence is written correctly, put a *C* in the blank. If the sentence is not written correctly, correct any possessive form errors in the sentence.

1. It's feathers are blue and green.

_____

2. Who's is it?

_____

3. My sisters-in-law's parties are usually dull.

_____

4. Aidas and Juarezs pictures are lovely.

_____

5. George's and Jim's room is very hot in the summer.

_____

6. The three attorneys-at-laws office is in my building.

_____

7. No ones coat is here.

_____

8. We went to her's party.

_____

9. This is our's.

_____

10. Mark said that he had used our's paper as well as anothers.

_____

Check answers at the end of Lesson 12.

LESSON 12 ANSWERS

Sentence Variety (pp. 173–177)

Practice A (sample paragraphs):

1. My brother, who is the oldest sibling in my family, is continuously in trouble with the law. It seems that he has always been in some sort of trouble or another, and my parents have never been able to control him. I'm afraid of him, and so are my brothers and sisters. I think that my parents are afraid of him also.

2. Now that his father had died, school was out of the question. All his mother ever did was complain about money and about how hard she worked. She was bitter about the small amount of insurance she collected, and never once did she mourn for his father. He just wanted to pack up and get out.

3. My biology instructor, who is a hypochondriac, comes to class late every class meeting. He does this on purpose because he does not want to mingle with any of the students. He uses a handkerchief to wipe the door knob before he opens it, and he never walks around the room. If anyone coughs or sneezes, he avoids that person; he doesn't allow anyone to come up to talk to him, and he makes us write any special or personal questions we may have. These questions are given to him at the end of the class period; he also applies in writing. Dr. Hypochondriac, who doesn't leave the classroom until after everyone has left, waits in the far corner of the room, while we leave.

4. When my friends and I found out that our biology professor was married, we couldn't believe it. We cannot imagine Mr. Hypochondriac with a wife. She, too must be a hypochondriac. Can you imagine them living together. They probably eat at opposite ends of a twenty-foot table, sleep in separate beds that are rooms apart, and make love ten feet apart. We also see them writing notes to each other whenever they have colds.

Practice B: 1. He uses a variety of sentence patterns.   2. He varies the beginnings of his sentences.   3. He varies his sentence lengths.   4. He uses different types of sentences.

Practice C: The sentence is very effective because it seems to set the stage for the rest of the story. The author's vivid description of an oppressive autumn day is carried over to the country in which he is traveling as well as to the House of Usher. The author's lengthy sentence as well as involved sentence structure also helps to portray a feeling of foreboding and gloom. By putting the most important point at the end of the sentence, the author is able to maintain suspense.

Word Usage: Troublesome Prepositions and Idioms (pp. 177–180)

Practice A: 1. on 2. for 3. at 4. at 5. from 6. of 7. with 8. about 9. to 10. with

Practice B: 1. in 2. from 3. for 4. of 5. of 6. of 7. against 8. of 9. to 10. with 11. of 12. of 13. from 14. with 15. with 16. on 17. with 18. to 19. to 20. of

Practice C: (sample answers) 1. I refuse to take the blame for something that I did not do. 2. I feel that everyone should be free from fear. 3. It is difficult for me to adapt to such primitive conditions. 4. My friend is going to argue against that proposal. 5. I can sympathize with you about that.

Practice D: 1. Please get your dirty shoes off the table. 2. Between you and me, I believe that he will get what is coming to him. 3. After waiting for more than a half hour outside my advisor's office, I left. 4. My parents live in Connecticut on Park Street. 5. He is chairman of the Board of Trustees.

Punctuation: Parentheses (pp. 180–182)

Practice A: 1. sic 2. parentheses 3. parentheses 4. brackets 5. sic

Practice B (sample sentences): 1. When you mark the papers, put a check (√) in front of all the correct answers and a cross (+) or an "ex" (x) in front of all the incorrect answers. (enclosing symbols) 2. My suite-mate at college is a very haughty (having great pride in oneself) person who is making my life miserable. (enclosing an added explanation) 3. After working for days on my English paper (I never want to look at another sheet of paper and pencil again), I finally finished it. (inserting loosely related material)

Practice C: (sample sentences) The writer said that his friend [the well-known comedian] would never appear on stage again. 2. "It seems peculiar that after all the trouble we went to, we will not be able to publich [sic] our report," said Mr. Brown in his statement to the press.

Spelling: Possessives II (pp. 182–184)

Practice A: 1. somebody's 2. no one's 3. one's 4. brother-in-law's 5. attorney-general's 6. jack-o-lantern's 7. anybody's 8. each one's 9. whose 10. its.

Practice B: 1. *Its* feathers are blue and green. 2. *Whose* is it? 3. C 4. *Aida's* and *Juarez's* pictures are lovely. 5. *George* and Jim's room is very hot in the summer. 6. The three *attorneys-at-law's* office is in my building. 7. *No one's* coat is here. 8. We went to *her party.* 9. This is *ours.* 10. Mark said that he had used *our* paper as well as *another's.*

UNIT III REVIEW CROSSWORD PUZZLE

Directions: Your knowledge of the material presented in Lessons 9–12 will help you to solve this crossword puzzle.

Across

1. To be fully aware of
7. A conjunction
8. An interjection
9. Said at wedding ceremonies
10. To enlarge
12. Used to form the plural of many words
13. Different from is a(n) _____
15. Abbreviation of certificate of deposit
17. Same as #12 Across
18. Abbreviation of evening
21. Abbreviation of Veterans Administration
22. An indefinite article
23. Abbreviation of Royal Academy
24. Used to indicate a misspelled word in a quote

Down:

1. An increase in wages
2. A period comes at the _____ of a sentence
3. Much_____about nothing
4. A personal pronoun
5. Aquarius is a sign of the _____
6. A prefix meaning out, forth, away
10. Happily, sadly, and very are examples of _____
11. Perform
13. Same as #4 Down
14. Independent clauses may also be called_____clauses
15. A person with marked mental deficiency
16. The_____is less limited than other punctuation marks

26. These modify nouns and pronouns
29. Same as #4 Down
30. Used in rowing
32. A rating symbol used by movie houses
33. Used to signal a noun
34. Abbreviation of Thursday
35. A male sheep
37. Referring to a metrical foot
41. A greeting
42. Same as #6 Down
43. Shows the relation or connection between a noun or pronoun and another word in a sentence
46. If_____is added to some verbs the verbs can act as adjectives
47. The comparative form of the adjective meaning coming after the due time
48. A direction
49. Roman numeral 1000
50. Opposite of admit
51. A person's possessions, property, etc.
55. Same as #22 Across
56. A preposition
57. Roman numeral 100
58. Abbreviation of International Harvester
59. An adjective meaning upper, higher, excessive
61. A prefix meaning from, down, away
62. A robber
65. The largest existing deer of Europe and Asia
66. When he comes is a(n)_____ clause
68. Abbreviation of Royal Mail Service

Check answers on the next page.

17. Yes in Spanish
19. This makes sentences more interesting
20. Ending for the past tense of regular verbs
24. A device that produces a warning sound
25. When she came home, she was very tired is a(n)_____ sentence
27. Skill in dealing with people
28. Roman numeral 5
31. Same as #22 Across
36. Same as #22 Across
38. Monkey
39. Word used with adjectives and adverbs to show the comparative degree
40. Abbreviation of inventory and inspection
41. A conjunctive adverb
44. To talk in a noisy or excited manner
45. A preposition
49. Punctuation_____help clarify meaning
50. The action
52. Right or left_____
53. Thick and_____
54. Same as #22 Across
56. Abbreviation of North Dakota
57. Irregular verb meaning able to
60. A tree
62. Intransitive verb meaning to exist
63. Same as #56 Down
64. Abbreviation of teletypewriter
67. Same as #6 Down

UNIT III CROSSWORD PUZZLE ANSWERS

¹R	²E	³A	L	⁴I	⁵Z	⁶E			

Crossword grid answers:

- Row 1: ¹R ²E ³A L ⁴I ⁵Z ⁶E
- Row 2: ⁷A N D · ⁸O
- Row 3: ⁹I D O · ¹⁰A D ¹¹D
- Row 4: ¹²S · ¹³I D I O ¹⁴M · ¹⁵C ¹⁶D
- Row 5: ¹⁷S · ¹⁸E ¹⁹V ²⁰E · ²¹V A · ²²A · ²³R A
- Row 6: ²⁴S I ²⁵C · ²⁶A D J E C ²⁷T ²⁸I V E S
- Row 7: ²⁹I · ³⁰O ³¹A R · ³²R · ³³A N · ³⁴T H
- Row 8: ³⁵R ³⁶A M · ³⁷I ³⁸A ³⁹M B ⁴⁰I C · ⁴¹H I
- Row 9: ⁴²E · ⁴³P ⁴⁴R E P O S I T ⁴⁵I O N
- Row 10: ⁴⁶N · ⁴⁷L A T E R · ⁴⁸N W · ⁴⁹M
- Row 11: ⁵⁰D E N Y · ⁵¹E ⁵²S ⁵³T ⁵⁴A T E · ⁵⁵A
- Row 12: ⁵⁶N E X T · ⁵⁷C · ⁵⁸I H · ⁵⁹O V ⁶⁰E R
- Row 13: ⁶¹D E · ⁶²B A ⁶³N D I ⁶⁴T · ⁶⁵E L K
- Row 14: ⁶⁶D ⁶⁷E P E N D E N T · ⁶⁸R M S

WORD PUZZLES

Word Puzzle 1

The following clues help you figure out the words to which they refer. Hint: All the words rhyme.

1. Something light that you can fly in a breeze.

2. Set close together.

3. Correct.

4. Power.

5. Lacking originality.

6. Disease of a plant.

7. Bad state or condition.

Answers:

1. kite 2. tight 3. right 4. might 5. trite 6. blight 7. plight

Word Puzzle 2

Following are clues to seven words. Each new word adds one letter and uses all the letters of the word preceding it. To form the new word you can rearrange the letters in any way.

1. An indefinite article. (one letter)

2. Another way for saying "father." (two letters)

3. A light blow. (three letters)

4. The crown of the head. (four letters)

5. Food is served on this. (five letters)

6. Part of the mouth. (six letters)

7. A leveling off. (seven letters)

Answers:

1. a 2. pa 3. tap 4. pate 5. plate 6. palate 7. plateau

Word Puzzle 3

Each sentence below gives you a clue to a letter. When you put the letters together, you will have the answer to the riddle, "What animal is a good timekeeper?"

1. My first letter is in "dwindle" but not in linden."

2. My second letter is in "weather" but not in "whether."

3. My third letter is in "rapport" but not in "parlor."

4. My fourth letter is in "placate" but not in "palate."

5. My fifth letter is in "polish" but not in "spoiled."

6. My sixth letter is in "raid" but not in "warrior."

7. My seventh letter is in "demeanor" but not in "remainder."

8. My eighth letter is in "salvage" but not in "valuables."

Answer:

watchdog

REVIEW TEST 1

A. Here are ten sentences. In the blank in front of each sentence, put an *S* if the sentence is a simple one, an *X* if the sentence is a complex one, a *C* if the sentence is a compound one, a *CC* if the sentence is a compound-complex one, and an *F* if the group of words is not a sentence but a sentence fragment.

_____ 1. Be patient, and try to work things out.

_____ 2. Last night my two brothers decided to break up their partnership of ten years and go their separate ways.

_____ 3. Five years ago, when I was still in my teens, my friend committed a crime, but he was never caught.

_____ 4. My conscience has been bothering me about the crime, but I swore that I would never betray him.

_____ 5. Last week some police were asking peculiar questions about my friend.

_____ 6. It seems that my friend just committed another crime similar to the one that he had committed five years ago.

_____ 7. I couldn't believe that he could be so stupid.

_____ 8. I feel stupid that I protected him all these years by keeping quiet.

_____ 9. I should have spoken up; then no one else would have gotten hurt.

_____ 10. Somehow, thinking back five years ago.

B. Follow the directions in the parentheses for each of the following.

1. (Write a complex sentence.) _____

_____

_____

2. (Write a compound-complex sentence.) _____

_____

_____

3. (Write a compound sentence using a semicolon without a linking word to connect the independent clauses.) _____

_____

_____

4. (Write a compound sentence using a linking word such as *however, moreover, then, therefore,* and so on.) _____

_____

_____

5. (Write a compound sentence using a coordinate conjunction to connect the independent clauses.)_____

_____

6. (Write a simple sentence.)_____

_____

7. (Write an exclamatory sentence.)_____

_____

8. (Write an interrogative sentence.) _____

_____

9. (Combine these three sentences to make a compound sentence. 1. At the beginning of every semester, I make certain resolutions. 2. I really try to keep them. 3. I just can't.)_____

_____

_____

_____

10. (Combine these four sentences to make a compound-complex sentence. 1. The guys I bunk with are the sloppiest persons you ever saw. 2. They never clean up. 3. It's difficult to find anything in our room. 4. Everything is buried under piles of books, clothes, and even left-over food.

_____

_____

_____

_____

C. Read each of the following sentences carefully. If the sentence is correct, put a "C" in the blank. If anything in the sentence is incorrect, rewrite it correctly.

1. I decided to go to the class, then I changed my mind._____

_____

2. He seems to be a happy person; even though he has had so many misfortunes in his short life. _____

_____

3. No one can play the game of showmanship better than you, and you know it said my father. _____

_____

4. I've given up smoking and drinking, so now I bite my nails. _____

_____

5. "I'll pay half your tuition," my father said. "You, however, will have to pay the rest." _____

_____

6. "If you continue your relationship with him," Marie said. "You should have your head examined." _____

_____

7. He is more intelligent than all of them. _____

_____

8. He does that very good. _____

_____

9. I tried to take the blame off of him; but I couldn't. _____

_____

10. No one went to their advisor for advice all semester. _____

_____

REVIEW TEST 2: A TRUE/FALSE TEST

Directions: This is a true/false test on Lessons 9-12. Read each sentence carefully. Decide whether it is true or false. Put a *T* for true or an *F* for false in the blank.

_____ 1. The comparative degree is used in making comparisons between three or more persons.

_____ 2. A complex sentence contains two independent clauses.

_____ 3. A dependent clause must always follow an independent clause.

_____ 4. Nouns can be used to describe or limit another noun.

_____ 5. A comma is a stronger punctuation mark than a semicolon.

_____ 6. *Very* can modify adjectives or other adverbs.

_____ 7. The endings *ing, ed, d,* and *en* can be used to form an adjective.

_____ 8. It is correct to say *most circular.*

_____ 9. *Ly* is never found at the end of an adjective.

_____ 10. The word *well* can be used as an adjective.

_____ 11. Conjunctive adverbs connect two independent clauses.

_____ 12. The possessive of *Jones* is Jone's.

_____13. The plural possessive of *Ross* is Rossess'.

_____14. The plural possessive of *Moses* is *Moses'*.

_____15. Parentheses are used to enclose added material in a sentence.

_____16. The term *sic* signifies that the misspelled word in a quote has been noted by you.

_____17. The plural of *brother-in-law* is *brothers-in-law.*

_____18. The possessive of *brother-in-law* is brother's-in-law.

_____19. An idiom always makes sense when it is translated word for word.

_____20. A prepositional phrase is made up of a verb and a preposition.

_____21. Conjunctive adverbs can be used as modifiers.

_____22. *Although* is a conjunctive adverb.

_____23. *Where* and *when* can function as subordinate conjunctions.

_____24. A participle may be used as an adjective.

_____25. The past participle of regular verbs is formed by adding *en* to the verb.

Lesson 13

Sentence Expansion Using Modifiers

1. Sentences can be expanded or enlarged by adding words that **modify** (describe or limit) nouns, verbs, adjectives, and adverbs. The descriptive words that modify nouns or pronouns are called **adjectives**. The descriptive words that modify verbs are called **adverbs**. Adverbs can also describe or limit an adjective or another adverb.

The more descriptive words that are used in a sentence, the less general and more specific the sentence becomes. For example, let's expand the sentence *The cat runs* to *The small, shaggy white cat runs swiftly.* The second sentence gives us much more information about the cat and its manner of running. Because the cat is *small, shaggy,* and *white,* all *tall, well-groomed,* and *other shades* of cats are eliminated.

2. **Modifiers** (words that describe or limit another word or groups of words) can consist of phrases or dependent clauses. *Examples:* Alfie is a dog *that never barks or bothers anyone.* (The dependent clause *that never barks or bothers anyone* describes Alfie.) A pen *that doesn't write* is useless. (The dependent clause *that doesn't write* limits pen to a particular pen.) The man *whose genius was acknowledged* couldn't balance his own checkbook. (The dependent clause *whose genius was acknowledged* limits *man* to a particular man.) The students *in the play* missed too many classes. (The phrase *in the play* limits *students* to particular students.) She majored *in economics.* (The phrase *in economics* describes the verb *majored.* It tells in what she majored.) We attended *for her benefit.* (The phrase *for her benefit* describes *attended.* It tells why we attended.) We saw a car *coming toward us.* (The phrase *coming toward us* describes *car.*) The girl, *chewing gum,* walked home. (The phrase *chewing gum* describes the girl.)

SPECIAL NOTE

> A **phrase** is a group of related words having either no subject or no predicate; it may lack both. There are many different kinds of phrases. A phrase can be used as a noun, a verb, an adjective, or an adverb. A phrase cannot stand alone as a sentence. *Examples:* The man *in the picture* was an infamous criminal. We all ran *into the building*. *Studying for exams* is very tiring. Our team *may have lost* the game. The mountain climbers saw a large boulder *rolling in their direction*.

3. A modifier can be a noun or pronoun with or without its own descriptive words that follows a noun or pronoun and gives additional information that identifies the noun or pronoun. Such a modifier is called an **appositive**. *Examples:* Jane, *my friend*, is very pretty. The author *Ernest Hemingway* was fascinated by the art of bullfighting. I, *myself*, will take over the job. Dr. Jones, *the speech professor*, discussed the course he was teaching. Cheryl, *an accomplished pianist*, is performing in the recital tonight. We traveled to Albany, *the state capital*, to visit my uncle.

SPECIAL NOTE

> Modifiers should be placed next to or near the word or words that they modify.
> *Examples of misplaced modifiers:* The man went into the car *wearing a gray flannel suit*. The professor delivered his lecture *in a cheerful mood*. Jane told her story *crying uncontrollably*. Jack went into the building *eating an ice-cream cone*. Sharon skated on the ice *dressed very warmly*.
> *Examples of properly placed modifiers:* The man *wearing a gray flannel suit* went into the car. The professor, *in a cheerful mood*, delivered his lecture. Jane, *crying uncontrollably*, told her story. Jack, *eating an ice-cream cone*, went into the building. Sharon, *dressed very warmly*, skated on the ice.

Practice A. Fill in each blank with a word that would give more information about the noun or verb.

1. The _____ _____ dog barked _____.

2. The _____ President spoke _____.

3. After the _____ _____ women entered, everyone in the room cheered _____.

4. Although I am a _____ man, I like to buy _____ cars.

5. The _____ princess spoke _____ to everyone.

6. _____ food is important for _____ health.

7. The _____ rainfall caused _____ floods.

8. The _____ rats ate _____.

9. Jennifer is a(n)_____,_____, and_____girl.

10. Terry is a(n)_____,_____, and_____boy.

Check sample answers at the end of Lesson 13.

Practice B. Give five descriptive words for each of the following.

1. car _____

2. student _____

3. food _____

4. man _____

5. woman _____

Check sample answers at the end of Lesson 13.

Practice C. Give five descriptive words for each of the following.

1. eat _____

2. work _____

3. play _____

4. drive _____

5. sleep _____

Check sample answers at the end of Lesson 13.

Practice D. Following are ten incomplete sentences. Complete each sentence by adding modifiers as specified in parentheses.

1. My train,_____, had another breakdown. (dependent clause)

2. Dr. Smith,_____, has a personality that matches his drill. (appositive)

3. My friend broke her leg_____. (phrase)

4. _____, the bells interrupted our thoughts. (phrase)

5. "Chicago",_____, is the subject of a poem by Carl Sandburg. (appositive)

6. Politicians_____ are hard to find. (dependent clause)

7. My brother,_____, started to work when he was ten years old. (appositive)

8. My father, _____, has a great amount of power. (dependent clause)

9. The student rally,_____, was a
   success. (dependent clause)

10. The employer,_____, interviewed
    fifty candidates for the one job. (appositive)

Check sample answers at the end of Lesson 13.

Practice E. Here are ten sentences with misplaced modifiers. Rewrite each sentence so that the sentence makes better sense.

1. John rushed to catch the bus shivering from the cold.

_____

2. Barbara rode her bike eating an ice-cream cone.

_____

3. Mary fell on the ice dressed in very light clothes.

_____

4. Jack rode his motorcycle wearing a helmet.

_____

5. The couple rode the escalator kissing passionately.

_____

6. The student wrote on the chalkboard chewing gum.

_____

7. The man walked rapidly to the bus yelling loudly.

_____

8. The miner dug for coal continuously coughing.

_____

9. Bob turned on the light working late.

_____

10. The fishermen caught fish telling jokes.

_____

Check answers at the end of Lesson 13.

Word Usage: Verb Tense

Tense refers to the changes that take place in a verb to show the *time* of the action of the verb.

1. Present Tense — You use the present tense of a verb to show that an action is taking place in the present and to show present facts. *Examples:* The children run in the park. Mother cooks dinner. It is snowing. The food smells delicious.

You generally use the present tense of a verb when reviewing a book. However, in writing about the events of the author's life, the past tense is used.　*Examples:* Lewis Carroll *writes* about Alice's dialogue with Humpty Dumpty in *Through the Looking Glass.* Helen Keller, who *was* deaf, mute, and blind, *recounts* in her autobiography how she *acquired* language.

You usually use the present tense of a verb when writing about general truths or about statements that are permanently true. These statements are presented in the present because of their timelessness.　*Examples:* The earth revolves around the sun. Geology is the study of the earth's crust. Biology is the science of living things.

2. Past Tense — You use the past tense of a verb to show that something has taken place in the past and that the action is completed.　*Examples:* I bought enough food to last all week. We went camping. My friend had a baby.

3. Future Tense — You use the future tense of a verb to show actions that have not happened yet.　The actions will take place at a future time. Words that are usually used to express future tense are *shall, will, is to be, about to,* and *going to.*　*Examples:* We will start our vacation next week. Tomorrow, we are going to have ten people for dinner. I shall wear my long blue dress for the dinner. "What are you going to be when you grow up?"

4. Words Describing Time — Many words, such as *yesterday, today, tomorrow, in a while, shortly, presently, at times, frequently, now and then, in a moment, always,* and *now,* are used to help give clearness to the writing. When those words define the time of the verb, they are *adverbs.*　*Examples:* Presently, I will begin to do my school work. Now is the time to do it. Yesterday we met one of my former buddies.

SPECIAL NOTES

a. Following are some examples of the present, past, and future tense formations of regular and irregular verbs.

Regular verb — *climb*　　　　Auxiliaries — *be, will*

Present　　　　　　　　　　　　　　　　**Past**

Singular	**Plural**	**Singular**	**Plural**
I climb (am climbing)	we climb (are climbing)	I climbed (was climbing)	we climbed (were climbing)

Future

Singular	**Plural**
I will climb (will be climbing)	we will climb (will be climbing)

Irregular verb — *go*　　　　Auxiliaries — *be, will*

Present　　　　　　　　　　　　　　　　**Past**

Singular	**Plural**	**Singular**	**Plural**
I go (am going)	we go (are going)	I went (was going)	we went (were going)

Future

Singular	Plural
I will go	We will go
(will be going)	(will be going)

b. The present participle, which is formed by adding -*ing* to the verb, is used with the auxiliary *be* to produce the progressive verb form. The progressive verb forms are used to show that an action is ongoing or continuing; that is, it is not fixed in time. *Examples:* am climbing; are climbing; were climbing. The progressive verb form occurs in all tenses. All examples of tense formations of regular and irregular verbs will include the progressive verb forms.

5. You just learned about the **present**, **simple past**, and **future** verb tenses, which are the most frequently used tenses. However, in speaking and writing we often use other tenses in order to be more precise.

When an action that started in the past is going on or continuing at any time up to the present, you use the word *have* or *has* with the past participle of the verb. This verb tense is called the **present perfect**. You cannot use the simple past tense to show this action because the past tense is used to show that something ended in the past. *Examples:* They *have gone* to the beach a number of times this month. This problem *has been going* on for some time now. I *have requested* the report five times already. He *has stalled* long enough.

SPECIAL NOTE

Following are some examples of the present, past, future, and present perfect tense formations of regular and irregular verbs.

Regular verb — *climb*   Auxiliaries — *be, will, have*

Present		**Past**	
Singular	**Plural**	**Singular**	**Plural**
you climb	you climb	you climbed	you climbed
(are climbing)	(are climbing)	(were climbing)	(were climbing)

Future		**Present Perfect**	
Singular	**Plural**	**Singular**	**Plural**
You will climb	you will climb	you have climbed	you have climbed
(will be climbing)	(will be climbing)	(have been climbing)	(have been climbing)

Irregular verb — *go*   Auxiliaries — *be, will, have*

Present		**Past**	
Singular	**Plural**	**Singular**	**Plural**
you go	you go	you went	you went
(are going)	(are going)	(were going)	(were going)

Future		Present Perfect	
Singular	**Plural**	**Singular**	**Plural**
you will go (will be going)	you will go (will be going)	you have gone (have been going)	you have gone (have been going)

6. When a tale of past events is interrupted with an event happening before the past events, the word *had* is used with the past participle of the verb.   *Examples:*   Some years ago I met a man who told me that he *had been* around the world three times in three years.   My friend said that she *had stopped* smoking.   Arthur explained his investment policies to me and told me he *had made* a fortune on the market.

7. An action that was completed before some other past action requires the word *had* with the past participle of the verb.   *Examples:*   The test that I took last week was not as hard as I *had expected* it to be.   We learned that the plane that we were waiting for *had crashed* in an unknown area.

8. When the verb *had* is used with the past participle of a verb, the verb tense is called the **past perfect**.

SPECIAL NOTE

Following are some examples of the present, past, future, present perfect, and past perfect tense formations of regular and irregular verbs.

Regular verb — *climb*   Auxiliaries — *be, will, have*

Present		Past	
Singular	**Plural**	**Singular**	**Plural**
he, she climbs (is climbing)	they climb (are climbing)	he, she climbed (was climbing)	they climbed (were climbing)

Future		Present Perfect	
Singular	**Plural**	**Singular**	**Plural**
he, she will climb (will be climbing)	they will climb (will be climbing)	he, she has climbed (has been climbing)	they have climbed (have been climbing)

Past Perfect

Singular	Plural
he, she had climbed (had been climbing)	they had climbed (had been climbing)

Irregular verb — *go*   Auxiliaries — *be, will, have*

Present		Past	
Singular	**Plural**	**Singular**	**Plural**
he, she goes (is going)	they go (are going)	he, she went (was going)	they went (were going)

Future		Present Perfect	
Singular	Plural	Singular	Plural
he, she will go (will be going)	they will go (will be going)	he, she has gone (has been going)	they have gone (have been going)

Past Perfect

Singular	Plural
he, she had gone (had been going)	they had gone (had been going)

Practice A.   Circle the verb that correctly completes each sentence.

1. Speaking of her own early years, my mother said that she (was/has been/had been) a perfect child.

2. He explained that he (knew/has known/had known) about the problem a month ago.

3. She (had been/was/has been) postponing her wedding for some time now.

4. The pilots claimed that their plane (had/has) never been late.

5. The doctors related to the reporters all that was known about the strange virus that (has/had) claimed so many lives.

6. Before I met my blind date, I knew that he (has/had) dark hair, dark eyes, and a moustache.

7. She (had been/is/has been) living here for a decade now.

8. I believe that the escaped zoo animals (have been/had been/were/are) missing for two days.

9. Yesterday I (had asked/have asked/asked) the campus beauty for a date.

10. I (had been/have been/was) studying for this exam since noon today.

11. (Are/Will) you be going with us?

12. I (saw/see) your best friend at work yesterday.

13. The Rocky Mountains (are/were) in western North America.

14. Oak (makes/made) a very good floor.

15. *Jaws* (is/was) a novel about a shark's effect on the people in a resort area.

16. The United States (has/had) a democratic form of government.

17. Soon I (travel/will travel/traveled) to Europe.

18. The moon (is/was) a satellite of the earth.

19. How old (are/were) you now?

20. *The Invisible Man* (is/was) a book by Ralph Ellison.

21. He (is helping/has helped/helped/will help) me a great deal the past three months.

22. They (buy/will buy/bought/have bought) a large mobile home yesterday.

23. My aunt (is/was/will be/has been) a great help to us during these years of crises.

24. Neither of you (is/was/are/were/has been/have been) available to help us this whole week.

25. My brother (is/was/has been) away at school for three months now.

26. It seems as though that movie (is/was/has been) playing for weeks.

27. I (am/has been/have been/was) interviewing some people for a job yesterday.

28. I (was/am/have been) delaying going to the dentist for one month.

29. The bell (is/was/has been) ringing for some time now.

30. Tony (is/was/has been) away on several business trips this month.

Check answers at the end of Lesson 13.

Practice B. Choose the verb that is correct for the given subject. Construct a sentence using the given subject and the chosen verb.

Subject	Verb
Tomorrow I	is/am/will/was
Yesterday we	is/are/will/were
Soon the price of movies	is/are/will
Now Jack and Herb	is/are/shall
The South Sea Islands	is/are/was/were

Check sample answers at the end of Lesson 13.

Practice C. In the following, if the sentence is correct, put a *C* in the blank. If the sentence is not correct, rewrite it correctly.

1. My present instructor was teaching at the college for twenty years.

2. Biology and geology were science courses that many students will elect.

_____

_____

3. In a moment it is storming.

_____

4. I mailed my letter yesterday.

_____

5. The postman has been coming at different times every day.

_____

_____

6. I think my years at camp have not been very happy ones, now that I look back on them.

_____

_____

7. This year is a good one, so far.

_____

8. The police searched for the sniper for three days and have not caught him yet.

_____

_____

9. Today is a beautiful day.

_____

10. The recently discovered primitive tribe lived in isolation for centuries.

_____

_____

11. The police feared that the child has been killed.

_____

12. The student said that his parents had been upset when he came home so late from school.

_____

_____

13. The crime rate in my city has been increasing steadily.

_____

14. Although I have seen him only once, I knew that I would never forget him.

_____

_____

15. My typewriter is not working properly for some time now.

_____

16. Violence in movies and television shows had increased in the past few years.

_____

_____

17. John said that he had met the President of the United States last year.

_____

_____

18. We were sure that the man with the scar was the villain in the movie.

_____

_____

19. We were surprised when we learned that we had made a mistake.

_____

_____

20. After my girlfriend and I have broken up, I became depressed.

_____

Check answers at the end of Lesson 13.

Punctuation: Italics

    1. Writers use a single straight line to show that something is to be put into italics.   *Example:* Be sure to dot your i's and cross your t's.

    2. Italics is a special kind of slant type that printers use.   *Example:* Throughout this book the word *Example* is in italics. *This entire sentence is in italics.*

    3. Here is a list of items that are usually put in italics.

        a. Titles of books   *Examples: Catcher in the Rye; War and Peace; All Quiet on the Western Front*

    b. Magazines, journals, newspapers   *Examples: News Tribune; Courier Post; Time Magazine; Newsweek; Playboy; Esquire; Cosmopolitan; English Journal*

    c. Plays, movies, and other works of art such as names of paintings   *Examples: Whistler's Mother; Mona Lisa; Macbeth; The Doll House; Dracula; Peter Pan; Yank*

    d. Names of ships   *Example: Queen Elizabeth II*

    e. Foreign words or abbreviations of foreign words   *Examples: Op. cit; ibid.; sic; petit fours*

    f. Words used as words or numbers used as numbers in a sentence   *Examples:* Students often confuse the contraction *who's* with the interrogative pronoun *whose.* One of my students reverses his *7's* and *9's.*

SPECIAL NOTES

    a. It is usually not a good idea to use italics to emphasize an important word or phrase that you are using in a sentence. It is better to present the idea in such a way so that the reader recognizes that you are emphasizing this point.

    b. The Bible and other religious works are usually not put in italics.

    c. Quotation marks rather than italics may be used when referring to special words or numbers in a sentence.

Practice A. Here are ten sentences. Determine whether the underlined word or words should be in italics. If the underlined word or words should be in italics, write *yes* in the blank. If the underlined word or words should not be in italics, write *no* in the blank.

_____ 1. My favorite food is ice cream.

_____ 2. Last night I read a hundred pages of my economics book.

_____ 3. Last year's issue of Playboy featured girls from Ivy League colleges.

_____ 4. Coming Home was a good movie.

_____ 5. The New York Times is so large that it takes me all week to read it.

_____ 6. I wrote ibid. and op. cit. many times in my paper.

_____ 7. My friend always misspells judgment.

_____ 8. Our instructor gives us key words to help us remember important ideas.

_____ 9. Almost every hotel or motel room has a copy of the New Testament.

_____ 10. Nonsense poems such as Eletelephony are fun to read.

Check answers at the end of Lesson 13.

Spelling: Homonyms or Homophones I

Homonyms or **homophones** are words that sound alike but are spelled differently and have different meanings. Following is a list of homonyms or homophones that are often substituted for one another. Because they are misspelled so often, they are called "homonym demons." Each is presented in a sentence so that you can see its correct usage. (Although some of the words presented here have more than one meaning, only one sentence and one meaning are given for each.)

one—I have only *one* pair of shoes.
won—I'm glad that you *won* the game.

meet—Let's *meet* after school.
meat—I like *meat* and potatoes.

hour—I have to wait an *hour* for my appointment.
our—*Our* brother is an artist.

write—I *write* a little every day.
right—Why are you always *right*?

sew—My mother can *sew* clothes very well.
so—Why are you *so* angry?

weigh—How much does the chicken *weigh*?
way—On the *way* to the store, I met my friends.

too—I like that, *too.*
to—Let's go *to* the movies after school.
two—I have *two* tickets to the game.

peace—When there is no fighting or tension, we have *peace.*
piece—That's a large *piece* of cake.

red—Cars stop at *red* lights.
read—I *read* a story to my brother.

know—My father seems to *know* a lot.
no—There was *no* way back.

wood—He needed *wood* for his fireplace.
would—I *would* go if I had the time.

I—*I* need to learn how to spell.
eye—I went for an *eye* examination because my eyes hurt.

bear—We met a *bear* in the woods.
bare—In the winter many trees are *bare* of leaves.

led—The guide *led* the way.
lead—I have a *lead* pencil.

heard—We *heard* all about it.
herd—The *herd* of cattle was delivered.

route—Which *route* did you take?
root—If the *root* of the plant dies, the whole plant will die.

dye—She used a strong *dye* to change the color of her hair.
die—All mortals *die.*

Practice A. Circle the correct word.

 1. She has only (one/won) friend.

 2. He (one/won) the game.

 3. I have to (meat/meet) my friend.

 4. I had (meat/meet) for dinner.

 5. This (hour/our) seems so long.

 6. (Hour/Our) picture is pretty.

 7. Arthur is always (write/right).

 8. I like to (write/right).

 9. It is fun to (sew/so) clothes.

10. I feel (sew/so) bad.

11. How much does that (weigh/way)?

12. Do you know the (weigh/way) to school?

13. I am going (two/to/too) tell him.

14. I want some, (two/to/too).

15. I have (two/to/too) friends.

16. It is good to have (peace/piece) in the world.

17. May I have a (peace/piece) of pie?

18. Have you (red/read) the latest novel?

19. (Red/Read) is my favorite color.

20. Do you (know/no) how to do the problem?

21. (Know/No), I will not go.

22. The men (would/wood) not go into the forest to gather the (would/
    wood).

23. (Eye/I) need to wear glasses because (Eye/I) have a problem with my
    right (I/eye).

24. The big (bear/bare) growled at us.

25. They were so poor that their cupboards were (bear/bare) of food.

26. When she (lead/led) us to the cave opening, we screamed with delight.

27. Children have gotten (lead/led) poisoning from eating paint containing (lead/led).

28. We (heard/herd) that the (heard/herd) had been in a stampede.

29. To get to Florida, take this (route/root).

30. I needed (route/root) canal work done on my teeth.

31. When we heard that he (would/wood) soon (dye/die) because of his illness, we cried.

32. I can't use any (dye/die) on my hair because I'm allergic to it.

Check answers at the end of Lesson 13.

Practice B. Change some words in each sentence so that the sentence makes sense.

1. Know, that is write.

2. Hour friend is sew hungry, two.

3. Meat him on the weigh.

4. Hour to friends red a book two their sisters at hour house for an our.

5. I red that a peace of meet had almost choked hour mayor to times, two.

6. Eye herd that the bare ran into the woods.

7. Eye will knot die my hare because eye herd a tail that said that dying is know good for your hare routes.

8. The heard that came on a different root was lead by a lean steer with only one horn.

Check answers at the end of Lesson 13.

Practice C. Here are a number of challenging homonym riddles. State the words that fit the two clues. The words sound alike but have different spellings and different meanings. (Many of the words were not presented in this lesson.)

1. a fruit; to trim _____   _____

2. a passageway; a tract of land surrounded by water _____

_____

3. to conceal; a fruit _____   _____

4. to sell; a foot lever _____   _____

5. to rob; a strong metal _____   _____

6. a song of joy; a place for individual study, which is usually found in a library _____   _____

7. vulgar; a subject _____   _____

8. a fish; something spiritual _____ _____

9. money; a Building _____ _____

10. a fruit; the swiftest part of a stream _____ _____

11. a slender threadlike outgrowth of the skin; an animal _____

_____

12. part of your body; an act of skill _____ _____

13. part of a horse; chief or principal _____ _____

14. a way of acting; the house of an estate _____ _____

15. an artillery piece; a rule _____ _____

16. very large; a frame of parallel bars _____ _____

17. an arab chief; sophistication of dress or manner _____

_____

18. a branch of a tree; the forward part of the ship _____

_____

19. forward; a number _____ _____

20. a movement smoother and slower than a gallop; a choir leader

_____ _____

21. a metal instrument; a solid artificial landing place for ships _____

_____

22. a signal; a waiting line _____ _____

23. to allot; food _____ _____

24. cleverly humorous; a hardy annual grass _____

_____

25. an illness; a strong hold _____ _____

Check answers at the end of Lesson 13.

Practice D.   What homonym is Alex confusing with *locks*?

ALEX IN WONDERLAND   **by Bob Cordray**

Answer: ©1978 by Bob Cordray

Check answer at the end of Lesson 13.

LESSON 13 ANSWERS

Sentence Expansion Using Modifiers (pp. 197–200)

Practice A (sample answers):   1. The *large black* dog barked *loudly.*
2. The *powerful* President spoke *firmly.*   3. After the *two old* women
entered, everyone cheered *enthusiastically.*   4. Although I am a *tall* man, I
like to buy *small* cars.   5. The *gentle* princess spoke *kindly* to everyone.
6. *Nutritious* food is important for *good* health.   7. The *heavy* rainfall
caused *many* floods.   8. The *hungry* rats ate *greedily.*   9. Jennifer is a
beautiful, charming, and *intelligent* girl.   10. Terry is a *handsome, athletic,*
and *intelligent* boy.

Practice B (sample answers):   1. car — compact, low-priced, good-looking, economical, smooth-riding   2. student — smart, hardworking, serious,
enthusiastic, thinking   3. food — tasty, bland, spicy, delicious, fattening
4. man — tall, bald, intelligent, stocky, friendly   5. woman — slender,
beautiful, blue-eyed, dark-haired, smart.

Practice C (sample answers):   1. eat — heartily, quickly, slowly, well,
excessively   2. work — hard, lazily, intelligently, sloppily, carelessly   3. play
— nicely, quietly, hard, fairly, properly   4. drive — carefully, well, recklessly,
carelessly, haphazardly   5. sleep — soundly, well, restfully, fitfully, uncom-
fortably.

Practice D (sample answers):   1. which is always late   2. my dentist
3. near the park   4. Clanging loudly   5. a midwestern city   6. who don't
talk "double talk"   7. James   8. who is president of his company   9. which
was called to gather support for a new student center   10. a well-dressed man.

Practice E: 1. John, shivering from the cold, rushed to catch the bus.
2. Barbara, eating an ice-cream cone, rode her bike.   3. Mary, dressed in very
light clothes, fell on the ice.   4. Jack, wearing a helmet, rode his motorcycle.
5. The couple, kissing passionately, rode the escalator.   6. The student, chewing gum, wrote on the chalkboard.   7. The man, yelling loudly, walked rapidly
to the bus.   8. The miner, continuously coughing, dug for coal.   9. Bob,
working late, turned on the light.   10. The fishermen, telling jokes, caught
fish.

Word Usage: Verb Tense (pp. 200–207)

Practice A: 1. had been   2. had known   3. has been   4. had   5. had
6. had   7. has been   8. have been   9. asked   10. have been   11. Will   12. saw
13. are   14. makes   15. is   16. has   17. will travel   18. is   19. are   20. is
21. has helped   22. bought   23. has been   24. has been   25. has been
26. has been   27. was   28. have been   29. has been   30. has been.

Practice B (sample answers):   1. Tomorrow I will fly to Rome.   2. Yesterday we were visiting my married sister.   3. Soon the price of movies will
be a small fortune.   4. Now Jack and Herb are very successful.   5. The South
Sea Islands are in the Pacific.

Practice C: 1. My present instructor has been teaching at the college for twenty years.   2. Biology and geology are science courses that many students will elect.   3. In a moment it will storm.   4. C   5. C   6. I think my years at camp were not very happy ones, now that I look back on them. 7. This year has been a good one, so far.   8. The police have been searching for the sniper for three days and have not caught him yet.   9. C   10. The recently discovered primitive tribe has been living in isolation for centuries. 11. The police feared that the child had been killed.   12. C   13. C   14. Although I had seen him only once, I knew that I would never forget him. 15. My typewriter has not been working properly for some time now. 16. Violence in movies and television shows has increased in the past few years.   17. C   18. C   19. C   20. After my girlfriend and I had broken up, I became depressed.

Punctuation: Italics (pp. 207–208)

Practice A: 1. no   2. no   3. yes   4. yes   5. yes   6. yes   7. yes   8. no 9. no   10. no

Spelling: Homonyms or Homophones I (pp. 209–212)

Practice A: 1. one   2. won   3. meet   4. meat   5. hour   6. Our 7. right   8. write   9. sew   10. so   11. weigh   12. way   13. to   14. too 15. two   16. peace   17. piece   18. read   19. Red   20. know   21. No. 22. would, wood   23. I, I, eye   24. bear   25. bare   26. led   27. lead, lead 28. heard, herd   29. route   30. root   31. would, die   32. dye

Practice B: 1. No, that is right.   2. Our friend is so hungry, too   3. Meet him on the way.   4. Our two friends read a book to their sisters at our house for an hour.   5. I read that a piece of meat had almost choked our mayor two times, too.   6. I heard that the bear ran into the woods.   7. I will not dye my hair because I heard a tale that said that dyeing is no good for your hair roots. 8. The herd that came on a different route was led by a lean steer with only one horn.

Practice C: 1. pear; pare   2. aisle; isle   3. bury; berry   4. peddle; pedal 5. steal; steel   6. carol; carrel   7. coarse; course   8. sole; soul   9. capital; Capitol   10. currant; current   11. hair, hare   12. feet, feat   13. mane, main 14. manner, manor   15. cannon, canon   16. great, grate   17. sheik, chic 18. bough; bow   19. fore; four   20. canter; cantor   21. key; quay   22. cue; queue   23. mete; meat   24. wry; rye   25. grippe; grip

Practice D: lox

UNIT IV

Lesson 14

Figures of Speech

Figures of speech are important because they give color, decoration, and life to language. We often use figures of speech without realizing it because they have become part of everyday language. *Examples:* the body of a letter, the foot of the class, the hands of the clock, the heart of the matter, take it on the chin.

Figurative Language

Figurative language represents an indirect way of saying something—the meaning is implied, not directly stated. Understanding figures of speech is necessary to an appreciation of most poetry as well as other literature. The figures of speech most commonly used in writing are *simile, metaphor,* personification, hyperbole,* and *oxymoron.*

1. A **simile** is a comparison between two unlike objects made by using the word *like* or *as.* A metaphor is also a comparison between two unlike objects, but the *like* or *as* is not used. Because a simile is signaled by the word *like* or *as*, it is easy to distinguish a simile from a metaphor.

Examples:

    a. The clouds were *like masses of whipped cream.*
    b. The lion was *as friendly as a kitten.*
    c. Her disposition is *like glass*; it breaks easily, and when it breaks, it cuts.
    d. Her mind works *like a computer programmed in the wrong language.*

---

* Often the term *metaphor* is used in a generic (general) sense to cover all forms of figures of speech. Therefore, simile, personification, and so on might be referred to as metaphor.

2. A **metaphor** may be more difficult to recognize because it is not signaled by an identifying word. The comparison is complete: one thing *is* another thing.

Examples:

    a. The clouds were *downy pillows* floating in the sky.
    b. The lion was a *friendly kitten.*
    c. Her *razor-edge* disposition is always sharpest in the morning.
    d. His mind is a *computer.*

3. **Personification** is the giving of human characteristics and capabilities to nonhuman things such as inanimate (nonliving) objects, abstract ideas, or animals. An excellent example of personification is this quote from Joseph Conrad: "The sun looked upon the ship all day, and every morning rose with a burning, round stare of undying curiosity."

Examples:

    a. The *clouds cried* a torrent of tears.
    b. *Winter's icy breath and cold fingers* chilled our bodies.
    c. *Vengence commanded* me and I was its tool.

SPECIAL NOTE

In writing you should be careful not to overdo or mismatch personifications. Expository writing (writing that explains or conveys information) probably should not include personification—unless personification is the best way to get your point across.

4. **Hyperbole** is another common figure of speech. It is the use of *excessive exaggeration* for effect. Whenever we say, "I'm so hungry I could eat a horse," or "I'm so tired I could sleep for a year," we are using **hyperbole**. Writers use hyperbole to stretch the truth because they want to make a point emphatically.

Examples:

    1. For the *five millionth time,* "No!"
    2. She *cried forever*!
    3. They have *tons* of expensive things.
    4. She's *smaller than my thumb.*
    5. His morals are *as upright as wet spaghetti.*

Writers also use hyperbole to portray their feelings. For example, when a writer says, "The Joneses prattled on for an eternity," he is not only telling us that the Joneses talked for a very long time, he is also giving us his feelings about it. If the writer had enjoyed the company of the Joneses, he would not say that they prattled on for an eternity.

SPECIAL NOTE

Hype is used often, especially by the advertising industry in connection with television and movie advertisements. Exaggerated words such as *blockbuster, death defying shocker, stupendous, stupefying, sensational, amazing,* and *unbelievable* are used to promote productions.

     5. **Oxymoron** is the combining of contraries (opposites) to portray a particular image or to produce a striking effect. Word contradictions attract our attention and present the author's feelings or ideas expressively. An oxymoron with which you may be familiar is "poor little rich girl." Most often this word contradiction is used sarcastically, that is, the speaker means to ridicule the girl while seeming to be sympathetic. However, it is possible for the phrase "poor little rich girl" to be meant sympathetically—that the girl has a lot of material possessions but does not have other things she needs such as love and understanding.

Examples:

    a. Parting is such *sweet sorrow.*
    b. A *loud silence* followed the improper remark.
    c. This is one of those occasions for *making haste slowly.*
    d. She lives in *happy ignorance.*
    e. He is suffering from *benign neglect.*
    f. She was *conspicuous* by her *absence.*

    The word contradiction "the dawn of night" could be used in connection with the adventures of Dracula.   *Example:* Dracula awoke at the *dawn*

©1960 United Feature Syndicate, Inc.

of night.   You can probably come up with some other interesting oxymorons in relation to Dracula.

An oxymoron can serve more than one purpose.   For example, Arthur Koestler's title *Darkness at Noon* is a word contradiction.   Noon is usually the brightest time of the day because the sun is at its highest point.   Obviously, Koestler intended his title to attract our attention, but he also had other reasons for using it.   Koestler was giving us some clue to what his novel is about.   Even if you haven't read his book yet, you get the feeling of something dark, ominous, or evil happening while it's light, the feeling of something evil but unnoticed, a dark cloud gradually covering the light while people are unaware of the gathering gloom.

Overworked Phrases

It is usually easier to use a common phrase than to think of a fresh and original way to say something.   A phrase that is used over and over again to describe something is called an **overworked phrase.**   *Examples:* pretty as a picture; white as a sheet; hard as nails; cold as ice; black as pitch; friendly as a kitten; blushing bride; soft as down; hungry as a bear; work like a dog; babbling brook; pearly teeth.

You can probably think of many more.   Try to avoid using overworked phrases in your writing.

Strong, active, and descriptive words are better than general and static ones.   For example, see how the sentence *They removed the obstacle* can be made into a more vivid and graphic sentence by changing the verb *removed* to one of the following verbs: *erased, demolished, obliterated, destroyed, liquidated, wiped out, deracinated, smashed, scattered,* or *displaced.*

Practice A.   Choose a word or phrase from the list below that most vividly completes these sentences with an expression of personification.

Phrase List: crept softly, straining, impatiently, opened, devour, wept huge tears, refused, felt naked, smiled, angry, spat fire, thirsty, begged, panting.

1. The rain clouds _____.

2. The _____ locomotives slowly climbed the hill.

3. The stalled car _____ to move.

4. The fog _____ along the ground.

5. The tunnel _____ its mouth to _____ the cars.

6. The _____ cars waited _____ for the light to change.

7. The _____ land _____ for water.

8. The trees _____ without their leaves.

9. The warm spring sun _____ at us.

10. The _____ volcano _____ .

Check answers at the end of Lesson 14.

Practice B. Choose a phrase from the list that most vividly completes a simile in these sentences.

Phrase List: a glowing orange ball; a frayed brown cord; a gorged buzzard; a rocky road; a light in the night; a seal; a waterfall; a swift bird; a telegraph; a tall bride.

1. The huge 747 lumbered toward its takeoff like _____

   _____ .

2. Her tears flowed like _____ .

3. The woodpecker's pecking sounded like _____

   tapping out a message.

4. From the airplane, the dirt road looked like _____

   _____ .

5. My math course is like _____ .

6. The doe is like _____ in flight.

7. The answer illuminated the subject like _____

   _____ .

8. He looked like _____ with his whiskers

   drooping from his upper lip.

9. The sun rose like _____ in the east.

10. The white poplar tree looked like _____ .

Check answers at the end of Lesson 14.

Practice C. Choose a phrase from the list below that most vividly completes a metaphor in these sentences.

Phrase List: a crewcut, a ghost, confetti; a lamb; hot potatoes; razor-sharp; living pincushions; a wolf; a smoking volcano; twisted pretzels.

1. My father's whiskers are _____ .

2. The cars in the accident became _____ .

3. He is _____ when it comes to girls.

4. He has lost so much weight that he is merely _____ of

   his former self.

5. Jane is _____ to allow you to get away with so much.

6. Our overheated car became _____.

7. Controversial issues are _____that most politicians try to avoid.

8. Her_____tongue lashed out at all who defied her.

9. The farmer gave his grain field _____.

10. The snow was _____ falling from the sky.

Check answers at the end of Lesson 14.

Practice D.   For these ten lines, taken from famous poems, underline the figure of speech, and then state what kind it is.

1. Her face is a garden of delight. (Thomas Campion)

_____

2. Her brows like bended bows do stand. (Thomas Campion)

_____

3. The Moon doth with delight look round her when the heavens are bare. (William Wordsworth)

_____

4. I wandered lonely as a cloud. (William Wordsworth)

_____

5. The daffodils are tossing their heads in sprightly dance. (William Wordsworth)

_____

6. The sea bares her bosom to the moon. (William Wordsworth)

_____

7. The wrinkled sea beneath him crawls. (Lord Tennyson)

_____

8. There's no frigate like a book to take us lands away. (Emily Dickinson)

_____

9. The sun is laid to sleep. (Ben Jonson)

_____

10. The stars threw down their spears and watered heaven with their tears. (William Blake)

_____

Check answers at the end of Lesson 14.

Practice E.   Name the figure of speech that Alex uses.

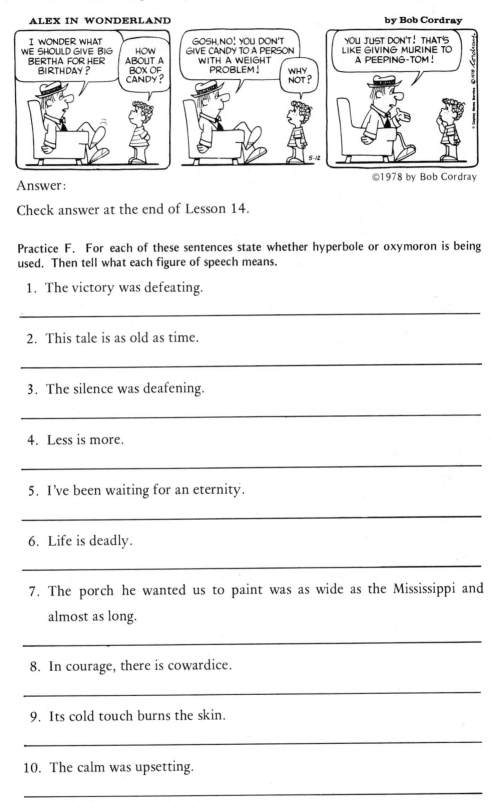

ALEX IN WONDERLAND   **by Bob Cordray**

©1978 by Bob Cordray

Answer:

Check answer at the end of Lesson 14.

Practice F.   For each of these sentences state whether hyperbole or oxymoron is being used.   Then tell what each figure of speech means.

1. The victory was defeating.

_____

2. This tale is as old as time.

_____

3. The silence was deafening.

_____

4. Less is more.

_____

5. I've been waiting for an eternity.

_____

6. Life is deadly.

_____

7. The porch he wanted us to paint was as wide as the Mississippi and almost as long.

_____

8. In courage, there is cowardice.

_____

9. Its cold touch burns the skin.

_____

10. The calm was upsetting.

_____

Check answers at the end of Lesson 14.

Practice G. Write a vivid phrase describing each of the following words or phrases.

1. fog _____

2. a cold winter day_____

3. a star-filled sky_____

4. a barbeque_____

5. a clock _____

Check sample answers at the end of Lesson 14.

Practice H. Write a vivid verb describing an action appropriate to each of the following words or phrases.

1. fog _____

2. a cold winter day_____

3. a star-filled sky_____

4. a barbeque_____

5. a clock _____

Check sample answers at the end of Lesson 14.

Practice I. In the following ten sentences, figures of speech that are used in everyday conversations are italicized. State their meanings.

1. Sharon is the *apple of his eye.*

_____

2. After what happened, I have a *bone to pick* with you.

_____

3. Let's all give her the *cold shoulder.*

_____

4. Life is no *bed of roses* if you have to work from dawn to dusk.

_____

5. I have to carry this *millstone about my neck.*

_____

6. I'm not going on a *wild-goose chase.*

_____

7. You can get a *bird's eye view* of the city from here.

_____

8. She spoke with *tongue in cheek* about her short life on the stage.

_____

9. When he didn't show up again, I said that it was the *last straw.*

_____

10. The *lame-duck* Congress was very inactive.

_____

Check answers at the end of Lesson 14.

Practice J. Write a sentence describing each word or phrase in parentheses.

1. (your shadow)_____

_____

2. (trees)_____

_____

3. (in the morning)_____

_____

4. (April)_____

_____

5. (frost)_____

_____

Check sample answers at the end of Lesson 14.

Word Usage:
Logical Sequence of Tenses

1. In writing sentences, you should make the verb in the independent clause logically consistent with the verb in the dependent clause.   *Examples:* The boss asked his secretary to come into his office because he wanted to dictate a letter to her. When the school bell rings, the children usually stop playing and start to line up. I have asked her for a date many times, but she has never accepted.

2. If the dependent clause is introduced by a verb of thinking, telling, or saying in the past tense, you should usually put the verb in the dependent clause in the past tense.   *Examples:* He said that he liked her. He explained to the registrar that he needed another course in order to graduate. She thought that she had completed her assignments satisfactorily.

3. The tense in which you start a story should be consistent throughout the story. That is, if you begin a tale in the past tense, then you should continue throughout with the past tense. If you begin your story with the present tense, then you should maintain the present tense throughout.   *Examples:* a. The price of meat was very high a month ago. As a result, my family decided to become vegetarians. We ate only vegetables, fruits, nuts

and dairy products. b. The big bear is sitting in the woods. Next to him are the mama bear and the baby bear. "I am hungry," says the baby bear. c. Last week I met someone that I had not seen for ten years. I was shocked that he was able to recognize me. Ten years ago, I was very skinny, wore braces, and had long pigtails.

Practice A. Circle the verb that completes the sentence correctly.

1. We showed him our new car when we (had seen/saw) him yesterday.

2. Because Tyrone (had been injured/was injured) in an automobile crash, he avoided driving.

3. I like going out to fancy restaurants, but my boyfriend (prefers/preferred/ has preferred/had preferred) homecooked meals.

4. I told my friends that I (am/was) not going to the game with them because I (have/has/had) to study for a final, but my friends (do/did) not believe me.

5. John thought that he (has completed/had completed/completed) his course requirements a long time ago.

6. The doctors said that they (have sent/had sent/sent/will send) the biopsy to the disease center in Atlanta, Georgia for analysis a week earlier, but since then they (heard/have heard/will hear) nothing.

7. The bank hired Jim a month ago to manage their mortgage department, but so far the employees in the mortgage department (had refused/are refusing/will refuse/have refused) to work for Jim.

8. We told them the good news when we (had seen/have seen/saw) them yesterday.

9. Although she (is/has been/had been) excellent in her part, the play closed because the audience and critics (do/did) not like it.

10. When the doctor (had told/told/has told) me that I had broken my leg, I (am/was) very upset because my coach had told me that the team (needs/need/had needed/has needed/needed) me to play in the semifinals.

Check answers at the end of Lesson 14.

Practice B. Choose words from column A to match with words from column B to make the most logically correct sentence. Fill in each of the blanks of column B with a verb.

Column A	*Column B*
1. Mary said	a. that he _____ gotten an A in chemistry.
2. Next semester I	b. what one _____ capable of doing.

3. The doctor said

c. that she _____ broken up with her boyfriend a month ago and that she _____ given him back his ring at that time.

4. He was sure

d. that it _____ difficult to see.

5. They told us

e. and _____ the nuts out of our hands.

6. Yesterday it rained so much

f. that they _____ finished building the boat about a month ago.

7. No one knows

g. _____ take all required courses.

8. None of my friends sat next to Bill at the game

h. that we still _____ a flooded basement.

9. The room is so dark

i. because he continually _____ played cruel jokes on many of us.

10. The squirrels came up to us

j. that the dog bite _____ not serious.

Check answers at the end of Lesson 14.

Punctuation: A Review—
Simple and Compound Sentences

Rules for Punctuating Simple Sentences (Only one Independent Clause)

A period, a question mark, or an exclamation mark is placed at the end of a simple sentence. A comma is not used to separate two different predicates. *Examples:* My name is Jennifer Smith. Who is that? That is great! The cat meows and chases the ball of yarn.

**Rules for Punctuating Compound Sentences
(Two or More Independent Clauses)**

1. A semicolon (;) is used at the end of the first independent clause if there is no linking word to join the two independent clauses. *Examples:* We no longer resent the new house blocking our view of the lake; it caught fire last night and burned down to the ground. I doubt that Sally will be very proud of her score on the test; she copied every answer from Sue. Hearing the quitting bell, the workers didn't waste a moment; they put down their tools and left immediately.

SPECIAL NOTE

When a semicolon joins two simple sentences, the two simple sentences must be so related to one another that they naturally go together. At times, the surrounding information necessitates the joining of the two simple sentences into one sentence. However, when sentences are taken out of context, the two simple sentences would stand as two sentences. *Examples:* The workers completed their jobs early. They went home. (out of context) The workers were told that they could leave as soon as they finished their work. What do you think happened? Naturally, the workers completed their jobs early; they went home. (in context)

2. A semicolon (;) is usually used at the end of the first independent clause if a word such as *therefore, however,* or *then* is used to link the two independent clauses. *Examples:* We went swimming for three hours; then it was time to go home. We waited for Jim a long time; however, he never arrived. My parents are going out tonight; therefore I have to stay home and take care of my little brother.

3. A comma is usually used at the end of the first independent clause if a word such as *and, or, but, nor, for,* or *yet* is used to join the independent clauses. *Examples:* Last week our professor explained some punctuation rules to us, but we are still having difficulty with them. The sun shone brightly, and the sky didn't have one cloud in it.

Practice A. Punctuate the following sentences.

1. The twins are nine years old

2. He has many friends but his brother is not liked by anyone

3. The exam was very easy however I did not do very well on it

4. We waited for him for hours then he arrived with his girlfriend

5. José and Maria have been dating for a long time

6. Jim likes to hunt and fish

7. Charles and Peter went on a hike and they went for a swim later

8. We bought a lot of food for the picnic but we forgot to buy the paper plates and napkins

9. We can't go to the movies with you however maybe Jane and Joyce can go with you

10. My parents came to this country eight years ago but they still have difficulty speaking English

Check answers at the end of Lesson 14.

Spelling: Homonyms or Homophones II

Following is a list of homonyms or homophones that may cause you some difficulty. Each is presented in a sentence so that you can see its correct usage. (Although some of the words presented here have more than one meaning, only one sentence and one meaning are given for each.)

pores—Cold water tends to close your *pores.*
pours—Every time she *pours* the milk, she spills it.

coarse—That material is very *coarse.*
course—The *course* I took in school was hard.

threw—He *threw* away all his old clothes.
through—I am *through* with her forever.

toe—My big *toe* is so large.
tow—When my car broke down, we needed to *tow* it to a garage.

air—I need *air* in all my tires.
heir—He is *heir* to the throne.

gait—The horse's *gait* was a trot.
gate—Please close the *gate.*

heel—The *heel* of my foot hurts.
heal—I hope your wound will *heal* quickly.

fair—That sounds *fair* to me.
fare—What is the bus *fare*?

ring—I wear a *ring* on almost all my fingers.
wring—Don't *wring* the clothes too much.

soars—The kite *soars* high in the sky.
sores—My feet have lots of *sores* from walking so much.

duel—He fights a *duel* in the film.
dual—He plays a *dual* role in the film.

sight—My *sight* is excellent.
cite—Please *cite* that for me again.
site—The building *site* was a good one.

principal—The school *principal* is very busy.
principle—I don't understand the *principle* involved.

due—That is long *due.*
dew—The grass was moist from the morning *dew.*

rode—We *rode* all night.
road—The *road* is in poor condition.

plain—I like *plain* things, nothing fancy.
plane—How many times have you flown in a *plane*?

hare—The *hare* ran into the woods.
hair—She has lovely blond *hair*.

knot—That's such a difficult *knot* to get out.
not—I will *not* attend the meeting.

tale—I enjoy hearing you tell that funny *tale*.
tail—The rabbit has a bushy *tail*.

hole—He fell into the *hole*.
whole—I want to buy the *whole* thing.

pane—The window *pane* was broken.
pain—She was in a lot of *pain*.

stake—Put the *stake* here to mark the spot.
steak—We eat *steak* for dinner once a week.

ate—I *ate* a lot yesterday.
eight—*Eight* is my lucky number.

Practice A.   Circle the correct word in parentheses.

1. I stubbed my (tow/toe)

2. (Stake/Steak) is good to eat.

3. Whenever she (wrings/rings) her hands, I know that she's worried.

4. I would like to (soar/sore) in the sky like a bird.

5. It is against the law to (duel/dual) in this country.

6. We had enough (fair/fare) to get us to the (fair/fare).

7. Fortunately for me, my (heel/heal) will (heel/heal)

8. If you park here, the police will (toe/tow) your car away.

9. He seems to walk with a superior (gait/gate).

10. The (principle/principal) called a student to his office to discuss a specific (principle/principal) concerning school fights.

11. I am (threw/through) fooling around.

12. His manners are so (course/coarse).

13. Did you choose the (cite/site/sight) for the new school?

14. I hate it when he starts to (sight/site/cite) those special (principles/ principals) to me.

15. On the golf (course/coarse) I met my best friend.

16. I don't think it's (fair/fare) that the (fair/fare) keeps going up.

17. (When are our reports (due/dew)?

18. Have you ever found (due/dew) on the ground in the early morning?

19. Cold water tends to close your (pours/pores).

20. Please (pour/pore) that carefully.

21. The (heir/air) to the throne was a woman who always had a superior (heir/air) about her.

22. The bumpy (rode/road) made our long journey very uncomfortable.

23. Last week we (rode/road) our bikes for five hours.

24. It's (plane/plain) to see that you are afraid of being in a (plane/plain).

25. How could you (knot/not) attend the meeting?

26. Unless you can untie this (knot/not), I'll have to cut it off.

27. That (tale/tail) about the dog's (tale/tail) is not very funny.

28. He couldn't believe that he had eaten the (hole/whole) pie.

29. They dug a large (whole/hole) in the ground.

30. The (pain/pane) was frosted.

31. The (pain/pane) in her leg was unbearable.

32. I have a large (stake/steak) in that investment.

33. (Steak/Stake) is an expensive cut of beef.

34. I (ate/eight) (ate/eight) pieces of candy.

35. I like short (hare/hair).

Check answers at the end of Lesson 14.

Practice B.   Change some words in each sentence so that the sentence makes sense.

1. Some principles site principals to their teachers.

_____

2. The fair two the circus cite was not fare.

_____

3. If my soar does not heel soon, eye will visit a doctor.

_____

4. The principle reason for the foul heir at the golf course was that the dump cite was won mile away.

_____

_____

5. He is soar because eye will play a duel roll in the play.

_____

6. When my I hurt on the plain, eye tried knot to show my pane, but my I made me feel as though eye wood dye.

_____

_____

7. After he eight the hole stake, he had a pane in his hole side.

_____

Check answers at the end of Lesson 14.

Practice C. Here are a number of challenging homonym riddles. State the words that fit the two clues. The words sound alike but have different spellings and different meanings. (Many of the words were not presented in this lesson.)

1. a number; what you did when you were hungry _____

_____

2. an insect; a relative _____ _____

3. part of your body; an animal _____ _____

4. an animal; what you bake with _____ _____

5. you bake with this; a blossom _____ _____

6. a part of something; freedom from disturbance _____

_____

7. a thoroughfare; to determine the heaviness of something

_____ _____

8. an animal; lacking clothing _____ _____

9. a number; a conjunction _____ _____

10. manner of walking; an opening in a fence _____

_____

11. yeses; important body organs _____ _____

12. part of a person's body; squander _____ _____

13. to trim; a fruit _____ _____

14. a vegetable; something that permits the escape of something else

_____ _____

15. up-to-date; a fruit _____ _____

16. a tree; a seashore area _____ _____

17. a vegetable; a unit of weight for precious stones _____

_____

18. fastening; the roof of a room _____ _____

19. blood runs through this; an instrument showing the direction of the wind

_____ _____

20. incline; a charge against property _____ _____

21. to kill; a snow vehicle _____ _____

22. money; intelligence _____ _____

23. a blow; an outer garment _____ _____

24. a soothsayer; to scorch _____ _____

25. a quick descent; a new growth of a plant _____

_____

26. an organized subdivision of the military; the central part _____

_____

27. an illness; a channel in a chimney _____ _____

28. a term used in mathematics; a signal _____ _____

29. arid land usually found in regions of extreme temperature ranges; a ladder rung _____ _____

30. a shellfish; a body tissue _____ _____

Check answers at the end of Lesson 14.

LESSON 14 ANSWERS

Figures of Speech (pp. 215–223)

Practice A: 1. wept huge tears   2. panting   3. refused   4. crept softly
5. opened; devour   6. straining; impatiently   7. thirsty; begged   8. felt naked
9. smiled   10. angry; spat fire

Practice B: 1. a gorged buzzard   2. a waterfall   3. a telegraph   4. a
frayed brown cord   5. a rocky road   6. a swift bird   7. a light in the night
8. a seal   9. a glowing orange ball   10. a tall bride

Practice C: 1. living pincushions   2. twisted pretzels   3. a wolf   4. a
ghost   5. a lamb   6. a smoking volcano   7. hot potatoes   8. razor-sharp
9. a crewcut   10. confetti

Practice D: 1. garden of delight (metaphor)   2. like bended bows
(simile)   3. with delight look round her (personification)   4. as a cloud
(simile)   5. tossing their heads in sprightly dance (personification)   6. bares
her bosom (personification)   7. wrinkled; crawls (personification)   8. like a
book (simile)   9. laid to sleep (personification)   10. threw down their spears
and watered heaven with their tears (personification)

Practice E: simile

Practice F: 1. Oxymoron—Although it was a victory, it brought losses
or other problems.   2. Hyperbole—The story is very old.   3. Oxymoron—It
was so quiet that it very vividly came to everyone's attention.   4. Oxymoron—
This refers to value. Something could be less in quantity but be worth more
than something greater in quantity.   5. Hyperbole—Someone has been waiting
for a very long time.   6. Oxymoron—Life can have many problems and difficulties.   7. Hyperbole—The person has a very large porch.   8. Oxymoron—It
may be that persons do something not because they are very brave but because they are afraid of the consequences if they don't do it.   9. Oxymoron—
Something can be so cold that it actually does burn the skin, e.g., dry ice.
10. Oxymoron—If it's quiet when there normally should be noise, the quiet-
ness can be frightening.

Practice G (sample answers):   1. ghostly gray   2. breathlessly cold
3. wavering pinpoints of light   4. smoky heat   5. relentless ticking.

Practice H (sample answers):   1. muddles   2. penetrates   3. dazzles
4. tempts   5. annoys.

Practice I: 1. apple of his eye—favorite; something highly cherished
2. bone to pick—grievance against; a cause for complaint; a matter to argue
about   3. cold shoulder—intentionally cold or unfriendly treatment
4. bed of roses—a place without trouble or discomfort; easy matter   5. millstone about my neck—hardship, heavy burden   6. wild-goose chase—futile
(useless), purposeless quest   7. bird's eye view—general view, an over-all
view, seen from above.   8. with tongue in cheek—jokingly, with insincerity
or whimsical exaggeration   9. last straw—the final thing   10. lame-duck—
coming to the end of a political term but still in office, even though the next
person to hold office has been chosen; helpless, ineffectual, disabled.

Practice J (sample answers): 1. your shadow—Your shadow is sunlight on a plate of silver. (Amy Lowell) 2. trees—The trees splash the sky with their fingers. (John Gould Fletcher) 3. in the morning—In the morning light drips through the shutters like the dew. (Conrad Aiken) 4. April—April comes like an idiot, babbling and strewing flowers. (Edna St. Vincent Millay) 5. frost—Frost, invisibly thorough, spreads its thickening stiffening lacquer. (Melville Cane).

Word Usage: Logical Sequence of Tenses (pp. 223–225)

Practice A: 1. saw 2. had been injured 3. prefers 4. was; had; did 5. had completed 6. had sent; have heard 7. have refused 8. saw 9. had been; did 10. told; was; needed.

Practice B: 1. (c) Mary said that she had broken up with her boyfriend a month ago and that she had given him back his ring at that time. 2. (g) Next semester I will take all required courses. 3. (j) The doctor said that the dog bite was not serious. 4. (a) He was sure that he had gotten an *A* in chemistry. 5. (f) They told us that they had finished building the boat about a month ago. 6. (h) Yesterday it rained so much that we still have a flooded basement. 7. (b) No one knows what one is capable of doing. 8. (i) None of my friends sat next to Bill at the game because he continually has played cruel jokes on many of us. 9. (d) The room is so dark that it is difficult to see. 10. (e) The squirrels came up to us and ate the nuts out of our hands.

Punctuation: A Review—Simple and Compound Sentences (pp. 225–226)

Practice A: 1. The twins are nine years old. 2. He has many friends, but his brother is not liked by anyone. 3. The exam was very easy; however, I did not do very well on it. 4. We waited for him for hours; then he arrived with his girlfriend. 5. José and Maria have been dating for a long time. 6. Jim likes to hunt and fish. 7. Charles and Peter went on a hike, and they went for a swim later. 8. We bought a lot of food for the picnic, but we forgot to buy the paper plates and napkins. 9. We can't go to the movies with you; however, maybe Jane and Joyce can go with you. 10. My parents came to this country eight years ago, but they still have difficulty speaking English.

Spelling: Homonyms or Homophones II (pp. 227–231)

Practice A: 1. toe 2. Steak 3. wrings 4. soar 5. duel 6. fare, fair 7. heel, heal 8. tow 9. gait 10. principal, principle 11. through 12. coarse 13. site 14. cite, principles 15. course 16. fair, fare 17. due 18. dew 19. pores 20. pour 21. heir, air 22. road 23. rode 24. plain, plane 25. not 26. knot 27. tale, tail 28. whole 29. hole 30. pane 31. pain 32. stake 33. Steak 34. ate, eight 35. hair.

Practice B: 1. Some principals cite principles to their teachers.   2. The fare to the circus site was not fair.   3. If my sore does not heal soon, I will visit a doctor.   4. The principal reason for the foul air at the golf course was that the dump site was one mile away.   5. He is sore because I will play a dual role in the play.   6. When my eye hurt on the plane, I tried not to show my pain, but my eye made me feel as though I would die.   7. After he ate the whole steak, he had a pain in his whole side.

Practice C: 1. eight; ate   2. ant; aunt   3. hair; hare   4. doe; dough 5. flour; flower   6. piece; peace   7. way; weigh   8. bear; bare   9. four; for 10. gait; gate   11. ayes; eyes   12. waist; waste   13. pare; pear   14. leek; leak 15. current; currant   16. beech; beach   17. carrot; carat   18. sealing; ceiling 19. vein; vane   20. lean, lien   21. slay; sleigh   22. cents; sense   23. rap; wrap 24. seer; sear   25. chute; shoot   26. corps; core   27. flu; flue   28. sine; sign 29. steppe; step   30. mussel; muscle.

Connotative Meaning
Word Usage: Active and Passive Voices of Verbs
Punctuation: A Review—Complex Sentences
Spelling: Some Spelling Generalizations I
Answers to Practices

Lesson 15

Connotative Meaning

When we speak or write we often rely more on the *connotative* meanings of words than on their *denotative* meanings to express our real position. The *connotative* meaning of a word includes its *denotative* meaning, the direct, specific meaning. However, the connotative meaning also includes all *emotional senses* associated with the word. The connotative use of a word therefore requires an understanding of more than a simple definition. When you respect a word's connotative meanings, you will use the word precisely and effectively.

1. *Credulous* and *trusting* are two words that have a similar denotative meaning: ready to believe or have faith in. However, if you refer to someone as "trusting," you are saying he or she has the admirable trait of believing the best of someone or something. If you refer to the same person as "credulous," you are saying that he or she lacks judgment, that he or she foolishly believes anything. Although both words have the same denotative meaning, in their very different connotative senses one is complimentary and the other belittling or insulting. Connotative meanings are obviously vital to saying the right thing the right way. Writers rely on connotative meanings all the time, especially when they want to influence their readers. Whether a word has a positive (*trusting*) or a negative (*credulous*) connotation makes a great difference to what is actually said.

SPECIAL NOTES

a. Words often have different overtones or associations for different people. For example, the term *mother* can bring forth images of apple pie, warmth, love, and kindness to one person; whereas for another it can mean beatings, hurt, shame, fear, and disillusionment.

b. Some words lend themselves more readily to emotional overtones or associations than others. For example, the term *home* can bring forth good or bad associations based on the past experiences of an individual. However, the term *dwelling*, which has the same specific definition as *home*, does not have the emotional overtones that *home* does.

2. A number of words have substitutes that more aptly express a particular meaning. For example, read these three sentences:

    a. The *girl* walked down the avenue.

    b. The *hussy* walked down the avenue.

    c. The *maiden* walked down the avenue.

Sentence (a) is more or less neutral. It probably does not evoke (bring forth) any emotional response.

Sentence (b) uses a derogatory (belittling) substitute for *girl*. The term *hussy* has strong negative overtones.

Sentence (c) uses a term that is more "refined," that is, has more positive overtones.

Practice A. Following are twelve pairs of statements. Determine the author's purpose in each one. Put a *P* in the blank if the author wishes you to feel *positively* and an *N* in the blank if the author wishes you to feel *negatively*.

For example: __P__ John is wearing a sharp suit.

                 __N__ John is wearing a flashy suit.

1. a. _____ Joan's hat was a glaring yellow.

   b. _____ Joan's hat was vivid yellow.

2. a. _____ The Demopluts are truly for the people.

   b. _____ The Demopluts are filled with radicals.

3. a. _____ Did you see Lucy's huge "barn"?

   b. _____ Did you see Lucy's mansion?

4. a. _____ What a gourmet feast that was!

   b. _____ What a vulgar display of a meal!

5. a. _____ The candidate, a solid citizen, looked over his constituents.

   b. _____ The candidate, cigar in mouth, leered at his puppets.

6. a. _____ Arthur is a candid person.

   b. _____ Arthur is tactless.

7. a. _____ Isn't Florence a friendly person?

   b. _____ Isn't Florence too familiar?

8. a. _____ That man has a sturdy body.

   b. _____ That man is too fat.

9. a. _____ What a helpful person!

   b. _____ What a fawning person!

10. a. _____ Marty is so openminded about everything.

    b. _____ Marty can never take a stand on anything.

11. a. _____ Every time he speaks, it's double talk.

    b. _____ His speech is technical and erudite.

12. a. _____ It's difficult to get anything done in the red tape of such a vast bureaucracy.

    b. _____ Systematic checks on all decisions are very important in large organizations.

Check answers at the end of Lesson 15.

Practice B. Following are some newspaper headlines on similar topics. Notice the headlines in each. Notice the words used by the writers to describe the players and the action. State whether the writer is neutral (has no favorites), has a favorite (state the favorite), or is negative. (Make one choice only for each headline.)

1. a. J. J. Downs N. J. _____

   b. J. J. Blasts N. N. Out of the Court_____

   c. N. N. No Match for J. J. _____

   d. N. N. Has Off Night — Loses to J. J._____

2. a. Farley Defeats Five Foes _____

   b. Farley, More Clown Than Fighter_____

   c. Farley, in Masterful Exhibition, Defeats Five Foes in Succession ____

   _____

3. a. K. James to Meet L. Mack in Ring_____

   b. K. James Cinch to Slaughter L. Mack_____

   c. Fight Rated a Toss-up by Most Experts_____

4. a. Country X Changes Its Regime_____

   b. Country X in the Grip of an Iron Hand_____

   c. Country X Enjoying Good Fortune_____

5. a. Civil War Ends in Country Y_____

   b. Government Troops of Country Y Surrender to Insurgent Forces

   _____ (*insurgent*—rising up against

   political or governmental authority)

c. Government Troops of Country Y Ruthlessly Annihilated by Insur-

gent Forces _____

(*annihilate*—to destroy wholly; demolish, with connotation of excessive violence)

Check answers at the end of Lesson 15.

Practice C. For each of these ten sets of words, use the following key to indicate whether
the word has a neutral, a positive, or a negative connotation. (1)—neutral; (2)—belittling
or negative; (3)—lofty or positive. A set may have more than one word in each category
or may have no words in one of the categories. Put the number in the blank.

1. A building people live in: (a) shack_____   (b) barn_____

   (c) castle_____   (d) house_____

2. One who upholds the law: (a) officer_____(b) policeman_____

   (c) pig_____   (d) cop_____

3. One engaged in military service: (a) mercenary_____ (b) warrior_____

   (c) soldier_____

4. A girl: (a) woman_____   (b) chick_____   (c) lady_____

   (d) female_____

5. A girlfriend: (a) date_____(b) prostitute_____ (c) whore_____

   (d) companion_____(e) call girl_____

6. A characteristic of an individual: (a) effeminate_____(b) weak_____

   (c) gentle_____(d) cowardly_____

7. A characteristic of an individual: (a) passive_____(b) submissive_____

   (c) patient_____

8. A characteristic of an individual: (a) miserly_____(b) niggardly_____

   (c) greedy_____(d) thrifty_____

9. A smell: (a) fragrance_____   (b) odor_____ (c) stink_____

   (d) scent_____

10. A piece of furniture: (a) old_____   (b) run-down_____

    (c) antique_____(d) obsolete_____

Check answers at the end of Lesson 15.

Word Usage: Active and Passive Voices of Verbs

    1. If the subject in a sentence is doing the action, the verb is in the
active voice.   *Example of active voice:* John hit the ball. (John [the sub-

ject is the doer of the action] hit [verb] ball [the noun receiving the action is the object of the action]). *Other examples:* Sharon baked a cake. Jennifer ate the cookie. Ernesto read a book. The men fixed the car.

2. If the subject in a sentence is receiving the action, the sentence is in the **passive voice**. *Example of the passive voice:* The ball was hit by John. (Ball [the subject is the receiver of the action] was hit [the verb phrase containing a form of the verb *to be*] John [a noun becomes part of the phrase beginning with *by*].) *Other examples:* A cake was baked by Sharon. The cookie was eaten by Jennifer. A book was read by Ernesto. The car was fixed by the men.

SPECIAL NOTE

In the sentence *The ball was hit by John,* John is object of the preposition *by. By John* is a prepositional phrase.

3. The passive voice should not be used when there is a strong and convenient subject to use with the active.

Examples:
(active)	The students applauded the speaker.
(passive)	The speaker was applauded by the students.
(active)	The student met the advisor.
(passive)	The advisor was met by the student.
(active)	Sharon baked a cake.
(passive)	A cake was baked by Sharon.

4. The active voice is generally preferred to the passive voice. The passive voice is usually not as direct as the active voice, and it often reduces the smoothness of the sentence.

Examples:
   a. His performance was loudly applauded by the audience. (passive voice)
   b. The audience loudly applauded his performance (active voice)

   a. The food was eaten with great pleasure by everyone. (passive voice)
   b. Everyone ate the food with great pleasure. (active voice)

   a. The reading of the book was enjoyed by me. (passive voice)
   b. I enjoyed reading the book. (active voice)

   a. The window was broken by John. (passive voice)
   b. John broke the window. (active voice)

Sentences (b) express more emphasis because they are more direct, and they are also smoother than sentences (a).

5. The passive voice is necessary when the doer of the action is unknown or the mention of a specific subject is not desirable.

Examples: The window was broken during the night. The store was robbed. The wealthy oil man was kidnapped. A pie was thrown at the speaker. Many stories have been told about the Lindbergh kidnapping.

6. The passive voice is necessary when the doer of the action (the subject) is less important than the action itself or the result of the action. *Examples:* The entire village was wiped out. Five women were assaulted in the same area. The people were cured.

7. A verb in the passive voice consists of some form of the auxiliary verb *to be* plus the past participle of the main verb. The past participle of a verb is a verb that usually ends in *-ed, -en,* or *-t* or is formed by a vowel change (*swept, claimed, broken, attacked, kept, sung,* and so on). *Examples:* It *was eaten* by me. The floor *was swept* by Mary. The game *was won* by the other team. The man was *killed* by the car. The book *is read* by Francis. The cookie *is being eaten* by the baby. The men *were attacked.* The factory *was shut down.* The building *was burned* to the ground.

SPECIAL NOTES

a. You should not confuse the past tense of a verb with the past participle of a verb. When the past participle is used as a verb, it is always used with an auxiliary such as *have* and *be*; whereas the past tense of a verb is always used alone as a single-word verb.

b. The past participle and the past tense of regular verbs are spelled the same.

Examples:

Past Tense	Past Participle
climbed	climbed
jumped	jumped
played	played
carried	carried

c. The past participle and the past tense of irregular verbs are usually not spelled the same.

Examples:

Past Tense	Past Participle
was	been
began	begun
chose	chosen
wrote	written

d. Writers cannot be as creative with the passive voice as with the active voice because of the need to use some form of the verb *to be* with the passive.

8. Only sentences that contain **transitive verbs** can be changed to the passive voice. *Examples:* John plays soccer (active voice). Soccer is played by John (passive voice). The verb *play* can take an object. *Play* is a transitive verb. The object of *play* in the sentence is *soccer.* The action [*play*] of the doer [*John*] goes to the object of the action [*soccer*] .

9. Sentences containing intransitive verbs cannot be put into the passive voice. *Examples:* Birds fly. John thinks. Mary is pretty. Anna walks. She is a lawyer. John became a doctor.

10.   There are times when the combining of the active and passive voices in the same sentence is beneficial. It is also helpful when you want a variation of pace.   *Examples:* Although the basement had been cleaned thoroughly a month before, it now needed cleaning again. (combining of passive in dependent clause and active in independent clause) The active and passive voices differ in force, emphasis, and pace, but they can be used in the same sentence. (combining of active in the first independent clause and passive in the second independent clause)

11.   There are times when the combining of the active and passive voices in the same sentence is awkward and should not be used. Sentences (a) use a combination of the active and passive voices. Sentences (b) use only one voice.

Examples:

a. Although the ball was thrown by him very swiftly, I hit it.
b. Although he threw the ball very swiftly, I hit it.

a. As we had waited a long time to see him, his visit last week was enjoyed by us.
b. As we had waited a long time to see him, we enjoyed his visit last week.

a. We were shocked by the news that a car had killed John.
b. We were shocked by the news that John had been killed by a car.

Practice A. Put a circle around the numbers of those sentences that can be put in the passive voice.

1. She went for a walk in the part.

2. My sister is a doctor.

3. I hope to become a lawyer.

4. The actors read the script with great feeling.

5. The cat drank the milk.

6. How old are you?

7. I will build that house.

8. Her name is Jennifer Alison Smith.

9. His father helped me with my math problem.

10. Nobody seems to be responsible for him.

11. The birds fly south at this time every year.

12. The deer ran swiftly in the woods.

13. The dog bit the child's arm.

14. The shark dived underwater.

15. That dress is pretty.

Check answers at the end of Lesson 15.

Practice B. Change each of the following sentences into the active voice.

1. The baseball game was played by us in the schoolyard.

_____

2. Trash was thrown all over the field by motorists.

_____

3. The school was closed by the Board of Education.

_____

4. All the classes that I wanted to take had been closed by the registrar.

_____

5. The concert was enjoyed by us.

_____

6. The complicated step was danced by the couple.

_____

7. The jet was bought by our company.

_____

8. The entire cast in the show was fired by the producer.

_____

9. The test was failed by half of the class.

_____

10. The food was eaten by everyone.

_____

Check answers at the end of Lesson 15.

Practice C. Write the following sentences in the passive voice.

1. The men fixed the leak.

_____

2. Lightning struck the house.

_____

3. The boy climbed the ladder so that he could get a better view of the roof.

_____

4. The campers cleaned the bunkhouse so that their counselor would give them a star.

_____

5. Yesterday, after we had eaten dinner, we played basketball in the park.

_____

Check answers at the end of Lesson 15.

Practice D. Read each sentence carefully. If the sentence is written awkwardly, rewrite it. If the sentence does not need to be rewritten, put *O* in the blank.

1. Although the basement had been cleaned by us a month ago, we needed to clean it again.

_____

_____

2. Television was watched by us for three hours; then we ate a snack.

_____

_____

3. My roommates and I play bridge every Wednesday night, but last Wednesday poker was played by us.

_____

_____

4. The meal was eaten by us in silence because we just heard that one of our friends had broken his neck in a car accident.

_____

_____

5. We shook our heads in amazement when we saw the three little dogs riding the white horse.

_____

_____

Check answers at the end of Lesson 15.

Practice E. Write two sentences that combine the active and passive voices effectively.

1. _____

_____

_____

2. _____

_____

_____

Check sample sentences at the end of Lesson 15.

Punctuation: A Review—
Complex Sentences

Rules for Punctuating Complex Sentences

Remember that a complex sentence is one with an independent clause and one or more dependent clauses.

1. A comma is used in a complex sentence if the dependent clause precedes (comes before) the independent clause. *Examples:* Although he tries very hard, he just doesn't seem to be able to understand the work. When the train stopped at the station, crowds of people rushed to board it. Since it is so late now, I'll read the assignment in the morning.

2. No comma is used in a complex sentence if the independent clause precedes (comes before) a dependent clause that is restrictive (that supplies necessary information by limiting or defining an element in the main clause). *Example:* The moving van arrived hours before we did because our car had a flat tire.

SPECIAL NOTES

a. Clauses introduced by *though* and *although* are always nonrestrictive.
b. Clauses introduced by *if* are restrictive.
c. Clauses introduced by *because* are usually restrictive, but they may be non-restrictive.
d. Clauses introduced by *unless* and *except* are usually restrictive.

Practice A. Place commas in those sentences that need them. If a sentence does not require a comma, put a O in the blank.

_____ 1. When James arrived home from college his whole family went to meet him at the airport.

_____ 2. We will have to wait until she arrives.

_____ 3. Unless we find an antidote for the poison the child will die.

_____ 4. Before you take the exam read the directions.

_____ 5. I do not know where the twins are going on their vacation.

_____ 6. As long as you are here you might as well help us prepare for the party.

_____ 7. I do not want to go to the basketball game tonight because my former boyfriend will be there.

_____ 8. We told her that she was being silly.

_____ 9. No one knew what to expect when the new instructor came into the classroom.

_____10. Whenever I am feeling unhappy I play some lively music to cheer myself up.

Check answers at the end of Lesson 15.

Spelling: Some Spelling Generalizations I

Keeping the Final Silent *e* Before Endings Beginning with Consonants

Rule: Most words ending in a final silent *-e* keep the *e* when adding endings beginning with consonants. *Examples:* arrangement, lately, excitement.

Exceptions: judgment, acknowledgment, argument, ninth, truly, wholly, awful.

Adding *-able* to Words Ending in Silent *e*

Rule: Drop the final silent *e* before adding the ending *-able.*

Most words ending in a final silent *-e,* except those ending in *-ce* and *-ge,* drop the *e* before adding *-able.* Words ending in *-ce* and *-ge* keep the *e* to maintain the soft sound. If the *e* were dropped in words ending in *-ce* and *-ge,* the words would have a hard sound rather than a soft sound. For example, the *g* in manage would sound like the hard *g* in *get* and the *c* in *enforce* would sound like the hard *c* in *cat. Examples:* love — lovable; manage — manageable.

SPECIAL NOTE

Verbs ending in *ee* keep both *e*'s before endings beginning with vowels. *Examples:* agreeable, agreeing, seeing, refereeing.

Adding *-ing* to Words Ending in Silent *e*

Rule: Drop the final silent *e* before adding *-ing.*

Most words ending in a final silent *-e,* including those ending in *-ce* and *-ge,* drop the *e* before adding *-ing. Examples:* hope — hoping; manage — managing.

Adding Endings to Final *-y* Words

Rule: When a word ends in *-y* and a consonant precedes (comes before) the *y*, the *y* is usually changed to *i* before the ending is added. If a vowel comes before the *y*, the *y* is usually retained (kept) before the ending is added. *Examples:* beauty — beautiful; crazy — crazier; busy — business; fly — flies; day — days; happy — happiness; relay — relays; cry — cries. *Exceptions:* lay — laid; say — said; pay — paid; day — daily.

SPECIAL NOTE

Words that end in *-y* usually do not drop or change the *y* before adding endings beginning with *i*. *Examples:* baby — babyish; hurry — hurrying; bury — burying; fly — flying.

Practice A. Add the ending *-ful* (full of) to the following words.

1. force_____   2. care_____

3. waste_____   4. peace_____

5. use_____   6. grace_____

7. awe_____   8. fate_____

9. hope_____   10. shame_____

Check answers at the end of Lesson 15.

Practice B. Add the ending *-ment* (act of, state of) to the following words.

1. acknowledge_____   2. judge_____

3. excite_____   4. achieve_____

5. appease_____   6. state_____

7. commence_____   8. require_____

9. enforce_____   10. advertise_____

Check answers at the end of Lesson 15.

Practice C. Add the ending *-ly* (like, manner of) to the following words.

1. whole_____   2. true_____

3. prince_____   4. complete_____

5. relative_____   6. separate_____

7. genuine_____   8. late_____

9. entire_____   10. sure_____

Check answers at the end of Lesson 15.

Practice D.   Add the ending -ly to the following words.

1. ready_____   2. merry_____

3. happy_____   4. necessary_____

5. noisy_____   6. easy_____

7. day_____   8. busy_____

9. body_____   10. crazy_____

Check answers at the end of Lesson 15.

Practice E.   Add the ending -able to the following words.

1. like_____   2. sale_____

3. believe_____   4. receive_____

5. pleasure_____   6. enforce_____

7. measure_____   8. insure_____

9. blame_____   10. excuse_____

11. salvage _____   12. advise_____

13. desire_____   14. notice_____

15. pronounce_____   16. change_____

17. discourage_____   18. package_____

19. use_____   20. trace_____

21. knowledge_____   22. challenge_____

23. achieve_____   24. value_____

25. arrange_____   26. encourage_____

27. bounce_____   28. lease_____

29. dodge_____   30. mortgage_____

31. love_____   32. service_____

33. excite_____   34. slice_____

Check answers at the end of Lesson 15.

Practice F.   Add the ending -ed to the following words.

1. dry_____   2. spy_____

3. ply_____   4. marry_____

5. play_____   6. annoy_____

7. deny_____   8. envy_____

9. hurry_____   10. pay_____

Check answers at the end of Lesson 15.

Practice G. Add the ending -*ing* to the following words.

1. ice _____   2. bake _____

3. love _____   4. make _____

5. slice _____   6. change _____

7. challenge _____ 8. notice _____

9. dodge _____   10. use _____

11. wage _____   12. judge _____

13. interfere _____ 14. force _____

15. come _____   16. indulge _____

17. sense _____   18. argue _____

19. guide _____   20. write _____

21. refuse _____   22. rake _____

23. bounce _____   24. encourage _____

25. salvage _____

Check answers at the end of Lesson 15.

LESSON 15 ANSWERS

Connotative Meaning (pp. 235–238)

Practice A: 1. a. N   b. P;   2. a. P   b. N;   3. a. N   b. P;   4. a. P   b. N;
5. a. P   b. N;   6. a. P   b. N;   7. a. P   b. N   8. a. P   b. N;   9. a. P   b. N;   10. a. P
b. N;   11. a. N   b. P;   12. a. N   b. P.

Practice B: 1. a. neutral   b. favors J.J   c. favors J.J.   d. favors N.N.;
2. a. neutral   b. negative   c. favors Farley   3. a. neutral   b. favors K. James
c. neutral;   4. a. neutral   b. negative   c. favors Country X;   5. a. neutral
b. neutral   c. negative toward insurgents.

Practice C:

    1. a. (2) b. (2) c. (3) d. (1)
    2. a. (3) b. (1) c. (2) d. (2)
    3. a. (2) b. (3) c. (1)
    4. a. (1) b. (2) c. (3) d. (1)
    5. a. (1) b. (2) c. (2) d. (1) e. (2)
    6. a. (2) b. (2) c. (3) d. (2)
    7. a. (2) b. (2) c. (3)
    8. a. (2) b. (2) c. (2) d. (3)
    9. a. (3) b. (1) c. (2) d. (1)
    10. a. (1) b. (2) c. (3) d. (2)

Word Usage: Active and Passive Voices of Verbs (pp. 238–243)

Practice A: 4, 5, 7, 9, 13.

Practice B: 1. We played the baseball game in the schoolyard.
2. Motorists threw trash all over the field.   3. The Board of Education
closed the school.   4. The registrar had closed all the classes that I wanted to
take.   5. We enjoyed the concert.   6. The couple danced the complicated
step.   7. Our company bought the jet.   8. The producer fired the entire cast
in the show.   9. Half of the class failed the test.   10. Everyone ate the food.

Practice C: 1. The leak was fixed by the men.   2. The house was struck
by lightning.   3. The ladder was climbed by the boy so that a better view of
the roof could be gotten by him.   4. The bunkhouse was cleaned by the
campers so that a star would be given to them by their counselor.   5. Yesterday, after dinner had been eaten, basketball was played in the park.

Practice D: 1. Although we had cleaned the basement a month ago, we
needed to clean it again. *or:* Although we had cleaned the basement a month
ago, it needed to be cleaned again.   2. We watched television for three hours;
then we ate a snack.   3. My roommates and I play bridge every Wednesday
night, but last Wednesday we played poker.   4. We ate the meal in silence
because we just heard that one of our friends had broken his neck in a car
accident.   5. 0

Practice E (sample sentences):   1. Although the man had been beaten
very badly, he insisted on talking to the police about his assailant.   2. All

persons who were exposed to the disease were taken to the infirmary because they needed a special inoculation.

Punctuation: A Review—Complex Sentences (pp. 244–245)

Practice A: 1. When James arrived home from college, his whole family went to meet him at the airport. 2. O 3. Unless we find an antidote for the poison, the child will die. 4. Before you take the exam, read the directions. 5. O 6. As long as you are here, you might as well help us prepare for the party. 7. O 8. O 9. O 10. Whenever I am feeling unhappy, I play some lively music to cheer myself up.

Spelling: Some Spelling Generalizations I (pp. 245–248)

Practice A: 1. forceful 2. careful 3. wasteful 4. peaceful 5. useful 6. graceful 7. awful 8. fateful 9. hopeful 10. shameful.

Practice B: 1. acknowledgment 2. judgment 3. excitement 4. achievement 5. appeasement 6. statement 7. commencement 8. requirement 9. enforcement 10. advertisement.

Practice C: 1. wholly 2. truly 3. princely 4. completely 5. relatively 6. separately 7. genuinely 8. lately 9. entirely 10. surely.

Practice D: 1. readily 2. merrily 3. happily 4. necessarily 5. noisily 6. easily 7. daily 8. busily 9. bodily 10. crazily.

Practice E: 1. likable 2. salable 3. believable 4. receivable 5. pleasurable 6. enforceable 7. measurable 8. insurable 9. blamable 10. excusable 11. salvageable 12. advisable 13. desirable 14. noticeable 15. pronounceable 16. changeable 17. discourageable 18. packageable 19. usable 20. traceable 21. knowledgeable 22. challengeable 23. achievable 24. valuable 25. arrangeable 26. encourageable 27. bounceable 28. leasable 29. dodgeable 30. mortgageable 31. lovable 32. serviceable 33. excitable 34. sliceable.

Practice F: 1. dried 2. spied 3. plied 4. married 5. played 6. annoyed 7. denied 8. envied 9. hurried 10. paid.

Practice G: 1. icing 2. baking 3. loving 4. making 5. slicing 6. changing 7. challenging 8. noticing 9. dodging 10. using 11. waging 12. judging 13. interfering 14. forcing 15. coming 16. indulging 17. sensing 18. arguing 19. guiding 20. writing 21. refusing 22. raking 23. bouncing 24. encouraging 25. salvaging.

Lesson 16

Word Meanings and Sentence Context

Because many words have more than one meaning, the meaning of the word is determined by how the word is used in a sentence. In writing sentences, you must be careful to use those words with many meanings correctly. In the following pairs of sentences, notice how the same italicized word conveys different meanings:

1. That is a large *stack* of books.
2. *Stack* the books here.

1. The *train* had a lot of passengers.
2. Do you *train* your own dog?

1. The dogs *bark* at night in my neighborhood.
2. The *bark* of the tree is peeling.

From these, you can see that the way the word is used in the sentence will determine its meaning. Words that are spelled the same but have different meanings are called **homographs**. Readers should be able to grasp the meaning of homographs from the sentence **context** (the words surrounding a word that can shed light on its meaning). In the listed sentences notice how run's placement in the sentence and the surrounding words help you to figure out the meaning of each use.

1. Walk, don't <u>run</u>.

2. I have a <u>run</u> in my stocking.

3. Senator Jones said that he would not <u>run</u> for another term.

251

4. The trucker finished his <u>run</u> to Detroit.

5. She is going to <u>run</u> in a ten-mile race.

6. The play had a <u>run</u> of two years.

In sentence 1 *run* means "go quickly by moving the legs more rapidly than at a walk."

In sentence 2 *run* means "a tear."

In sentence 3 *run* means "be or campaign as a candidate for election."

In sentence 4 *run* means "route."

In sentence 5 *run* means "take part in a race."

In sentence 6 *run* means "continuous course of performances."

Some homographs are spelled the same but do not sound the same. For example, *refuse* means "trash"; *refuse* means "to decline to accept." In sentence a in the examples *refuse* (ref' use) meaning "trash" is pronounced differently from the term *refuse* (re fuse') meaning "to decline to accept" in sentence b. In reading you can determine the meaning of *refuse* from the way it is used in the sentence (context clues). *Examples:*

    a. During the garbage strike there were tons of uncollected *refuse* on the streets of the city.

    b. I *refuse* to go along with you.

©1978 by Bob Cordray

Practice A. In each of the following sentences, fill in the blanks with *one word* that will make sense in each place.

1. The _____ of the United States is Washington, D.C., but I don't think that it's a _____ idea to start a business there with so little _____ .

2. I'm glad that we ate a _____ meal and left while it was still _____ .

3. In the _____ , I watch the fish in the _____ _____ out of the water.

4. They ordered another _____ of soda in _____ more people than they expected showed up at the party to celebrate the winning of the _____ .

5. It's safer to change a_____tire on a _____road than on a hill.

6. At my father's army_____, there is a crooked _____that holds the letter box in which you _____your letters.

7. I must_____that we were in a happy_____when we left the_____in which my grandparents live.

8. I listened with great_____as the banker told me how much _____ I would receive.

9. My friend tells me that he can_____curve balls when it's _____dark.

10. The woman said that she would cast a _____on any-one who couldn't_____her name.

11. We tried to_____a taxi when it started to_____.

12. In the_____the robbers bury the gold in a_____in the cemetery.

13. The president of the _____said that his position was_____.

14. A_____error was made in calculating my_____pay for selling a_____of pens.

15. Mr._____said that he would not_____permission for the large_____that was requested.

16. The man, looking_____, said that a(n)_____error had caused the accident in which a person ended in a(n)_____.

17. It is_____knowledge that persons with _____manners lack refinement.

18. He couldn't even_____it at_____writing, so he decided to become a_____driver.

19. Although I am not in the_____of wearing such a(n)_____, it is the_____here to wear one.

20. At the_____, the_____player dropped the ball right in the_____of the basket.

21. The_____man always seems to break out in a(n)_____.

22. After the football player made a first_____, he fell_____on what felt like a bed of_____.

23. The_____man said that we should_____his name off

the list because there was no_____ next to his name.

24. I need to_____up on the_____structure of certain animals for my biology exam.

25. Although I do not like to_____opinions on what is proper _____, I think that the_____of the marriage service that you are planning should be changed.

Check answers at the end of Lesson 16.

Practice B. Following you will find two sets of sentences for each word. Each sentence uses the word in different ways. Read the sentences in set A carefully. Then read the sentences in set B. Match the sentence in set B to a sentence in set A that uses the word in the same sense.

Group I

       Set A

_____1. The workers went on *strike.*

_____2. The player made a *strike.*

_____3. *Strike* the match carefully to light it.

_____4. Don't *strike* that child.

_____5. When do you expect the enemy to *strike?*

       Set B

a. At dawn the soldiers prepared to *strike.*

b. If you *strike* him, you'll be arrested.

c. You have only one *strike*; so you're not out yet.

d. Why are you on *strike?*

e. *Strike* it lightly.

Group II

       Set A

_____1. My mother needs a few *rests* during the day.

_____2. His body *rests* in a sacred place.

_____3. The future *rests* in your hands.

_____4. The bundle *rests* on a table.

_____5. After the summation the defense lawyer *rests* his case.

       Set B

a. We hope he *rests* in peace.

b. In Greek architecture the column *rests* on a pedestal.

c. The defense *rests*, your honor.

d. The decision *rests* with you.

e. *Rests* are necessary for young children.

Group III

Set A

_____ 1. They've gone down to the *point* to dig for clams.

_____ 2. It was at that *point* that Arthur decided to intervene.

_____ 3. He scored a *point* in the game.

_____ 4. I can see no *point* in his going there.

_____ 5. That has a sharp *point*.

_____ 6. The witness was asked to *point* out the assailant.

_____ 7. What is the *point* of your story?

Set B

a. I need one *point* to graduate.

b. She said that there was no *point* in going on.

c. The lighthouse on the *point* guided them back to shore.

d. She reached a critical *point* in her life.

e. All the arrows on the trail were used to *point* out the right direction.

f. He never seems to be able to get his *point* across.

g. When the *point* of the needle touched me, I fainted.

Check answers at the end of Lesson 16.

Practice C. Following are sets of meanings for each word. State the word that corresponds to each set of meanings. Then construct a sentence using the word in at least two different ways. *Example:* bad smelling; unfair play. *Answer:* foul. He claimed that the *foul* air caused him to make a *foul*.

1. To cause to appear tidy; to train or develop; a man or boy whose work is tending horses; the husband of a bride. _____

_____

2. Social position; a state of peace; a state in which everything is in place; a group of men in a brotherhood; an arrangement of things; a fixed or definite plan; a command; to request things. _____

_____

3. The sea border of a country; the incline down which a slide is taken; to

keep going on acquired momentum. _____

---

4. Full of pluck; any specific sport or amusement; wild birds, fish, or other animals that are pursued. _____

---

5. A mathematical term referring to average; stingy; poor or inferior; to think, imagine; to have in mind. _____

Check answers and sample sentences at the end of Lesson 16.

Practice D. Find one word that fits the blanks in each set of phrases.

1. A _____ ing match; _____ the breeze; _____ pool.

2. _____ yourself; made of _____; nerves of _____.

3. A royal _____; _____ of a seed; _____ of a tooth; at the _____; hit in the _____.

4. The _____ hill; _____ ed in a subject; let it _____ for a while.

5. A _____ of grain; a state of _____; to meet with a _____; a _____ of hair.

6. _____ a little on the rules; _____ ed the figures; to _____ on delicate matters; delicious _____.

7. _____ the tide; _____ of a word; _____ of a plant; _____ of a musical note.

8. A _____ horse; a _____ aunt; a ship's _____ voyage.

9. A _____ of the industry; an extinct _____; of _____ size.

10. The flight _____; the _____ of events; frost _____; a dressmaker's _____; _____ yourself after.

11. The _____ of the problem; a decayed _____; the _____ of all evil; the _____ of a word; the _____ of a tooth.

12. _____ at any chance; my _____ is broken; _____ your fingers; _____ the lock shut.

13. _____ the salad; I will _____ the report with research data.

14. _____the bill; the _____of the hill; on _____;
    the _____of the bed.

15. _____for an exam; _____an ax; _____her teeth;
    _____out material.

16. The factory is in_____; the _____was a success; it's a
    simple_____.

17. Post_____; _____water; a _____for animals;
    _____out; the _____of a typewriter; the _____
    of a pail.

18. _____the odds; the _____is small; perfect _____.

19. Set in_____; a _____example; _____poetry.

20. _____out; an important _____; as a _____;
    _____a line; _____a country.

Check answers at the end of Lesson 16.

Word Usage: Verb Mood

The **mood** of a verb refers to the way that the writer or speaker views the action of a verb. It expresses the writer's or speaker's mood or state of mind. There are three different kinds of verb moods. You are probably very familiar with the first two.

1. Mood stating a fact or asking a question (indicative mood). This includes all statement (declarative) and question (interrogative) sentences. Most verbs are in this mood. *Examples:* I have a great amount of work to do. How much time do we have left to finish the exam?

2. Mood expressing a command, a desire, or an urgent request (imperative mood). *Examples:* Do it now. Please help us. Go at once to the hospital. Stop.

3. Mood expressing a wish or a condition contrary to fact, that is, a condition that does not exist at the moment (subjunctive mood). *Examples:* If I *were* to win the lottery, I would be a millionaire. If you *were* more mature, I would consider marrying you. If he *were* all those things, I would probably go out with him. I wish I *were* in the South Sea Islands. The subjunctive is also used in a dependent clause in a sentence expressing a demand, request, or requirement. *Examples:* It is important that you *be* present at the reading of the will. It is necessary that he *be* elected. He requested that you *be* there. He requested that the teacher *be* present at the meeting. He demanded that he *be* given the money.

SPECIAL NOTES

    a. In the subjunctive, *were* is used in place of *was* for the past tense and *be* is used in place of *are* in the present tense. However, *be* is not used very often in an *if* clause expressing a condition contrary to fact. *Be* is used more often in the dependent clause of a sentence expressing a demand, request, or requirement.

    b. The subjunctive mood usually requires coupling with the conditional forms *would* and *could*. In the subjunctive, you do not say, "If I were to win the lottery, I *will* be a millionaire," but, "If I were to win the lottery, I *would* be a millionaire." The subjunctive declares a state that is imagined rather than one that is or will be fact. The verbs of statements related to that subjunctive must reflect the unfulfilled quality of the state of action. On the other hand, if the "if clause" expresses a state of action that may come to pass, then related verbs are not in the subjunctive mood but in the indicative. *Examples:* If I am elected, I shall carry out my campaign promises. (indicative) If I am elected, I will not let that man stay in politics. (indicative)

Practice A. Fill in the blank in each sentence with a word that correctly completes the sentence.

1. The hijackers demanded that their requests_____ met.

2. We wish we_____ in Bermuda.

3. I wish I_____ a famous author.

4. If he_____ the candidate, he could win the election.

5. It is necessary that you_____ in good shape for the tennis match tomorrow.

6. The people demanded that the killer_____ captured.

7. If I were you, I_____ not go to that party.

8. We insist that you_____ present tomorrow to hear the results.

9. If I_____ wealthy, I would help make life easier for my family.

10. The instructor requested that the student_____ given another examination.

Check answers at the end of Lesson 16.

Punctuation: Revision and Proofreading

    Both revision and proofreading are important and needed for a polished final copy of a paper, but they involve different processes. Revision refers to the creative improvement of an existing script; whereas proofreading has to do with the correcting of technical writing errors such as punctuation errors, capitalization errors, spelling errors, and so on. As this book is primarily concerned with the writing of sentences, the discussion of revision and proofreading will be confined mostly to this area.

Checklist for Revision

1. Reread your sentences. Do they make sense to you? (React as an uninformed reader to your topic rather than as the writer.)
2. Is the way you have written your sentences the *best* way to present your ideas?
3. Do all your sentences begin in the same way?
4. Have you used variety in sentence structure?
5. Have you used different types of sentences to portray your ideas?
6. Have you varied sentence lengths?
7. Is the tone of your sentences the one you want; that is, do you sound overbearing, preachy, sarcastic, or angry?
8. Are your sentences too wordy; that is, can you say the same thing in fewer words or more succinctly?
9. Do you present your ideas in a direct rather than round-about manner?
10. Have you used overworked phrases in your writing?
11. Have you overused certain words or phrases?
12. Are you pleased with what you have written?

Checklist for Proofreading

1. Have you checked your spelling and looked up any words you are not sure of in the dictionary?
2. Do you have a period at the end of your sentences that should have periods?
3. Do you have a question mark at the end of your sentences that ask a question?
4. Do you have a capital letter at the beginning of all of your sentences?
5. Do you have a capital letter at the beginning of all names and names of things?
6. Have you capitalized "I" whenever you used it?
7. Have you put in commas when you are listing lots of things?
8. Have you put the apostrophe in the proper place in making contractions—such as *can't, don't, isn't, hasn't, I'm*?
9. Have you used the apostrophe in the correct place in writing possessives—such as *Charles's, Joneses', enemies', deer's*?
10. Have you checked for agreement of subject and verb?
11. Have you checked for proper agreement of pronouns with their antecedents?
12. Have you used the active voice whenever possible?
13. Have you overused dashes, brackets, or parentheses?
14. Have you used semicolons in the correct places?
15. Have you checked for run-on sentences?
16. Do you have the proper verb tenses?
17. Do you have the proper verb mood?
18. Are your sentences parallel?
19. Are your sentences complete sentences?

Spelling: Some Spelling Generalizations II

Double Consonant Rule for Closed Syllables (One-Syllable Words)

Before you study the double consonant rule for closed syllables, read over this explanation of syllables.

Explanation of Syllable

A **syllable** is a vowel or group of letters that has one vowel sound. *Examples:* a; bet; coat; bell; the; cle; bi; man.

Explanation of Closed Syllables

Look at the following nonsense syllables. State what they all have in common.

cos   shen   han   prat   blan   slin   wan   dof   il   em   os   ut

Answer: They *all* end in a consonant. They all have only *one* vowel and end in one consonant. They are all only one syllable. Words or syllables that have only one vowel and end in one consonant are called **closed syllables**. The vowel sound in a closed syllable is usually short.

Vowels: a e i o u and sometimes y and w
Consonants: All the other letters in the alphabet

The ending *-ed* has been added to the nonsense syllables presented earlier. Can you state a rule for adding endings to one-syllable closed syllables?

cossed   shenned   hanned   pratted   blanned   slinned   wanned   doffed illed   emmed   ossed   utted

Rule: One-syllable words that are closed syllables usually double the consonant before adding endings beginning with a vowel. (This rule does not apply to words that end in *-y* or *-w* because *y* and *w* act as vowels in words such as *say, fly, cry, vow, draw, grow, throw, know,* and *sew.*)

Double Consonant Rule for Multisyllabic Words Ending in Closed Syllables

Rule: A **multisyllabic word** (word with more than one syllable) that ends in a **closed syllable** (a syllable ending in one consonant and containing only one vowel) usually doubles the consonant before an ending beginning with a vowel *if* the accent falls on the final syllable. *Examples: a.* Recurring (*recur* doubles the *r* because *cur* is a closed syllable and the accent falls on *cur,* the final syllable). *b.* Detained (*detain* does not double the *n* because *tain* is not a closed syllable). *c.* Reasoning (*reason* does not double the *n* because the accent falls on the first syllable rather than on *son.*)

SPECIAL NOTE

Some words such as *travel* and *signal* can be spelled *traveled* or *travelled* and *signaled* or *signalled*.

The *ie* Rule

©1966 United Feature Syndicate, Inc.

Rule: 1. In words having *ei* or *ie* when the sound is long *e*, it's usually *i* before *e* except after *c*.

Examples: receive, believe, yield, achieve, ceiling, field, thief, shriek, fierce.   *Exceptions:* weird, either, neither, sheik, leisure, codeine, protein, caffeine, seize.

2. In words having *ei* or *ie* when the sound is long *a*, it's *e* before *i*. *Examples:* neighbor, rein, eight, veil, freight, vein, weigh.

SPECIAL NOTES

a. In words having *ei* or *ie* when the vowel sound is other than long *e*, it's usually *e* before *i*.   *Examples:* foreign, sovereign, height.   *Exceptions:* friend, view.

b. When a vowel is long, it sounds like its letter name.   For example, long *e* sounds like the *e* in *me* and long *a* sounds like the *a* in *bake*.

Practice A.   Add the ending *-ed* to the following words:

1. can_____

2. chat_____

3. beg_____

4. trap_____

5. look_____

6. trim_____

7. pin_____

8. cook_____

9. steam_____

10. bat_____

11. broil_____

12. mail_____

13. tan_____

14. step_____

15. shop_____

16. fan_____

17. sail_____   18. pet_____

19. chop_____   20. trot_____

21. pat_____   22. fail_____

23. stop_____   24. fit_____

Check answers at the end of Lesson 16.

Practice B. Add the ending *-ing* to the following words:

1. can_____   2. bat_____

3. load_____   4. sun_____

5. fit_____   6. beg_____

7. look_____   8. trim_____

9. pin_____   10. cook_____

11. cut_____   12. let_____

13. step_____   14. steam_____

15. boil_____   16. mail_____

17. fry_____   18. trot_____

19. tan_____   20. shop_____

21. sew_____   22. pet_____

23. set_____   24. grow_____

25. chat_____   26. pat_____

27. wrap_____   28. get_____

29. fail_____   30. stop_____

31. drop_____   32. sit_____

33. hit_____   34. sail_____

35. run_____   36. boil_____

Check answers at the end of Lesson 16.

Practice C. Add the ending *-ing* to the following words.

1. recur_____   2. retain_____

3. develop_____   4. refer_____

5. commit_____   6. occur_____

7. happen_____   8. permit_____

9. begin_____   10. confer_____

Check answers at the end of Lesson 16.

Practice D. Add the ending -ed to the following words.

1. limit_____   2. contain_____

3. commit_____   4. remit_____

5. reveal_____   6. impel_____

7. compel_____   8. label_____

9. model_____   10. refer_____

Check answers at the end of Lesson 16.

Practice E. Check each of the following words carefully. If the word is spelled correctly, put a *C* in the blank. If the word is spelled incorrectly, put a line through it, and spell it correctly.

1. concieted_____

2. wiegh_____

3. weird_____

4. receipt_____

5. neigh_____

6. cieling_____

7. feild_____

8. siege_____

9. riegn_____

10. eight_____

11. brief_____

12. height_____

13. foriegn_____

14. niether_____

15. liesure_____

16. shriek_____

17. belief_____

18. fierce_____

19. cheif_____

20. grief_____

21. theif_____

22. viel_____

23. freight_____

24. friend_____

25. rien _____

26. relieve _____

27. view _____

28. soveriegn _____

29. decieve _____

30. sheik _____

Check answers at the end of Lesson 16.

LESSON 16 ANSWERS

Word Meanings and Sentence Context (pp. 251–257)

Practice A: 1. capital   2. light   3. spring   4. case   5. flat   6. post
7. state   8. interest   9. pitch   10. spell   11. hail   12. plot   13. firm   14. gross
15. grant   16. grave   17. common   18. hack   19. habit   20. center   21. rash
22. down   23. cross   24. bone   25. form

Practice B: Group I: 1. d   2. c   3. e   4. b   5. a;   Group II: 1. e
2. a   3. d   4. b   5. c;   Group III: 1. c   2. d   3. a   4. b   5. g   6. e   7. f.

Practice C (sample answers):   1. groom — The *groom* told his bride that
she would have to help the *groom groom* the horses.   2. order — In our *order*
we have strict rules about law and *order* and no one can *order* anyone to
order things that he or she doesn't want to *order*.   3. coast — On the West
Coast where we live it's too dangerous to *coast* downhill in your car.
4. game — It's no *game* for me to shoot *game*.   5. mean — What did the
mean man *mean* when he referred to the arithmetic *mean*?

Practice D: 1. shoot   2. steel   3. crown   4. steep   5. shock   6. fudge
7. stem   8. maiden   9. mammoth   10. pattern   11. root   12. snap   13. pepper   14. foot   15. grind   16. operation   17. bail   18. balance   19. concrete
20. rule.

Word Usage: Verb Mood (pp. 257–258)

Practice A: 1. be   2. were   3. were   4. were   5. be   6. be   7. would
8. be   9. were   10. be.

Spelling: Some Spelling Generalizations II (pp. 260–264)

Practice A: 1. canned   2. chatted   3. begged   4. trapped   5. looked
6. trimmed   7. pinned   8. cooked   9. steamed   10. batted   11. broiled
12. mailed   13. tanned   14. stepped   15. shopped   16. fanned   17. sailed
18. petted   19. chopped   20. trotted   21. patted   22. failed   23. stopped
24. fitted.

Practice B: 1. canning   2. batting   3. loading   4. sunning   5. fitting
6. begging   7. looking   8. trimming   9. pinning   10. cooking   11. cutting
12. letting   13. stepping   14. steaming   15. boiling   16. mailing   17. frying
18. trotting   19. tanning   20. shopping   21. sewing   22. petting   23. setting
24. growing   25. chatting   26. patting   27. wrapping   28. getting   29. failing
30. stopping   31. dropping   32. sitting   33. hitting   34. sailing   35. running
36. boiling.

Practice C: 1. recurring   2. retaining   3. developing   4. referring
5. committing   6. occurring   7. happening   8. permitting   9. beginning
10. conferring.

Practice D: 1. limited   2. contained   3. committed   4. remitted 5. revealed   6. impelled   7. compelled   8. labeled   9. modeled   10. referred

Practice E: 1. conceited   2. weigh   3. C   4. C   5. C   6. ceiling   7. field 8. C   9. reign   10. C   11. C   12. C   13. foreign   14. neither   15. leisure 16. C   17. C   18. C   19. chief   20. C   21. thief   22. veil   23. C   24. C 25. rein   26. C   27. C   28. sovereign   29. deceive   30. C.

UNIT IV REVIEW CROSSWORD PUZZLE

Directions: Your knowledge of the material presented in Lessons 13–16 will help you to solve this crossword puzzle.

Across

1. Went is the _____ tense of go
5. An auxiliary verb
8. The self
11. To strike; to talk
12. To be in debt
14. Usual plural ending for nouns ending in ch, sh, s, ss, or x
15. Aid
16. A musical syllable intermediate between fa and sol
17. A group of similar things; a bird's home
19. A suffix meaning having, full of, like, or somewhat that signals an adjective
20. A poetic exclamation
21. Words that describe or limit another word or groups of words
24. A linking verb
25. Another way of saying "mother"
27. A fish; part of your foot, alone
28. You use this to obtain a photograph of some part of the body

Down

1. A tree; part of your hand
2. Follows a noun and gives additional information about the noun
3. Usually indicates a noun plural
4. You need _____ _____ your taxes by April 15th
5. A plural pronoun
6. An indefinite article
7. Same as #3 Down
8. The superlative ending for adjectives
9. The seventh letter of the alphabet
10. A figure of speech that uses contradictions
11. A prefix meaning back
13. Husband and _____
14. Found in a subjective test
15. Rode is a _____ of road
17. A preposition meaning adjacent to
18. To make a mistake
22. A male's name; to put on
23. A singular pronoun

30. Same as #20 Across
31. Same as #20 Across
32. Comes from grapes
33. A preposition
34. Has 365 or 366 days
36. Homonym of know
38. Abbreviation of temperature
39. Roman numeral 1000
40. Same as #6 Down
41. Homonym of too
42. Abbreviation of year
43. A form of slant type used for titles of books, magazines, journals, and so on
48. May signal an adjective
49. A pronoun
50. Used to describe adjectives and adverbs
51. A preposition
54. The verb phrase have been is in the present _____ tense
56. Shows the way a writer or speaker views the action of the verb

Check answers on this page.

24. Same as #6 Down
26. Same as #6 Down
29. A conjunction used to show contrast.
32. The twenty-third letter of the alphabet
33. French for friend
35. To inspire with dread
37. A mineral containing a valuable constituent
40. A poisonous snake
44. Abbreviation of territory
45. A characteristic sound of a dog
46. A strong alkaline solution
47. A _____ back
52. Abbreviation of order of merit
53. Same as #36 Across
55. Roman numeral 100
57. Same as #20 Across
58. Used with an apostrophe in a contraction to mean had, did, or would

UNIT IV CROSSWORD PUZZLE ANSWERS

WORD PUZZLES

Word Puzzle 1

See how many of the word riddles you can solve.

1. I am a person with supernatural powers; take away one of my letters, and I will make you very uncomfortable.
2. I am a small demon; add three letters to me, and you will become very small yourself or an edible shellfish.
3. I have magic power; take away two of my letters, and you have something so vital that you could not live without it.
4. I'm a folklore character; take away one of my letters, and you will have something good to eat.
5. I'm something you use for weaving; add a letter to me, and I become something that attracts bees.
6. I'm used to tie things together; take away one of my letters, and you will think that you're seeing double.
7. I'm sinister and not well-liked; add one letter to me, and you'll know who causes me.
8. I'm a thick dark substance that's hard to get off; take away one of my letters, and you'll know what'll happen to you if you get stuck in me.
9. My first word is the home of a wild animal; my second word is what teachers do to test papers. Put us together, and I become a country.
10. My first word helps you to get away; my second word means the same as "decay." Put us together, and you have a vegetable.
11. My first word is another way of saying "mother"; my second word refers to small insects. Put us together, and you have the opposite of "charity."
12. My first word is a metric unit; my second word means "to spoil." Put us together, and you'll have a subject that is studied in school.
13. My first word is the opposite of "old," and my second word is a boat or ship. Put us together, and you have a city.
14. My first word means "to make a mistake," and my second word is a conjunction that is often used. Put us together, and you will send someone on a short trip for another.
15. My first word is a baby goat, and my second word is what you do when you're tired. Put us together, and act quickly to prevent a crime.
16. My first word is something you wear on your head; my second word is a cereal grass. Put us together, and you have the opposite of "steadfastness."

Answers:

1. witch–itch 2. imp–shrimp 3. fairy–air 4. troll–roll 5. loom–bloom 6. twine–twin 7. evil–devil 8. pitch–itch 9. den–mark–Denmark 10. car–rot–carrot 11. ma–lice–malice 12. gram–mar–grammar 13. new–ark–Newark 14. err–and–errand 15. kid–nap–kidnap 16. cap–rice–caprice

Word Puzzle 2

The following clues help you figure out the words to which they refer. (Hint: The last two letters of each preceding word are the first two letters of the next word.)

1. to form an opinion
2. a spring that throws forth at intervals jets of heated water and steam
3. wandering
4. frozen water
5. a person who takes out material he feels is harmful
6. elaborately decorated
7. rash boldness

Answers:

1. judge 2. geyser 3. erratic 4. ice 5. censor 6. ornate 7. temerity

Word Puzzle 3

Two words are combined to make a scrambled set. The letters for each word in the scrambled set are presented in order, and a clue is given for each set.

1. tforaodg   — amphibians (land and water animals)
2. lhoaownk   — birds
3. npuetpmpeegr   — spices
4. faulnggiae   — plants
5. omuysssetelr   — mollusks (shellfish)
6. scnrocaokdiele   — reptiles
7. rehliepnhoacnerots — pachyderms

Answers:

1. toad, frog 2. loon, hawk 3. nutmeg, pepper 4. fungi, algae 5. oyster, mussel 6. snake, crocodile 7. rhinoceros, elephant

REVIEW TEST 1

A. Expand each of the following sentences so that they become complex sentences.

1. Joe caught the ball._____

_____

2. The ball hit someone._____

_____

3. The robber left the bank._____

_____

4. The teller gave the robber the money._____

_____

5. The police arrived on the scene._____

_____

B. Follow the directions in the parentheses for each of the following.

1. (Write a sentence that contains a simile.)_____

_____

2. (Write a sentence that contains a statement of personification.)_____

_____

3. (Write a sentence that contains a metaphor.)_____

_____

4. (Write a sentence that contains an oxymoron.)_____

_____

5. (Write a sentence that contains a hyperbole.)_____

_____

C. Follow the directions in the parentheses for each of the following.

1. (Write a sentence in which the dependent clause is restrictive.)_____

_____

2. (Write a sentence in which the dependent clause is nonrestrictive.)_____

_____

3. (Write a sentence which has a nonrestrictive modifier.)_____

_____

4. (Write a sentence which has a restrictive modifier.)_____

_____

5. (Write a sentence which has a phrase modifying a noun.)_____

_____

6. (Write a sentence which contains at least three adjectives and two adverbs.)

_____

7. (Write a sentence which uses a homograph in at least three different ways.)

_____

8. (Write a sentence which contains a verb in the present perfect.)_____

_____

9. (Write a sentence which contains a verb in the past perfect.)_____

_____

10. (Write a sentence which contains a statement of *timelessness*.)_____

_____

D.   Read each of the following sentences carefully. If anything in the sentence is incorrect, correct it. If the sentence is correct, put a *C* in the blank.

1. The cat climbed the tree meowing. _____

_____

2. My oldest sister Jane is getting married next month._____

_____

3. Last week someone told me that he has figured out how to stretch the
   dollar and that he had patented his device. _____

_____

4. I didn't know that you could patent a counterfeiting machine._____

_____

5. My hare grows very fast because my hare is healthy hare._____

_____

6. The ate principles meat every weak. _____

_____

7. My father has always worked very hard, but he never made a lot of
   money. _____

_____

8. Jim Jack and George attended the party without their girlfriends._____

_____

9. The beautiful black cat sat and purred. _____

_____

10. John tells all his dates that they have to pay for dinner when they go
    out to eat. _____

_____

REVIEW TEST 2: A TRUE/FALSE TEST

Directions: This is a true/false test on Lessons 13–16. Read each sentence carefully. Decide whether it is true or false. Put a *T* for true or an *F* for false in the blank.

_____ 1. *Liesure* is spelled correctly.

_____ 2. An action that started in the past and is continuing requires a verb in the past perfect tense.

_____ 3. The word *had* is used with the past participle of the verb when an action that started in the past is continuing in the present.

_____ 4. Italics are used for foreign words.

_____ 5. *Her stories are like a broken record* is an example of a simile.

_____ 6. Oxymoron is the combining of similes to make a point.

_____ 7. Personification is the giving of human characteristics and capabilities to nonhuman things such as inanimate objects, abstract ideas, or animals.

_____ 8. "She's as thin as a toothpick" is an example of both simile and hyperbole.

_____ 9. "The wind's heavy breathing" is an example of hyperbole.

_____10. The verb in the dependent clause is usually not in the same tense as the verb in the independent clause.

_____11. The tense of a story should be consistent throughout the story.

_____12. The dictionary definition of a word is more closely related to the denotative meaning of a word than to the connotative meaning of a word.

_____13. The term *pirate* has negative overtones.

_____14. Writers use the connotative meanings of words to influence us in some way.

_____15. Writers try to influence us only negatively.

_____16. The sentence *She walks* can be put into the passive voice.

_____17. The sentence *Jim cheered when his favorite team won* can be put into the passive voice.

_____18. *He hugged everyone in sight* can be put into the passive voice.

_____19. The active voice is usually preferred to the passive voice.

_____20. The past participle of a verb does not have to be used with an auxiliary when it is used as a verb.

_____21. A comma is usually used if a dependent clause precedes an independent clause.

_____22. When an ending beginning with a consonant is added to words ending with a final silent *e* the *e* is usually retained.

_____23. Context refers to the words surrounding a word that can throw light on the meaning of the word.

_____24. The mood of a verb expresses the writer's state of mind.

_____25. In the subjunctive, *was* is used in place of *were* for the past tense.

APPENDIX I

Some Troublesome Verbs

Following are some verbs that seem to cause a great amount of difficulty for writers.

1. Leave — let.

Leave means *to cause to remain, to have remaining, to permit to remain undisturbed.* *Examples:* Leave your boots outside because they are covered with mud. My parents left me alone in the house.

Let means *to allow, to permit.* *Examples:* Please let me go to that party. My parents let me stay alone in the house.

In the sentence *My parents left me alone in the house,* the child remained in the house while the parents left. In the sentence *My parents let me stay alone in the house,* the child was allowed to stay alone in the house.

2. Sit — set.

Set means *to put, to place, to lay, to deposit.* When you *set* something, you are putting something in a place. *Examples:* He set the table. Set the books on my desk. Set the child down.

The verb *set* is considered a transitive verb (a verb that can take an object). However, *set* is commonly used to refer to hens laying eggs, as *setting hens.* It is used in speaking of the *setting sun,* the *sun sets,* or the *sunset.*

Sit means *to rest the body in a vertical position, usually on a chair.* *Examples:* Sit down. Sit next to me. Sit the child down.

Notice that the sentence *Set the child down* has a different meaning from *Sit the child down.* In the first sentence the child is put down, not necessarily in a sitting position. However, in the second sentence the child is put in a sitting position.

3. Lay — lie.

Lie (lay, have lain) means *to rest* or *to recline.* *Examples:* I must lie down because I am so tired. Last week I lay in bed every day until seven o'clock in the morning. I could have lain in bed all day.

Lay (laid, have laid) means *to put down* or *to place.* *Examples:* Lay the bundles on the table. The hens lay eggs. He can't remember where he laid his wallet yesterday.

Persons generally confuse the verbs *lie* and *lay* because of the closeness in spelling of the two verbs. Remember that when you lay something down, you are putting something down. When you lay down yesterday, you were reclining. If you laid something down, you put something down. If you have lain for a while, you have been reclining for a while.

4. Can — may.

Can means *being able to* do something.   *Examples:* I can swim very well.   I can play the piano.

May means *having permission to* do something.   *Examples:* May I go swimming at the shore? May my friends visit us for the weekend? You may go to the party.

5. Teach — learn.

Teach means *to cause to know a subject* or *to cause someone to know how to do something.*   *Examples:* My teacher taught the children to read and write.   He taught me how to swim.

Learn means *to gain knowledge or understanding.*   *Examples:* I learned all about rocks and rock formations in my geology class.   In anthropology, I learn about cultures different from ours.

Do not use *learn* in place of *teach.* Remember, you learn something that is taught to you by someone, or you can teach yourself something.

APPENDIX II

Some Often Used Irregular Verbs

Present	Past	Past Participle
arise	arose	arisen
be	was	been
beat	beat	beaten
begin	began	begun
bet	bet	bet
bite	bite	bitten
blow	blew	blown
break	broke	broken
cast	cast	cast
catch	caught	caught
choose	chose	chosen
come	came	come
cost	cost	cost
cut	cut	cut
do	did	done
drink	drank	drunk
drive	drove	driven
eat	ate	eaten
fall	fell	fallen
flee	fled	fled
forget	forgot	forgotten
freeze	froze	frozen
get	got	got
grow	grew	grown
hit	hit	hit
know	knew	known
lay	laid	laid
lead	led	led
leave	left	left
let	let	let
lie (recline)	lay	lain
lie	lied	lied
lose	lost	lost
put	put	put

Present	Past	Past Participle
ride	rode	ridden
ring	rang	rung
rise	rose	risen
run	ran	run
see	saw	seen
set	set	set
shake	shook	shaken
shrink	shrank	shrunk
shut	shut	shut
sing	sang	sung
sink	sank	sunk
sit	sat	sat
slay	slew	slain
slide	slid	slid
speak	spoke	spoken
spring	sprang	sprung
stand	stood	stood
steal	stole	stolen
swear	swore	sworn
swim	swam	swum
swing	swung	swung
take	took	taken
tear	tore	torn
throw	threw	thrown
wear	wore	worn
win	won	won
write	wrote	written

APPENDIX III

Diagnostic Tests

Part 1: Sentences

A. *Directions:* Read each sentence carefully. Put a *O* in front of those that are not sentences.

_____ 1. Come here.

_____ 2. Go.

_____ 3. Who are you?

_____ 4. Which is?

_____ 5. Because of them.

_____ 6. Out of the yard.

_____ 7. The girl ran far, and she.

_____ 8. The persons, whom we met.

_____ 9. This is good.

_____10. Help!

B. *Directions:* Underline the clauses in each of the following sentences that are independent clauses.

1. Terry doesn't want to go to an out-of-state college.

2. When he left for school, we missed him very much.

3. The workers stopped work at six o'clock when the whistle blew.

4. Although he was badly hurt in the automobile accident, he still wanted to become a racer.

5. The people at the picnic ate first, and then they played bridge.

C. *Directions:* Combine the following two sentences to make a compound sentence.

The child is crying. She wants to be held.

D. *Directions:* Combine the following three sentences to make a complex sentence.

The child is crying. She wants to be held. She is spoiled.

_____

_____

E. *Directions:* Combine the following four sentences to make a compound-complex sentence.

The child is crying. She wants to be held. She is spoiled. Her mother can't carry her all the time.

_____

_____

_____

F. *Directions:* Expand each sentence using descriptive words.

1. The man walks. _____

2. Dogs eat. _____

3. Cats drink milk. _____

G. *Directions:* This is a multiple-choice test. Circle the correct answer for each question.

1. Choose the sentence that is a complex sentence.
   a. John and Mary have been friends since elementary school.
   b. Jeff went on a trip to Florida during the semester break.
   c. The high cost of gasoline prices has forced me to give up my car and bicycle to school instead.
   d. My buddy, however, will not trade in his car for a bike because he wants to be a car racer.

2. Choose the sentence that is a simple sentence.
   a. If tuition costs keep rising, I may have to drop out of school.
   b. No one seems to be able to answer questions in a straightforward manner at my school.
   c. I have one instructor who seems to produce more heat than light in his classes.
   d. However, I have another instructor who is such an excellent lecturer that no one notices when the period is over.

3. Choose the sentence that is a compound sentence.
   a. If Bruce doesn't go to the concert, I'm not going either.
   b. My best friend and my girl friend went away together.
   c. At first, I was in a state of shock, but I got over it when I met Sal.
   d. It is distressing not to be able to trust your friends, but I can't.

4. Choose the sentence that is a compound-complex sentence.
   a. I feel that Woody Allen is very egotistical because almost all of his films deal with himself.
   b. Many writers write about themselves because they feel that they know themselves the best, but I prefer to read novels in which the writer keeps himself or herself in the background.

c. There must be something wrong with me because I never seem to like the films that everyone else likes.

d. I felt great when I met Susan and found out that she shares the same feelings that I do about films.

5. Choose the sentence fragment.
   a. I have too much to do, and I don't have enough time.
   b. When he arrives.
   c. My busy schedule prevents me from doing all the things that I should do.
   d. After one week of classes, my friend needs rest and recreation.

6. Choose the sentence with the dependent clause.
   a. I would like to go, but I can't go.
   b. She's fun to be with because she has a good sense of humor.
   c. No one else would do it; therefore I did it.
   d. However, I volunteered.

7. Choose the sentence that has an intransitive verb.
   a. I feel nervous when I take tests.
   b. I will fly the plane.
   c. Al needs help in math.
   d. Debbie offered her help to Al.

8. Choose the sentence that has both an object and an indirect object.
   a. The dorms are too noisy for me.
   b. Jim helped Judy move out of the dorm.
   c. Judy gave Jim a huge hug for his help.
   d. Jim immediately asked Judy for a date.

9. Choose the sentence with a linking verb.
   a. I need at least five more days to complete my paper.
   b. My brother Dan is editor of the school paper.
   c. Not one of my friends failed a course last semester.
   d. Unfortunately, I flunked gym.

Part 2: Word Usage

A. 1. *Directions:* For each sentence, put an *S* in front of it if it has a simple subject and a *C* in front of it if it has a compound subject. Also, underline the simple or compound subject.

_____ 1. Mary, John, and Jack are friends.

_____ 2. We chose Jim and Herb to represent us.

_____ 3. Are you going tomorrow to visit Mary and Joe?

_____ 4. José and Flores can't go with us.

_____ 5. Are you and the baby going?

2. *Directions:* For each sentence, put an *S* in front of it if it has a simple predicate and a *C* in front of it if it has a compound predicate. Also, underline the simple or compound predicate.

_____ 1. The lawyer is helping his client.

_____ 2. She laughed and then cried.

_____ 3. The students arrived late for their class.

_____ 4. Help us.

_____ 5. They gave aid and comfort to the accident victims.

B. *Directions:* Circle the verb that correctly completes the sentence.

1. Clara (cooks/cook) very well.

2. They (plays/play) nicely together.

3. Roses and tulips (is/are) pretty flowers.

4. Not one of my friends (is/are) going to the dance.

5. Neither my teacher nor my principal (was/were) present at the school dance.

6. Either the schools or the clubs (offers/offer) the evening programs.

7. There (is/are) no one here I know.

8. There (is/are) too many people here.

9. None of my relatives (was/were) present at my party.

10. Everybody (is/are) welcome.

11. Neither of the courses (is/are) appealing to me.

12. The importance of the studies (has/have) been discussed by many scientists.

13. The husband, as well as his wife, (was/were) sued.

14. My brother, together with his friends, (was/were) hurt.

15. The estimate of the damages (is/are) too high.

16. Physics (was/were) a hard course for me.

17. Seven from ten (equals/equal) three.

18. Fifty dollars (is/are) too much to pay for that.

19. Those scissors (is/are) too sharp.

20. Athletics (is/are) important in our school.

21. The *Morning Call* (is/are) an Allentown, Pennsylvania newspaper.

22. *Gaining Word Power* (is/are) a vocabulary book.

23. *Hamlet* (is/are) a play by Shakespeare.

24. Sharon, not Susan, (is/are) going.

25. The Browns' daughter (is/are) staying with us.

C. *Directions:* Circle the correct pronoun for each sentence.

1. Each individual must do (his/their) work.

2. Each of the guests at the dinner had brought (his/their) own favorite dish.

3. No one can tell what (his/their) future will be.

4. My younger brothers have to do (his/their) homework before they can go out to play.

5. Neither Dick nor Jim has decided on what (he/they) will be majoring in at school.

6. Everybody is studying hard for (his/their) exams.

7. Some person in the audience had to be asked to leave because (he/they) became very noisy and rude.

8. My brother and my father work together in (his/their) store.

9. Not one of the people I know can afford (his/their) own apartment.

10. The class as one greeted (its/their) new teacher.

D. *Directions:* Fill in each blank with the word that you think was left out.

When to Study

Some students only study just before an announced test.
(1)_____ stay up all night (2)_____ cram. All of us
(3)_____ probably done this once (4)_____ twice. However, if this (5)_____ your steady way of (6)_____ things,
you will not (7)_____ well in school. Cramming (8)_____
not bring about lasting (9)_____ . It should only be (10)_____
as a last resort. (11)_____ order to be a (12)_____ student,
you must plan (13)_____ study time and spread (14)_____
out over a period (15)_____ time. In planning your (16)_____
make sure that you (17)_____ for social and physical (18)_____ .
Remember that a rhythm (19)_____ activities is important. It
(20)_____ not important whether you (21)_____ in the
evening before (22)_____ after dinner or right (23)_____
class during free periods. (24)_____ important thing is that
(25)_____ have a schedule that (26)_____ follow and that
your (27)_____ is spread out over (28)_____ week.

E. *Directions:* Circle the verb that correctly completes each sentence.

1. Whom did you say you (have/has/had) seen only once?

2. The Great Wall (is/was/were) in China.

3. *Psychological Principles* (is/was/were) a psychology book.

4. During the past three months I (had received/have received/will receive) a great amount of help from my colleagues.

5. Neither of you (has been/have been/is/was/were) in class all week.

6. She (is/has been/have been/was) gone all week.

7. I (had/have) met him before I met my husband.

8. The scientists claimed that they (have/has/had) found a cure for a dreaded disease.

9. I enjoy skiing but my fiance (refused/refuses/had refused) to go with me.

10. So far my freshmen year at college (has been/had been) difficult, but I am managing to survive.

11. If I were to receive an *A* in the course, I (will/would) be very happy.

12. I wish I (was/were) in some other place.

13. Professor Jones (learns/teaches) courses in speech at a university.

14. (Can/May) we borrow your tape recorder?

15. The sun (sits/sets).

16. My friends are (lying/laying) in the sun.

17. (Let/Leave) the package where it is.

18. Jim (lie/lay/laid) in bed all day yesterday because he (is/was) ill.

19. The chicken (lay/laid) an egg yesterday.

F. *Directions:* Put a circle around the number of those sentences that can be put in the passive voice.

1. My father is a salesman.

2. She eats too much meat.

3. Our club held a dance.

4. What is your name?

5. The airplane made a forced landing.

6. This year's homecoming queen is smart as well as beautiful.

7. We ate a large meal.

8. She seems like a nice person.

9. He broke his toe.

10. The whale attacked an unsuspecting swimmer.

G. *Directions:* **Change the following two sentences into the active voice.**

1. The excellent lecture was given by the professor.

_____

2. A cake was baked by us.

_____

H. *Directions:* **Change the following words into adjectives.**

1. help_____   2. force_____

3. enjoy_____   4. comfort_____

5. salt_____   6. hero_____

7. excite_____   8. break_____

9. hide_____   10. sing_____

I. *Directions:* **Insert a noun to act as an adjective for the following nouns.**

1._____ windows

2._____ bowl

3._____ coat

4._____ tray

5._____ music

J. *Directions:* **Change each of the following adjectives into adverbs.**

1. noisy_____

2. angry_____

3. cheerful_____

4. careful_____

5. graceful_____

6. heavy_____

7. great_____

8. good_____

9. real_____

10. thankful_____

K. *Directions:* Write a sentence using an adverb according to the directions in parentheses.

1. (Construct a sentence with an adverb describing a verb.)

_____

_____

2. (Construct a sentence with an adverb describing another adverb.)

_____

_____

3. (Construct a sentence with an adverb describing an adjective.)

_____

_____

4. (Construct a sentence with an adverb used as a linking word.)

_____

_____

Part 3: Punctuation and Capitalization

A. *Directions:* Correctly punctuate the following sentences.

1. How marvelous that is

2. What's her name

3. Give me one

4. The man arrived to fix the sink because it had a leak

5. Although I enjoy playing the piano I wouldn't want to be a concert pianist

6. The train came to a sudden halt and then two gunmen quickly boarded it

7. There were many clouds in the sky but it didn't rain

8. We played ball and then went for a swim

9. We were sorry that you didn't get into the school of your choice

10. This play is exciting and interesting

11. However it's a good idea

12. They were disappointed for they had failed the exam

13. The day was hot and clear therefore we went to the beach

14. I'd like him to go with us because he's so much fun

15. Of course you can spend the night with us

16. Playing in a tournament can be very tiring proper nourishment and adequate sleep are essential to winning

17. The cable car stopped in the middle of its run it was stuck

18. As a worker he was unhappy however as an employer he was happy

19. He said Go away

20. I eat fruit vegetables and nuts

21. The dog wearing the flea collar was hit by a car

22. The author Samuel Clemens wrote many satirical essays

23. We ourselves will do it

24. Jim Taylor an excellent teacher is well-liked

B. *Directions:* Correct the following sentences.

1. Arthur mowed the lawn wearing his bathing suit

   _____

2. José sat down in front of the examiner trembling with fear

   _____

3. The professor gave a brief description of the ancient Roman Senate speaking without notes _____

C. *Directions:* Put an *R* in front of any run-on sentence. If the sentence is a run-on sentence, correct it.

_____ 1. The band stopped playing, we stopped dancing.

   _____

_____ 2. Our school officers are doing an excellent job, they have saved us a lot of money this year.

   _____

   _____

_____ 3. She is an excellent athlete, but she is a little too heavy.

   _____

_____ 4. No one would say anything about the cheating; however, everyone knew about it.

   _____

   _____

_____ 5. As a singer, he is very good, as a dancer, he is not.

D. *Directions:* Punctuate the following sentences.

1. Although I did well in school I have had difficulty getting a job

2. The singer spent six hours taping her song finally she called it quits

3. I don't feel that it's a good idea to send away for that however I will if

   you want it

4. Jane said that she would do it because she was a friend of mine

5. I like to shop at that store but the prices are too high

6. As the workers refused to accept their employer's offer they continued

   their job action

7. It's a good idea nevertheless and I think you should consider it

8. Jane my best friend said that she would back me up

9. The man who attacked the woman ran down the street but a policeman

   caught him

10. The students drew up a petition to protest the scanty selection of courses

    that were being offered and they presented it to the college president

11. I bought my niece a beautiful little toy kitchen stove

12. My friend has a new stylish red winter coat

13. My friend's pet is a thick long slimy snake

E. *Directions:* Read each of the following. If the punctuation marks are correct, write a *C* in the blank. If the punctuation marks are incorrect, underline what is incorrect and put in the correct punctuation mark(s).

_____ 1. 7;15 P.M.

_____ 2. Dear Sir.

_____ 3. The following are: apples, bananas and pears;

_____ 4. Dear Peggy:

_____ 5. *The Art of Love; Another Look*

F. *Directions:*

1. Construct two sentences using the dash in two different ways.

   a. _____

   _____

b. _____

_____

2. Construct two sentences using parentheses in two different ways.

a. _____

_____

b. _____

_____

3. Construct one sentence using brackets.

_____

_____

_____

G. *Directions:* Circle all words in the following sentences that should be capitalized.

1. on saturdays jennifer would visit the rev. john smith.

2. during january we go to washington, d.c., to visit the smithsonian institution.

3. we read *national geographic* and *newsday.*

4. the secretary of the elks club said that president brown would be speaking on monday at the johnson company at twentieth street.

5. in the summer my brother and i visited the empire state building.

6. in our history class, we're studying the colonial period and about the signing of the declaration of independence.

7. when aunt barbara and uncle mike visit us in the fall, we go to the football games.

8. we listened to senator jones's talk on politics.

9. in the spring semester i'm taking sociology 101, geology 120, and a history and an english course.

10. the state of texas is in the southwest.

Part 4: Spelling

A. *Directions:* Make each of the following words plural.

1. fish_____   2. pass_____

3. fox_____   4. can_____

5. rock_____   6. stamp_____

7. cheese_____   8. Jones_____

9. bunch_____   10. Smith_____

11. rash_____   12. tray_____

13. volley_____   14. monarchy_____

15. penny_____   16. cherry_____

17. leaf_____   18. child_____

19. salmon_____   20. elf_____

21. domino_____   22. mother-in-law_____

23. tariff_____   24. man_____

25. tree_____   26. tune_____

B. *Directions:* Circle the correct word(s) in each sentence.

1. After (one/won) of (hour/our) friends (one/won) the tennis match, we took him out to a (steak, stake) dinner.

2. (Eye/I) (no/know) that it is good to have (piece/peace).

3. (Eye/I) do not (no/know) the (weigh/way) to her house.

4. (Eye/I) (red/read) that the (fair/fare) opens tomorrow.

5. The (heal/heel) of her shoe got stuck in my (gait/gate).

6. The (air/heir) to the throne wears a special (wring/ring).

7. That has a (duel/dual) meaning so it's not (fare/fair) to give it in isolation.

8. The (principal/principle) said that the reason (eye/I) failed the (course/coarse) was because (eye/I) never handed in my papers when they were (due/dew).

9. The (site/sight) for the new building will be on the golf (course/coarse).

10. Will you (so/sew) that rip for me (so/sew) that it doesn't get worse.

C. *Directions:* Add the ending *ed* to the following words.

1. pat_____   2. chat_____

3. bake_____   4. mail_____

5. trim_____   6. wrap_____

7. toil_____   8. help_____

9. limit_____   10. occur_____

11. reason_____   12. commit_____

13. admit_____   14. retain_____

15. employ_____

D. *Directions:* Add the ending *-able* to the following words.

1. love _____

2. sale _____

3. pleasure _____

4. manage _____

5. challenge _____

6. package _____

7. enforce _____

8. encourage _____

9. dodge _____

10. mortgage _____

E. *Directions:* Add the ending *-ing* to the following words.

1. like _____

2. slice _____

3. argue _____

4. salvage _____

5. indulge _____

F. *Directions:* Add the ending *-ful* to the following words.

1. force _____

2. peace _____

3. use _____

4. awe _____

5. shame _____

G. *Directions:* Add the ending *-ment* to the following words.

1. judge _____

2. excite _____

3. acknowledge _____

4. state _____

5. commence _____

H. *Directions:* Add the ending -*ly* to the following words.

1. whole_____
2. true_____
3. state_____
4. late_____
5. sure_____
6. ready_____
7. easy_____
8. busy_____
9. noisy_____
10. day_____

I. *Directions:* Add the ending -*ed* to the following words.

1. dry_____
2. annoy_____
3. hurry_____
4. pay_____
5. convey_____

J. *Directions:* Check each of the following words carefully. If the word is spelled correctly, put a *C* in the blank. If the word is spelled incorrectly, put a line through it and spell it correctly.

1. receive_____
2. believe_____
3. liesure_____
4. foriegn_____
5. hieght_____
6. brief_____
7. viel_____
8. theif_____
9. decieve_____
10. riegn_____

K. *Directions:* Form the singular possessive for the following words.

1. Polly_____
2. woman_____

   3. Ms. Jones_____

   4. Mr. Lass_____

   5. class_____

L. *Directions:* Form the plural possessive for the following words.

   1. ox_____

   2. man_____

   3. baby_____

   4. knife_____

   5. potato_____

   6. cargo_____

   7. mouse_____

   8. child_____

   9. Jones_____

10. glass_____

M. *Directions:* Put the following words into their possessive forms.

   1. sister-in-law_____

   2. no one_____

   3. anybody_____

   4. who_____

   5. it_____

N. *Directions:* Fill in the blank with the abbreviation that makes the best sense. Abbreviations: i.e., e.g., etc. P.S., Inc., Co., A.M., P.M., B.C., A.D.

   1. Socrates, a noted philosopher lived in ancient Greece in about 400

      _____ .

   2. Johnson Brothers,_____ is a very large company.

   3. The Pierson Building Supply_____ owns most of the lumber mills in this area.

   4. In the year_____ 2001, we will have arrived at a new century.

   5. All my letters seem to contain a(n)_____ , because I always seem to have to add something more to them.

   6. I have taken courses in history, geography, English, sociology, biology,

      _____ .

   7. Because of the high crime rate in our city, I try to get home by about

      7:00_____ , before it gets dark.

8. There are a number of famous comedians whom I have admired, _____ , Jack Benny, Red Skeleton, and Bob Hope.

9. Every morning I awaken at 7:00_____ .

10. Dachshunds, beagles, fox terriers, schnauzers, and German Shepherds are all dogs,_____ , they all have four legs, fur, a tail, and a bark.

O. *Directions:* Write the contractions for the following words.

1. I am _____   2. He will _____

3. They are _____   4. I have _____

5. Are not _____   6. Would not _____

7. There is _____   8. It is _____

9. Has not _____   10. Who is _____

P. *Directions:* Correct any errors in each of the following sentences.

1. Who's house is that?

_____

2. He has'nt any more, but Ill try to get some for you.

_____

3. Do'nt do that.

_____

4. Its mine, but who's is that?

_____

5. The toy was in it's box.

_____

Q. *Directions:* Give the comparative for the following adjectives.

1. bad_____

2. good_____

3. happy_____

4. much_____

5. little_____

R. *Directions:* Give the superlative for the following adjectives.

1. tall_____   2. big_____

3. little_____   4. peculiar_____

5. mean_____   6. truthful_____

7. cute_____   8. darling_____

9. good_____   10. bad _____

S. *Directions:* Give the comparative and superlative for the following adverbs.

1. quickly_____

2. much_____

3. hard_____

4. peacefully_____

5. cheerfully_____

T. *Directions:* **Look at each word carefully. If the word is spelled correctly, put a C in the blank. If the word is not spelled correctly, put a line through it and spell it correctly.**

1. absense_____

2. alright_____

3. alot_____

4. although_____

5. apparent_____

6. amatur_____

7. apearance_____

8. excellant_____

9. athlete_____

10. calender_____

11. arguement_____

12. commited_____

13. cemetary_____

14. finally_____

15. definte _____

16. expecialy_____

17. exagerate_____

18. existance_____

19. Febuary_____

20. fourty_____

21. goverment_____

22. humurous_____

23. guidence _____

24. independence _____

25. intelligence _____

26. ficticious _____

27. liesure _____

28. gurantee _____

29. heros _____

30. likly _____

31. laboratory _____

32. magazenes _____

33. mathametics _____

34. bachalors _____

35. ninty _____

36. pastimes _____

37. ridiculus _____

38. significent _____

39. suceed _____

40. tradgedy _____

41. vegtables _____

42. writen _____

APPENDIX IV

Extra Practice

Lesson 1

Simple Sentences

Practice A. In the following list, underline the complete sentences.

1. Don't go.

2. Out of the woods.

3. Help.

4. When he came.

5. Who was that?

6. The large dog attacked the child.

7. Not in the school.

8. About the course.

9. Why is that necessary?

10. The professor who helped us.

11. The car, when it arrived.

12. No one can go.

Practice B. Write three simple sentences.

1. _____

2. _____

3. _____

Word Usage: Nouns

Practice A. Give a noun for each of the endings given in parentheses and then write a simple sentence for each of the words that you gave.

1. (tion)_____

_____

2. (ance)_____

_____

3. (er)_____

_____

4. (ism)_____

_____

5. (ment)_____

_____

Punctuation

Practice A. Put in the proper punctuation for the following sentences.

1. What do you want
2. Stop
3. My psychology paper is due tomorrow
4. Is the ski trip to Switzerland very expensive
5. My geology class is going caving
6. I refuse to do that
7. Why are you so stubborn
8. Go immediately
9. No one can help them now
10. That is a formidable task

Spelling: Noun Plurals

Practice A. Make each of the following words plural.

1. fox_____   2. princess_____
3. hostess_____   4. host_____
5. church_____   6. miser_____
7. Ross_____   8. rose_____
9. Sharon_____   10. kiss_____
11. bunch_____   12. furnace_____
13. onion _____   14. glass_____
15. lash_____   16. lock_____

17. mix_____   18. lamp_____

19. shade_____   20. dish _____

Practice B. Make each of the following words plural.

1. ferry_____   2. money_____

3. eddy_____   4. clay_____

5. crayon _____   6. boy_____

7. Monday_____   8. autocracy_____

9. baby_____   10. candy_____

Lesson 2

Sentence Patterns

Practice A. Write three simple sentences that conform to Sentence Pattern 1 (N/P V).

1. _____

_____

2. _____

_____

3. _____

_____

Word Usage: The Subject of a Sentence

Practice A. Circle the simple subject in each sentence.

1. Several huge dogs attacked the student.

2. The pack of dogs roamed the city streets in search of food.

3. Nobody was available to help.

4. The student was badly hurt.

5. Some passers-by finally rescued the student.

Practice B. Circle the compound subject in each sentence.

1. John, Jim, and George are suitemates at college.

2. Harvard, Yale, and Princeton are universities in the Northeast.

3. Vegetables and fruits are low in cholesterol.

4. Lemons, oranges, and grapefruits are a good source of vitamin C.

5. Coffee and tea contain caffeine.

Practice C. Circle the complete subject in each sentence.

1. The battered child was taken from his parents.

2. The raging winds reached tornado strength.

3. The French supersonic jet was allowed to land in the United States.

4. The deans, faculty members, and students joined together to work out their differences concerning student representation at meetings.

5. Dry roasted sunflower nuts are José's favorite midday snack.

Practice D. Complete each sentence by inserting a simple or compound subject.

1. _____ knows who the killer is.

2. _____ , _____ , and _____
saw someone running down the dormitory hall after midnight.

3. The running _____ was identified.

4. The _____ did not feel that they had enough evidence to arrest him.

5. The _____ has not yet been caught.

Capitalization

Practice A. Circle all words in the following sentences that should have capital letters.

1. the last wednesday in february, sharon, carol, jennifer, and i are going to england.

2. pedro just finished reading mark twain's "baker's blue-jay yarn."

3. i read *sports illustrated, psychology today,* and *playboy.*

4. ms. smith listened to the rev. charles jones as he discussed the new proposal.

5. president brown of bensen college said that senator ortez would give the opening address in spanish.

Spelling: Noun Plurals

Practice A. Give the plural of the following words.

1. domino   2. cargo

3. tomato_____   4. mother-in-law_____

5. Negro_____   6. sheep _____

7. woman_____   8. veto _____

9. shelf _____   10. tooth_____

11. piano_____   12. chief_____

13. roof_____   14. bison _____

15. grouse_____   16. salmon_____

17. mouse_____   18. hero_____

19. tornado_____   20. silo_____

Lesson 3

Sentence Patterns

Practice A.   Write two simple sentences that conform to Sentence Pattern 2 (N/P V N/P).

1._____

_____

2. _____

_____

Practice B.   Write two simple sentences that conform to Sentence Pattern 3 (N/P V N/P N).

1._____

_____

2._____

_____

Practice C.   Write two simple sentences that conform to Sentence Pattern 4 (N/P LV N/P).

1. _____

_____

2. _____

_____

Practice D.   Write two simple sentences that conform to Sentence Pattern 5 (N/P LV Adj.).

1. _____

_____

2. _____

_____

Word Usage: Verbs

Practice A. Underline the nonsense word in each of the following nonsense sentences that is a verb.

1. The zebe rebbed.

2. Some very bloob glams glebbed the mouille.

3. A flome fleps.

4. Who vetts the holp?

5. Pland that cand.

Practice B. Write a simple sentence that contains a linking verb.

_____

_____

Practice C. Write a simple sentence that contains a transitive verb.

_____

_____

Capitalization

Practice A. Capitalize each word in the following sentences that should be capitalized.

1. i'm taking three social science courses, one arts and humanities course, and english literature 301.

2. when we visited my grandparents last tuesday, my aunt joan and uncle joe were there.

3. i drove for three miles on route 23 before i saw the sign for blakely college.

4. my spanish speaking friends are bilingual because they can speak and write english and spanish equally well.

5. in history we studied about president washington, the declaration of independence, and the constitution.

6. the student government is revising its constitution and moving to the georgian building.

7. jennifer said, "i want to visit my grandparents and my aunt sharon."

8. chicago's o'hare airport is always very crowded.

9. alexander pope's line, "a little learning is a dangerous thing" is so true.

10. in history we studied about world war I, world war II, and the korean war.

Spelling: Abbreviations

Practice A. Write what each of the following abbreviations stand for.

1. i.e._____

2. e.g._____

3. A.M._____

4. P.M._____

5. etc._____

6. A.D._____

7. P.S._____

8. Inc._____

9. Co._____

10. B.C._____

Practice B. Write a sentence using each of the following abbreviations.

1. i.e._____

_____

2. e.g._____

_____

3. A.D._____

_____

4. A.M._____

_____

5. Inc._____

_____

Lesson 4

Sentence Patterns

Practice A. Write two sentences that conform to Sentence Pattern 6 (N/P V N/P N).

1._____

_____

2. _____

_____

Practice B. Write two sentences that conform to Sentence Pattern 7 (N/P V N/P Adj.).

1. _____

_____

2. _____

_____

Word Usage: The Predicate of a Sentence

Practice A. Circle the simple predicate in each sentence.

1. The basketball star broke his arm.

2. My friends and I are practicing our skit for the amateur show.

3. They have gone with everyone to the picnic.

4. We will be working late tonight.

5. Help me.

Practice B. Circle the compound predicate.

1. The screaming child picked up a toy and threw it at the stranger.

2. The continuous rain destroyed dams and flooded cities.

3. The young child vocalizes, babbles, gurgles, and coos.

4. A mother's rapid speech can overload and hinder her child's language learning.

5. We will eat, drink, and have fun.

Practice C. Circle the complete predicate in each sentence.

1. The stonemason's work was very artistic.

2. No one knew the name of the accident victim.

3. The accident victim had no identification on her.

4. She was dressed in jeans, a sweater, and sneakers.

5. She was so young and pretty.

Compound Words

Practice A. Here are ten words. Combine these to make fifteen compound words.
Words: in, brother, sister, father, mother, step, grand, law, up, down

_____   _____
_____   _____
_____   _____
_____   _____
_____   _____
_____   _____
_____   _____
_____

Spelling: Contractions

Practice A. Give the two words that were combined to form the following contractions.

1. it's_____

2. you're_____

3. he'll_____

4. there's_____

5. haven't_____

6. wouldn't_____

7. can't_____

8. aren't_____

9. isn't_____

10. doesn't_____

Practice B. Write contractions for the following words.

1. here is_____

2. what is_____

3. have not_____

4. will not_____

5. we are_____

6. he is_____

7. there are_____

8. who is_____

9. were not_____

10. they are_____

Lesson 5

Compound Sentences

Practice A. Put a *C* in front of the following sentences that are compound sentences and an *S* in front of those that are simple sentences.

1. _____ It's difficult to get good food in the college cafeteria, but I try.

2. _____ Last year two girls tied for homecoming queen.

3. _____ Being away at college has its advantages and disadvantages.

4. _____ I would like to go to the concert, but I really can't afford to at this time.

5. _____ My parents may send me some extra money to help me out.

6. _____ Sometimes I find it difficult to express my real feelings or to speak candidly.

7. _____ We are going skating and then to a movie.

8. _____ It has been raining for ten straight days, and it will probably rain for ten more.

9. _____ All the students brought rubbers, umbrellas, and raincoats to keep from getting wet, cold, and sick.

10. _____ They helped us, and we helped them.

Practice B. Following are pairs of simple sentences. Choose a coordinate conjunction such as *and, but, or,* or *for,* and combine each pair into one compound sentence.

1. I was invited to a party. I couldn't go.

   _____

   _____

2. Don't put off doing your work. It will just pile up.

   _____

   _____

3. I borrowed my friend's car to visit my girlfriend. It ran out of gas half-way there.

   _____

   _____

4. My buddy received an *A* for his theme. I received only a *C.*

   _____

   _____

5. The star quarterback called the signals. The action began.

   _____

   _____

Practice C.   Write three compound sentences.

1._____

_____

2._____

_____

3._____

_____

Word Usage: Agreement of Subject and Verb I

Practice A.   Circle the verb that correctly completes the sentence.

1. She (practice/practices) the piano three hours every day.

2. She (read/reads) two books a week for our English Literature course.

3. José, Pedro, Maria, and I (are/is) good friends.

4. Everyone (get/gets) the same treatment here.

5. Neither my mother nor my father (try/tries) to influence me.

6. Either you or the twins (is/are) lying.

7. The branches and leaves (is/are) all over my driveway.

8. Neither my friends nor I (ski/skis).

9. You and I (need/needs) to talk.

10. Neither you nor she (need/needs) help with the math assignments.

Punctuation: The Comma

Practice A.   Shorten the following sentences with the use of commas.

1. The men and the women and the children rushed to leave the flooded area.

2. After five years and four months and two weeks and three days, I finally had my braces removed.

3. I love peanut butter and jelly and peanut butter and marshmallows and peanut butter and bananas.

4. Maine and New Hampshire and Connecticut are all New England states.

5. She got up and dressed and worked and ate.

Practice B.   Insert commas where needed in the following sentences. If a sentence does not require any comma, put a *0* in front of it.

_____ 1. One of our large storm windows was broken.

_____ 2. I can't afford another coat like my pretty blue winter coat.

_____ 3. My new white cat is a gift from my mother.

_____ 4. They are desperate hardened criminals.

_____ 5. I eat grapefruit for breakfast lunch and dinner.

Spelling: Some Often Misspelled Words I

Practice A. Look at each word carefully. If the word is spelled correctly, put a C in the blank. If the word is not spelled correctly, put a line through it and spell it correctly.

1. around_____

2. excelent_____

3. begining _____

4. commitee _____

5. consience _____

6. calender _____

7. disatisfied_____

8. separate _____

9. develop _____

10. disappoint _____

Lesson 6

Combining Similar Sentence Patterns to Form Compound Sentences

Practice A. Combine two similar sentence patterns to form a compound sentence.

Practice B. Combine two similar sentence patterns to form a compound sentence. (This sentence pattern should be different from the one in Practice A.)

Word Usage: Agreement of Subject and Verb II

Practice A. Circle the verb that correctly completes the sentence.

1. My pants (needs/need) cleaning.

2. His spectacles (is/are) so dirty.

3. My riches (consists/consist) of all that I have here.

4. The mumps (is/are) a dangerous illness for young adults, especially males.

5. The vaccine for measles (has/have) prevented many children from contracting the measles.

6. Ethics (deals/deal) with the areas of morality and goodness.

7. Fifty years of marriage (is/are) a long time.

8. Fifteen from twenty (is/are) five.

9. Ninety dollars (is/are) not too much to pay for a coat today.

10. The class (has/have) a special fund for parties.

Practice B. Circle the verb that correctly completes the sentence.

1. The strength of various medicines (depend/depends) on the dosage.

2. The importance of the experiments (is/are) hard to judge.

3. Games of chance (is/are) risky.

4. Five of the students (is/are) absent.

5. The carton of eggs (was/were) broken.

6. The students, including the faculty, (has/have) come to an agreement.

7. Children with birth defects (need/needs) special help.

8. The number of problems (seem/seems) infinite.

9. The chief, together with his wives, (watch/watches) the soldiers.

10. Not one of our friends (has/have) a car.

Punctuation: The Semicolon

Practice A. Insert a comma or semicolon in each of the following sentences.

1. When the fullback received the ball all the players of the opposing team tackled him.

2. I'm a vegetarian but my fiancé hates vegetables.

3. The meeting in the Student Center turned out to be a shouting spree therefore my friends and I left.

4. When the police discovered that the burglars were a group of men and women who pretended to sell vacuum cleaners the police warned the community about them.

5. Our basketball team won every game they played this season and our football team lost every game they played this season.

6. Since that unfortunate incident I am afraid to go out alone at night.

7. Because I am rather stocky my doctor put me on a diet.

8. I have one friend who has a hawk as a pet and I have another friend who has a boa constrictor as a pet.

9. I do not visit either of my friends too often and I do not allow them to bring their pets to my house.

10. Because falcons are on the endangered species list you must not hurt them.

Spelling: Some Often Misspelled Words II

Practice A. Look at each word carefully. If the word is spelled correctly, put a C in the blank. If the word is not spelled correctly, put a line through it and spell it correctly.

1. espesialy _____

2. exaggerate _____

3. fasinating _____

4. guarantee _____

5. imaginery _____

6. influntial _____

7. irelevant _____

8. ficticious _____

9. lisense _____

10. likly _____

Lesson 7

Combining Different Sentence Patterns to Form Compound Sentences

Practice A. Write four compound sentences in which each compound sentence consists of different sentence patterns.

1. _____

_____

_____

2. _____

_____

_____

3. _____

_____

_____

4. _____

_____

_____

Practice B. Here are ten compound sentences. In front of each compound sentence, write an *S* if the compound sentence uses similar sentence patterns or a *D* if the compound sentence uses different sentence patterns.

_____ 1. John kissed his wife, and then he dashed away.

_____ 2. No one voted James the winner, for James had made many errors.

_____ 3. Jeff considers himself a swinger, but the girls consider him a conceited bore.

_____ 4. One of my friends has had open heart surgery, but he is still very active.

_____ 5. My friends never play tricks on one another; however, they play lots of tricks on others.

_____ 6. She is personable, but she is not too bright.

_____ 7. The instructor called Betty a lazy person, and she called him an unfair teacher.

_____ 8. Jane is the genius in her family, and her sister is the beauty.

_____ 9. My sister is a doctor, and my brother is a lawyer.

_____ 10. I can't go with you, but you should go anyway.

Word Usage: Agreement of Subject and Verb III

Practice A. Circle the verb that correctly completes the sentence.

1. One of us (is/are) guilty.

2. None of them (is/are) going.

3. There (is/are) ten people present.

4. Each of the club members (is/are) responsible for planning a session.

5. Neither of the styles (is/are) very attractive.

6. Not one of the new members (seem/seems) very interesting.

7. Not one of the people I know (want/wants) to go.

8. There (is/are) only one problem that we have.

9. The group of people at the party (is/are) very lively.

10. Everyone of my friends (is/are) here.

Practice B. Circle the verb that correctly completes the sentence.

1. *The Hobbit* (is/are) a good book to read.

2. The Joneses' friend, not the Joneses, (has/have) a huge, frightening dog.

3. *The Morning Call* (carries/carry) the column "Let's Do It Together."

4. The *Detroit News* (is/are) a daily newspaper.

5. "The Most Dangerous Game" (is/are) a story by Richard Connell.

6. The Education Department, not the other departments, (is/are) being moved to another building.

7. It (is/are) sunny today.

8. She, not I, (is/am) going.

9. "Satan and Sam Shay" (is/are) written by Robert Arthur.

10. "Three Fables" (is/are) written by Robert Louis Stevenson.

Punctuation: The Colon

Practice A. Read each of the following. If the punctuation marks are correct, write a *C* in the blank. If the punctuation marks are incorrect, put in the correct punctuation mark(s).

_____ 1. The following are given as samples; toothpaste, powder, Kleenex, cologne, and so on

_____ 2. Dear Maggie:

_____ 3. Dear Father:

_____ 4. Dear Sir:

_____ 5. 9;10 A.M,

_____ 6. She explained: that she would be late.

_____ 7. "Fog" is a short poem.

_____ 8. "Listening; An Essential Skill"

_____ 9. They yelled: Hurry!

_____10. The shopping list has the following items, bread, butter, milk, cake, vegetables, fruit, and so on.

Spelling: Some Often Misspelled Words III

Practice A. Look at each word carefully. If the word is spelled correctly, put a *C* in the blank. If the word is not spelled correctly, put a line through it and spell it correctly.

1. bachalers_____

2. relize_____

    3. mathmatics _____

    4. necessary _____

    5. ninth _____

    6. pastimes _____

    7. peaceful _____

    8. instructar _____

    9. ridiculus _____

10. sophimore _____

Lesson 8

Combining Sentence Patterns to Form Compound Sentences

Practice A. Write two compound sentences. To form each compound sentence, combine *different* sentence patterns with a semicolon without a linking word.

    1. _____

_____

_____

    2. _____

_____

_____

Practice B. Write two compound sentences. To form each compound sentence, combine *similar* sentence patterns with a semicolon without a linking word.

    1. _____

_____

_____

    2. _____

_____

_____

Word Usage: Pronouns and Their Antecedents

Practice A. Circle the correct pronoun for each sentence.

    1. Neither of us has bought (his/their/our) textbooks yet.

    2. The thief told (his/their) story to the police.

    3. No one was able to give (his/their) name after the accident.

4. Jane, Sue, and Mary, my roommates, do (her/their) studying in the library.

5. Nobody knows what (he/they) will be doing a year from now.

6. Every person must make up (his/their) own mind.

7. Is anyone ready to give (his/their) talk?

8. Sue or Maria must make up (her/their) mind.

9. Neither John nor José has completed (his/their) project.

10. She told us, Maria and (I/me), to visit her tomorrow.

Punctuation: Quotation Marks

Practice A. Insert quotation marks where they are needed. Put a *0* in front of those sentences that require no quotation marks.

_____ 1. The following statements were overheard at a student center from three different persons: Professor M is too hard. You don't learn anything from Professor X. Professor Y is good, but he is a hard marker.

_____ 2. They said that they would work at the radio station.

_____ 3. Yes, I'll help you, she said.

_____ 4. What do you want? asked the man.

_____ 5. Eletelephony by Laura Richards is a delightful poem that children love.

_____ 6. Stopping by Woods on a Snowy Evening is one of my favorite Robert Frost Poems.

_____ 7. I always get chills running up and down my spine whenever I read The Masque of the Red Death by Edgar Allan Poe.

_____ 8. This year I'm going to work really hard, said Mary, and I'm going to hand in everything on time.

_____ 9. She asked whether she could go on the archaeology expedition.

_____10. No, only archaeology majors can go on the expedition, he said, because it is too dangerous for inexperienced persons.

Spelling: Some Often Misspelled Words IV

Practice A. Look at each word carefully. If the word is spelled correctly, put a *C* in the blank. If the word is not spelled correctly, put a line through it and spell it correctly.

1. apparattus_____

2. appetite_____

3. compliment _____

4. criticize_____

5. exerbitant_____

6. harrass_____

7. proffessor_____

8. polutants _____

9. resevoir _____

10. sacrafice_____

Lesson 9

Complex Sentences

Practice A. Put an *S* in front of the following sentences that are simple sentences, a *C* in front of those that are compound sentences, an *X* in front of those that are complex sentences, and a *0* in front of those that are not sentences.

1. _____ Go into the house with your things.

2. _____ The man who helped.

3. _____ I read the story to my students, and they liked it.

4. _____ When Jane arrived, we all left for the party.

5. _____ No one took the time to listen to Jim, and now he's dead.

6. _____ I went shopping but forgot to buy many things.

7. _____ Although I had accepted a date with Philip, I went out with James.

8. _____ When will he arrive?

9. _____ Whenever he is present.

10. _____ A good speaking voice should express meaning and mood, as well as be pleasing and easily heard.

Practice B. Following are groups of sentences. Combine the sentences into a complex one using a subordinate conjunction.

1. The baby cried. She was hungry.

_____

_____

2. Jack needs help. He will not ask for it.

_____

_____

3. Some courses lend themselves more to essay tests. In others you can use objective tests successfully.

_____

_____

_____

4. An objective test is easier to grade. On an objective test there is usually only one correct answer for a given question.

_____

_____

_____

5. We worked night and day. We wanted to finish our project.

_____

_____

Practice C. Write three complex sentences. Use a different subordinate conjunction for each sentence.

1. _____

_____

2. _____

_____

3. _____

_____

Word Usage: Adjectives

Practice A. Change the following five words into adjectives. Then put each into a compound or complex sentence. State which type of sentence you have written.

1. health _____

_____

2. trust _____

_____

3. love _____

_____

4. friend _____

_____

5. stick _____

_____

Practice B.   Change the following words into adjectives.

1. sick_____

2. rust_____

3. coward_____

4. snow_____

5. service_____

6. study_____

7. comprehension_____

8. nomad_____

9. power_____

10. anecdote_____

Punctuation: More Uses of the Comma

Practice A.   Insert commas where needed in each sentence. Put a *0* before those sentences that do not require a comma.

1. _____ My brother a hard worker owns his own business.

2. _____ Although she eats a lot she doesn't gain any weight.

3. _____ I like to go to parties but I won't go alone.

4. _____ She said moreover that she never wanted him to phone her again because he had embarrassed her at the party.

5. _____ When the bus arrived we all boarded it to go to the football game.

6. _____ The man in the faded gray suit was picked up by the police for questioning.

7. _____ I can always depend on George my college buddy to help me when I run out of money but I can't depend on him for anything else.

8. _____ My brother together with my sister planned a special celebration for me when I got into the college of my choice.

9. _____ When the firemen arrived at the scene of the fire they were unable to do anything.

10. _____ The woman who looks very embarrassed forgot to pay for an item in her grocery cart.

Spelling: Positive and Comparative Degrees of Adjectives

Practice A.   Give the comparative for the following adjectives.

1. poor_____

2. cheap_____

3. dark_____

4. stupid_____

5. hot_____

6. serious_____

7. dangerous _____

8. late_____

9. sorry_____

10. far_____

Practice B. Put the following adjectives in a comparative form, and then use each in a sentence.

1. pleasant_____

_____

2. powerful_____

_____

3. foolish_____

_____

Lesson 10

Compound-Complex Sentences

Practice A. In the following sentences, put an *S* in front of those that are simple sentences, a *C* in front of those that are compound sentences, an *X* in front of those that are complex sentences, and a *CC* in front of those that are compound-complex sentences.

1. _____ The college students constructed some informal tests, which they administered to third-graders.

2. _____ Nobody knows for sure whether the vaccine will work, but everyone hopes that it will prevent the spread of the deadly virus.

3. _____ Let's go away for the weekend and just relax.

4. _____ I'd love to go, but I have too much work to do.

5. _____ Although there is a time for work, and there is a time for play, you do not seem to understand this.

6. _____ My parents have supported me for all these years, and now I'm going to help them, although they don't want me to.

7. _____ I can't audition for the play because I have to work after classes.

8. _____ When we visited Italy, we met a number of people from our college who were on a different tour.

9. _____ The gunman entered the bank and demanded money from the bank tellers.

10. _____ Everyone froze because each person was frightened that the gunman would shoot someone.

Practice B. Write three compound-complex sentences.

1._____

_____

2._____

_____

3._____

_____

Word Usage: Using Nouns, Pronouns, and Verbs As Adjectives

Practice A. Change the words in parentheses into adjectives.

1. the (talk) doll _____
2. the (fall) tree _____
3. the (whistle) kettle_____
4. the (borrow) book _____
5. the (can) food _____
6. the (close) door_____
7. the (bend) wheel_____
8. the (heat) room _____
9. the (torment) man _____
10. the (smash) car _____

Practice B. State a noun to act as an adjective for the given nouns.

1._____ bean
2._____ worker
3._____ puzzle
4._____ lamp
5._____ counter
6._____ bread
7._____ frame
8._____ drawer

9. _____ socks

10. _____ lawyer

Punctuation: Comma Errors

Practice A. In the following sentences put a *C* in front of those that have no comma errors. Correct the comma errors in the other sentences.

_____ 1. "My career comes first", said my friend.

_____ 2. The strong, steel, doors were blasted open.

_____ 3. The man, who was peculiarly dressed, not the other fellow, suddenly began to throw confetti everywhere.

_____ 4. My brothers, sisters, aunts, and, uncles gave a party for my parents.

_____ 5. Jogging, and walking are my only sports.

_____ 6. The Dean said that, freshmen could not have cars on campus.

_____ 7. The wine, and cheese parties, are lots of fun.

_____ 8. Betty, my former roommate, is leaving school.

_____ 9. No one knows why but she said, that she had some personal problems.

_____ 10. Last semester she took only sociology, French, and, English.

Practice B. Correct the following run-on sentences.

1. The stock market went down four days in a row, I lost a lot of money.

_____

_____

2. The rain is flooding my basement, everything is getting ruined.

_____

_____

3. A ten-year-old child was picked up by the police for picking pockets, he has been picking pockets for two years.

_____

_____

Spelling: Superlative Degree of Adjectives

Practice A. Give the superlative for each of the following adjectives.

1. cheerful_____

2. sad_____

3. good_____

4. less_____

5. pleasant_____

6. insistent_____

7. unfortunate_____

8. rude_____

9. phony_____

10. reliable_____

Practice B. Put each of the following adjectives in a superlative form, and then use each in a compound-complex sentence.

1. high_____

_____

2. disastrous_____

_____

3. peculiar_____

_____

Lesson 11

Sentence Combining and Parallel Construction

Practice A. Combine each set of sentences into one sentence. You may change or add some words in combining your sentences.

1. A good book satisfies intellectual hunger. A good book helps persons awaken to the world around them.

_____

_____

2. It was a rainy day. It was a good day to work. I worked all day.

_____

_____

3. The gray-haired man walked into the restaurant. He was old and tired-looking. He looked around. He saw someone he knew.

_____

_____

4. No one was in the room. Something did not feel right. It felt as though someone was there.

_____

_____

5. I like to eat meat. My fiance likes to eat fish.

_____

_____

6. George is home for the holidays. Jane is home for the holidays. Susan is home for the holidays.

_____

_____

7. A group of men approached a stocky short man. The man looked frightened. He clutched his large black attaché case to his chest. The man shoved past the group of men. He ran away.

_____

_____

8. My roommate at college is Judy. Judy is very pretty. Judy is very popular. Judy is a pain in the neck.

_____

_____

9. The dance was boring. We left the dance. We went to a party.

_____

_____

10. The College Placement Office said that they had no jobs. They said that I should go to outside agencies. They said that I should advertise.

_____

_____

Practice B. Write four sentences that have parallel construction. The phrase in parentheses after each number tells you what kind of series the sentence should have.

1. (verb series)

_____

_____

2. (clause series)

_____

_____

3. (phrase series)

_____

_____

4. (noun series)

_____

_____

Word Usage: Adverbs

Practice A. Change each of the following adjectives into adverbs.

1. careful_____

2. courageous_____

3. safe _____

4. beautiful_____

5. splendid _____

6. hopeful_____

7. quick_____

8. soft_____

9. calm_____

10. bad _____

Practice B. Fill in each blank with *well* or *good*.

1. She had a_____day yesterday.

2. I do not feel very_____today.

3. You do your work very_____.

4. That is a_____report.

5. My sister is_____in mathematics.

Practice C. Write two sentences according to the directions in parentheses.

1. (Construct a sentence with a conjunctive adverb connecting two independent clauses.)_____

_____

2. (Construct a sentence with an adverb as a transitional word between sentences.)_____

_____

_____

Practice D. Write the comparative and superlative for each of the given adverbs.

1. quickly_____   _____

2. loudly_____   _____

3. peculiarly_____   _____

4. pleasantly_____   _____

5. properly_____   _____

Punctuation: The Dash

Practice A. Construct three sentences using the dash in three different ways. Construct the type of sentence stated in the parentheses.

1. (compound)_____

_____

2. (complex)_____

_____

3. (simple)_____

_____

Spelling: Possessives I

Practice A. Form the singular possessive for the following words.

1. woman_____

2. fox_____

3. house_____

4. Mrs. Jones _____

5. James_____

6. Mr. Burns_____

7. money_____

8. lady_____

9. Ms. Lass _____

10. knife _____

Practice B. Form the plural possessive for the following words.

1. woman _____

2. box _____

3. child _____

4. deer _____

5. mouse _____

6. datum _____

7. tooth _____

8. potato _____

9. baby _____

10. Jones _____

Practice C. Read each sentence carefully. If the sentence is written correctly, put a *C* in front of it. If not, correct any errors in the sentence.

_____ 1. Mrs. Jone's cake won the prize at the benefit.

_____ 2. The foxes' speed was no match for the dog's.

_____ 3. Charles' Dickens' books are read all over the world.

_____ 4. We are studying Keats' poems in our literature class.

_____ 5. My class's picnic will be in two weeks.

Lesson 12

Sentence Variety

Practice A. Rewrite this paragraph so that the sentences have more variety.

The man was obviously on the run. He wore a hat that covered his eyes. He wore a trench coat with the collar turned up. He wore glasses. He wore dark glasses. He carried a tattered bag. He walked swiftly. He kept looking over his shoulder. He kept one hand in his pocket. He heard a noise. He hid in the shadows of the night.

Word Usage: Troublesome Prepositions and Idioms

Practice A. Write a sentence for each idiom in the parentheses.

1. (identical with) _____

_____

2. (different from) _____

_____

3. (argue against) _____

_____

4. (superior to) _____

_____

5. (annoyed at) _____

_____

Punctuation: Parentheses

Practice A. Construct three sentences using parentheses in three different ways. Construct the type of sentence stated in the parentheses.

1. (compound) _____

_____

_____

2. (complex) _____

_____

_____

3. (simple) _____

_____

_____

Spelling: Possessives II

Practice A. Put the following words into their possessive forms.

1. anybody_____

2. one_____

3. who_____

4. it_____

5. attorney-general_____

6. sister-in-law_____

7. each other_____

8. nobody_____

9. another_____

10. boys_____

Lesson 13

Sentence Expansion Using Modifiers

Practice A. Give five descriptive words for each of the following.

1. meat_____

2. flower_____

3. wind_____

4. child_____

Practice B. Give five descriptive words for each of the following.

1. cook_____

2. swim_____

3. dance_____

Practice C. Following are five incomplete sentences. Complete each sentence by adding modifiers as specified in the parentheses.

1. The stranger,_____, looked very suspicious. (dependent clause)

2. Manuel,_____, is always getting into peculiar situations. (appositive)

3. Professor Brown,_____, gave a lecture on *Hamlet*. (appositive)

4. The meeting,_____, was a success. (dependent clause)

5. Everyone usually studies_____. (phrase)

Word Usage: Verb Tense

Practice A. Circle the verb that correctly completes the sentence.

1. Yesterday, my classes (are/were) all cancelled.

2. Who (sees/saw) what happened in the dormitory?

3. Three groups of students (are/be) going to Florida during the winter break.

4. Mt. Everest (is/was) the highest known mountain in the world.

5. Two persons I know (try/tried) to climb Mt. Everest last year.

6. A while ago, my boyfriend (lends/lent) me his car for the week.

7. James Thurber (is/was) the author of "The Secret Life of Walter Mitty."

8. Astronomy (is/was) the science of heavenly bodies.

9. Astrology (deals/dealt) with the reading of the stars.

10. *Charlotte's Web* by E. B. White (is/was) a favorite children's book.

11. I (have/has/had) met the victim ten years ago.

12. I (had been/have been) going to that doctor for years now.

13. It appeared from the autopsy that the victim (was/has been/had been) killed about three days earlier.

14. Recently, more descriptive sex scenes (had been/have been) increasing.

15. The trip that I went on two weeks ago was not as exciting as I (have/had) expected it to be.

16. We heard what (has/had) happened.

17. They told my brother that he (has/had) made the team.

18. Although my friend said that he (has/had) stopped gambling, I didn't believe him.

19. Everyone (had been/has been) very kind to me during these three difficult months.

20. We just learned that the murderer of three women (had been/has been) a student in our college for part of last year.

21. I (am/have been) studying for hours.

22. Yesterday, we (went/have gone) skiing.

23. We (bought/have bought) all the supplies yesterday.

24. My sister (is/has been) studying art in Paris for the past three months.

25. No one knows how long they (are/have been/were) in the caved-in mine before we missed them.

26. William Gilbert (is/was) usually looked upon as the founder of the modern science of electricity.

27. Last year (is/was/has been) a good year.

28. They (are/were/have been) working night and day to get the machine ready for today's race.

29. I (have paid/will pay/paid) my bill before I checked out.

30. Benjamin Franklin (is/was) considered America's first great name in science.

Practice B.   Construct five sentences according to the directions given in parentheses after each number.

1. (Construct a sentence containing a verb in the future tense.)

_____

_____

2. (Construct a sentence containing a verb in the present tense.)

_____

_____

3. (Construct a sentence containing a verb in the past tense.)

_____

_____

4. (Construct a sentence containing a statement of timelessness.)

_____

_____

5. (Construct a sentence containing a verb in the present perfect tense.)

_____

_____

Punctuation: Italics

Practice A.   Write three sentences in which italics would be used.

1._____

_____

2._____

_____

3._____

_____

Spelling: Homonyms or Homophones I

Practice A. In the following sentences circle the correct word.

1. She (one/won) the game.

2. I ate (meet/meat) for dinner last night.

3. That is (right/write).

4. (Hour/Our) friend will be here soon.

5. I need to (sew/so) this.

6. Tell him (to/too/two) stay.

7. I like her, (to/too/two).

8. This is a good (peace/piece) of cake.

9. What have you (read/red) lately?

10. I don't (know/no) her.

Practice B. In the following sentences circle the correct word.

1. I need (wood/would) for my fireplace.

2. The little old lady's cupboards were (bear/bare).

3. In the past, many children have gotten (lead/led) poisoning from eating paint.

4. (The heard/herd) of cattle is very large this year.

5. What color will you (die/dye) my blouse?

6. The (root/route) of the plant draws water and nourishment from the soil.

Practice C. Change some words in each sentence so that the sentence makes sense.

1. Hour friend one too read pillows.

_____

2. Know, to peaces of meet are two much.

_____

3. I no the write weigh two hour house.

_____

Lesson 14

Figures of Speech

Practice A. Here are ten sentences. Underline the figure of speech and then state what kind it is.

1. My heart was pounding like a racing motor car. _____

2. Her life is an open book. _____

3. The trees begged for mercy when the heavy snow crippled them.

   _____

4. The conspicuous silence embarrassed us. _____

5. His affront made me feel like an insect. _____

6. That basketball player is twenty feet tall. _____

7. The room was suffocating from the smoke, but the smokers ignored its sufferings. _____

8. The sky spoke to us in a menacing manner. _____

9. They were puppets in his hands. _____

10. He is the millionth person that I said *no* to today. _____

Practice B: Write a vivid word or phrase describing each of the following words or phrases.

1. life _____

2. a tree _____

3. forests _____

Practice C. Write a vivid verb describing an action appropriate to each of the following words.

1. life _____

2. a tree _____

3. forests _____

Word Usage: Logical Sequence of Tenses

Practice A. Circle the verb that completes the sentence correctly.

1. He replied that he (is/was) changing his major.

2. He told his instructor that he (doesn't/didn't) have his paper ready.

3. Although I (had studied/have studied) very hard for that exam, I didn't do very well on it.

4. When I work hard all day, I (can't/couldn't) study at night.

5. I have worked part time at this job for four years, but I (had received/have received) only two raises.

6. Although my mother has a terrible fear of heights, she (is trying/has tried/tried/had tried) over the years not to convey this fear to us.

7. I really can't stand people who (are/were) hypocrites. They pretend to be something that they are not.

8. Prehistoric man (smashes/smashed) rocks into small bits and wore the shiny bits and pieces as jewelry.

9. Man (is/was) supposed to be a rational animal who thinks things through.

10. Primitive man probably (has learned/learned/learns) by accident that cooked meat tasted better than raw meat.

Punctuation: A Review—Simple and Compound Sentences

Practice A. Punctuate the following sentences.

1. That is great

2. The firemen tried to save the victims their efforts were futile

3. John is leaving for school tonight however he will not be going until after dinner

4. First we went to the ball game then we went out to eat

5. With whom are you going to the dance

6. I've taken three years of French but I still can't hold a conversation in it

7. I can't go at this time and no one else is able to do the job

8. I cannot help you nevertheless you're free to ask someone else

9. I'm not dieting anymore so I can come to your dinner party

10. Hearing the bell the children didn't hesitate for a moment they all ran out of the building

Spelling: Homonyms or Homophones II

Practice A. In the following sentences circle the correct word.

1. She lost her (ring/wring) in the sink.

2. They had to (toe/tow) our car away.

3. It is illegal to fight a (dual/duel) in the United States.

4. I didn't have enough money to pay my (fair/fare).

5. You can recognize him by his (gait/gate).

6. He (through/threw) my best sweater out by mistake.

7. She is so (coarse/course) at times.

8. The (cite/site/sight) we chose for our house is beautiful.

9. Must I (sight/site/cite) that again for you?

10. The (principle/principal) in our high school used to hold faculty meetings every Wednesday.

Practice B. Change some words in each sentence so that the sentence makes sense.

1. The fare on the old golf coarse cite is dew two open soon.

_____

2. It is knot fare four you to play the principle duel roll.

_____

3. The principle weigh two kill a vampire is too put a steak threw its heart.

_____

4. Eye herd that he eight to stakes, two.

_____

5. My died hare always gets in my I or falls into nots.

_____

6. After eye eight, eye road my bike on root 47 two view the bare that had been found in the woulds.

_____

Lesson 15

Connotative Meaning

Practice A. For each of the following words give two substitute words, one with a positive and one with a negative connotative meaning.

1. house_____

2. trash collector _____

3. writer_____

4. judge _____

5. businessman_____

6. lawyer_____

7. doctor_____

8. recruiter _____

9. salesperson _____

10. work _____

Word Usage: Active and Passive Voices of Verbs

Practice A. Put a circle around the number of each sentence that can be put into the passive voice.

1. Who are you?

2. She will become a lawyer in a few years.

3. The muggers beat the old man.

4. No one saw the mugging of the old man.

5. The police captured the muggers.

6. The police took the old man to the hospital.

7. My brother is in medical school.

8. The air controllers put the planes in a holding pattern.

9. The workers demanded more pay.

10. The planes were flying too low.

Practice B. Write each of the following sentences in the active voice.

1. The window was broken by the children.

_____

2. The show was seen by us.

_____

3. The child's life was saved by the operation.

_____

4. Many books were read by us last semester.

_____

5. Nothing of value was taken by the burglars.

_____

Practice C. Write two sentences in the passive voice.

1. _____

_____

2. _____

_____

Practice D. Write two sentences that combine the active and the passive voice in a beneficial way.

1. _____

_____

2._____

_____

Punctuation: A Review—Complex Sentences

Practice A. Place commas in those sentences that need them. If a sentence does not require a comma, put a *0* in the blank.

_____ 1. After waiting for them for three hours we left.

_____ 2. No one told us that our friends had taken a later flight.

_____ 3. Although we were furious about wasting so much time we were not angry with them.

_____ 4. He was unhappy because his girlfriend had left him.

_____ 5. Because the room is so warm I can't do any work.

_____ 6. My heart skipped a beat when the professor returned my midterm to me.

_____ 7. While everyone was out celebrating I was home finishing a paper.

_____ 8. Whenever I wear red I feel cheerful.

_____ 9. When the students learned that their classes had been cancelled they went to the Student Center and played bridge.

_____ 10. As soon as my professor returns from his trip I will meet with him to discuss my independent study project.

Spelling: Some Spelling Generalizations I

Practice A. Add the ending *-able* to the following words.

1. sale _____   2. love _____

3. enforce _____   4. manage _____

5. mortgage _____   6. agree _____

7. knowledge _____   8. desire _____

9. receive _____   10. believe _____

Practice B. Add the ending *-ly* or *-ed* to the following words:

1. happy _____   2. say _____

3. rely _____   4. crazy _____

5. carry _____   6. satisfactory _____

7. reply _____   8. pray _____

9. study _____   10. ordinary _____

Practice C. Add the ending *-ing* to the following words.

1. force _____   2. charge _____

3. mortgage _____   4. discourage _____

5. like _____   6. make _____

7. forge _____   8. forgive _____

9. age _____   10. practice _____

Practice D. Add the ending *-ful, -ment,* or *-ly* to the following words.

1. fate _____   2. love _____

3. care _____   4. arrange _____

5. grace _____   6. polite _____

7. late _____   8. hope _____

9. retire _____   10. concise _____

Lesson 16

Word Meanings and Sentence Context

Practice A. For each of the following sentences, think of *one word* that will go in all the blanks of the sentence.

1. My mind goes_____ everytime I have to fill in a(n)

   _____ .

2. In England, I paid two_____ for a book to help me shed

   some_____ .

3. The lawyer knew that he had won his_____ when he pro-

   duced the _____ containing the murder weapon.

4. A certain_____ of dogs is easier to_____

   than others.

5. After he had drunk a lot of_____ , he wasn't in very

   good_____ because he thought that he saw_____ .

6. Part of the_____ was to_____ a course that

   no one could follow after we hid the jewels in the chosen cemetery

   _____ .

7. The police said that they would_____ everyone who was stand-

   ing by the barbeque_____ at the time of the murder.

8. I always_____ by some_____when I deliver a

speech about my_____on an issue.

9. Everytime I_____ , I get a(n)_____in

my stockings.

10. I don't_____ _____ing my little brother because he has

such a brilliant_____ .

11. My basketball_____said that he would_____ me in

math while we were riding in the _____.

12. While riding our horses on the _____we saw in _____

view a very_____house.

13. He was a(n)_____at the party because his_____

had won the game when he_____ the ball so hard.

14. It is the_____ of the custom officials to see to it that you

pay_____ on certain things that are brought into the

United States.

15. A(n)_____of persons wearing _____s around their

heads made fun of our school _____ .

Word Usage: Verb Mood

Practice A. Fill in the blank in each sentence with a word that correctly completes the sentence.

1. She wishes she _____a famous writer.

2. If I _____ elected, I would carry out all

my campaign promises.

3. It is important that you_____

present tomorrow for the reading of the will.

4. If only it_____ a dream, rather

than a reality.

5. The man demanded that his money _____

returned.

6. My boss requested that I_____ at the

special meeting.

7. I'm sure that you _____ finish your

paper on time.

8. What _____ you doing?

9. I would consider your offer, if you _____

more trustworthy.

10. I wish my mother _____ well.

Spelling: Some Spelling Generalizations II

Practice A. Check each of the following words carefully. If the word is spelled correctly, put a *C* in the blank. If the word is spelled incorrectly, put a line through it and spell it correctly.

1. concieve _____

2. protien _____

3. weird _____

4. either _____

5. beleive _____

6. cieling _____

7. rein _____

8. concieted _____

9. vien _____

10. cheif _____

11. weigh _____

12. neighbor _____

Practice B. Add the endings *-ed* and *-ing* to the following words.

1. rake _____

2. bat _____

3. can _____

4. dry _____

5. nag _____

6. ban _____

7. gain _____

8. plot _____

9. clap _____

10. knit _____

Practice C.   Add the endings *-ed* and *-ing* to the following words.

1. occur_____

2. repel_____

3. defer_____

4. quiz _____

5. remit_____

6. maintain_____

7. report_____

8. confer_____

9. counsel_____

10. admit_____

APPENDIX V

Glossary

ABBREVIATION. An abbreviation is a shortened form of a word or phrase. A period often follows an abbreviation. *Examples:* P.S. (post-script); A.M. (before noon); P.M. (after noon); B.C. (before Christ); A.D. (anno Domini = in the year of the Lord); etc. (and so on); e.g. (for example); i.e. (that is); Inc. (Incorporated); Co. (Company).

ADJECTIVE. A word that describes or limits nouns and pronouns is called an adjective. Descriptive words make sentences less general and more specific. (See modifier.) *Example:* The shaggy-haired brown dog is mine.

1. Suffixes — Certain suffixes (endings added to words) signal that a word is an adjective. By adding certain suffixes to nouns or verbs, you can change the words into adjectives. *Examples:* virtue — virtuous; beauty — beautiful; person — personable; rain — rainy. (See 7.)

2. Positive degree — The Positive degree is the simplest and most commonly used form of an adjective. It does not involve any comparisons. *Example:* The big black dog is barking. The working man went home.

3. Comparative degree — The comparative degree of an adjective is used to show a difference of quantity, quality, or manner between two and only two persons or things. To show that something is more than something else, *-er* is usually added to the end of the adjective. *Examples:* He is taller than she. This problem is easier than the other one.

Longer adjectives and many adjectives ending in *-ive, -ful,* and *-ish* show degree by placing the word *more* or *less* in front of the adjective. *Examples:* more bountiful; more protective; less sluggish.

A few adjectives change their spelling to form the comparatives. *Examples:*

Positive	Comparative
good	better
bad	worse
much	more

4. Superlative degree — The superlative degree is used when making a comparison involving more than two people or things. The superlative shows that the adjective used to describe quality, quantity, or manner is at its extreme. To show that something is the "most," *-est* is added to almost all

one-syllable and many two-syllable adjectives.   *Examples:* She is the friendliest person I know. He is the tallest person that I've every seen.

Longer adjectives and many adjectives ending in *-ive, -ful,* and *-ish* usually do not add *-est* to show the superlative degree. They show the superlative degree by placing the word *most* or *least* in front of the adjective. *Examples:* She is the most selfish person I know. He is the most powerful executive in the company. They are the least helpful salespeople that I've ever met.

A few adjectives change completely to form the superlative.   *Examples:* bad — worst; good — best; many — most.

5. Using nouns as adjectives — Nouns can be used to describe or limit a noun.   *Examples:* tea kettle; kitchen sink.

6. Using pronouns as adjectives — Pronouns can be used to describe or limit adjectives.   *Examples:* our new car; my beautiful baby.

7. Using verbs as adjectives — If *-ing* is added to a verb, it can act as an adjective.   *Examples:* the running dog; the sleeping baby. (See Participle.)

If *-ed, -d, -en,* or *-n,* is added to some verbs, they can act as adjectives. *Examples:* the broken toy; the dreaded moment. (See Participle.)

8. After verbs such as *be, become, smell, sound, taste, feel, look, appear,* an adjective rather than an adverb is used. These verbs are called linking verbs because they connect a subject with a word that in effect renames the subject or describes the subject.   *Examples:* That sounds good. He appears fine. He is nice. (See Linking Verb.)

9. *Good* and *well* are often confused with one another. *Good* is an adjective. *Good* is used to describe a person, place, or thing. *Well* is an adverb. *Well* is used to describe how something is done. However, *well* is used as an adjective when it describes someone's health.   *Examples:* That is good coffee. I do not feel well. He rides very well.

ADVERB. An adverb generally tells how, when, where, and how much. (See Modifier.)   *Examples:* The train moved *slowly.* (how) School starts *soon.* (when) They went *away.* (where) She runs *very* fast. (how much).

1. Adverbs usually describe or limit verbs.   *Examples:* They played *nicely.* She sews *beautifully.*

2. Adverbs can describe or limit an adjective or another adverb.   *Examples:* The *carefully* constructed plan was put to a vote. (*Carefully* describes the adjective *constructed.*) He drives *too* fast. (*Too* describes the adverb *fast.*)

3. Many adverbs end in *-ly.*   *Examples:* noisily, busily, quietly.

4. Some adverbs do not end in *-ly.*   *Examples:* always, never, later afterward, today.

5. Some adverbs have both *-ly* and non *-ly* endings.   *Examples:* deep — deeply; loud — loudly.

6. Adverbs, as adjectives, have degrees of comparison. The comparisons of adverbs are formed in the same way that comparisons of adjectives are formed.

Examples:

Positive	Comparative	Superlative
fast	faster	fastest
well	better	best
carefully	more carefully, less carefully	most carefully, least carefully

7. Conjunctive adverbs are used both as modifiers and linking words. They connect two simple sentences to form a compound sentence. *Examples of conjunctive adverbs:* nevertheless, then, therefore. (See Linking Word.)

8. Words such as *then, however, nevertheless, therefore,* and *besides* are usually called adverbs rather than conjunctive adverbs when they do not connect two simple sentences. (See Linking Word.)

AGREEMENT OF SUBJECT AND VERB. A verb and its subject should agree in number.

1. When a subject in a sentence is a single subject and names only one thing or person, the verb is singular. *Examples:* Jane is nice. The tomato tastes good.

2. When a subject in a sentence is a compound subject or names more than one thing or person, the verb is plural. *Examples:* Jim and Susan are partners. The flowers are beautiful.

3. A singular verb is used with a singular pronoun. *Example:* She is nice.

4. A plural verb is used with a plural pronoun. *Example:* They are partners.

5. When two or more singular subjects are joined by *or* or *nor,* the verb is singular. *Examples:* Neither Paula nor Paul *is* going to the picnic tomorrow. Either you or Peter *plays* the piano at the party.

6. When two or more subjects are joined by *or* or *nor* and one subject is singular and the other is plural, the verb agrees with the subject closest to it. *Example:* Jim or his friends are shopping for the party.

7. The verb agrees with the subject of the sentence and not with the noun in the complete predicate of the sentence. *Examples:* Oranges are a good source of vitamin C. Vitamin C is found in all citrus fruits.

8. The words *there is* should be followed by a singular noun. The words *there are* should be followed by a plural noun. *Examples:* There is a lot of noise in the room. There are too many people here.

9. A singular verb is used with such words as *neither, either, nobody, anybody, somebody, everybody, anyone, someone, one,* and *no one. Examples:* Either of you is welcome. Someone is out there.

10. The words *none* and *all* may be either singular or plural, but the plural meaning is more commonly used. Usually, when *none* is singular, the words *nobody, no one,* or *not one* could be used. *All* is singular when it means the whole amount of something. *Examples:* None of the records were broken. Not one of the records is broken. All is lost. All are accounted for.

11. When *each* is used with singular nouns connected by *and,* the verb is singular. *Example:* Each boy and each girl is eligible to enter the contest.

12. When a sentence has a singular subject with a plural modifier (a word or phrase that describes or limits), the verb is singular. *Example:* The price of cherries is very high.

13. When a subject is joined to other words by *with, together with, including, as well as,* or *no less than,* the verb agrees with the subject. The verb is not influenced by the words joined to the subject. *Examples:* The captain, together with his men, was able to bring the ship to safety. The students, as well as their professor, are going to the meeting.

14. A noun that is plural in form but singular in meaning usually requires a singular verb. *Examples:* mathematics, economics, physics, ethics, measles, mumps. Mathematics is an easy course for me. Ethics deals with questions of right and wrong.

15. A noun that is plural in form and plural in meaning usually requires a plural verb. *Examples:* athletics, spectacles, scissors, pants, riches. Riches are not easy to acquire.

16. When the subject of the sentence is a group of words describing a quantity or number, and the subject is thought of as whole, the verb is usually singular. *Examples:* One thousand dollars is a fair price to pay for that. Ten from forty is thirty.

17. When the subject of the sentence is the name of a television show a book, a poem, a newspaper, a film, a play, etc., a singular verb is used. *Examples: The Exorcist* was a frightening movie. The *New York Times* is read by people all over the world.

18. The word *it* requires a singular verb. *Example:* It is a nice day today.

19. When a sentence has both a negative and positive subject, the verb agrees with the subject in the positive. *Examples:* He, not you, is going. She, not I, is washing the dishes.

ANTECEDENT. (See Pronoun.)

APPOSITIVE. (See Modifier.)

AUXILIARY. An auxiliary is a helping verb. When an auxiliary accompanies a verb, it gives the tense (time) of the verb, person, number, and so on. *Examples:* am, have, will, be, may, did. I will bake the cake soon. She is going now. He has been gone a long time. (See Predicate of a Sentence.)

CAPITALIZATION. The following are capitalized.

1. Names of persons — Charles Brown
2. Titles of persons — Mr., Mrs., Ms.
3. Days of the week — Monday, Tuesday
4. Months of the year — January, February
5. Titles of books — *Gaining Word Power*
6. Titles of plays — *The Taming of the Shrew*
7. Titles of magazines and journals — *Time, Esquire*
8. Titles of poems — "The Death of the Hired Man"
9. Titles of movies — *Star Wars*
10. Names of countries — the United States of America, France, England
12. Names of cities — Nashville, Chicago, New York
13. Names of streets, avenues, and roads — Tenth Ave., 14th St., Stuart Road
14. Names of languages — English, Spanish, French, Chinese
15. Names of companies — Ford Motor Co., General Motors
16. Names of institutions — the Smithsonian Institution
17. The title *president,* and the words *presidential,* or *presidency* when they refer to the President of the United States.
18. Historical periods — the Middle Ages
19. Names of wars — World War II
20. Buildings — the World Trade Towers, the Empire State Building

21. Documents — the Bill of Rights
22. The first person singular pronoun — I
23. The first word of every line in poetry (except for the poetry of some modern poets)

> A word is dead
> When it is said,
> Some say.

24. Names of God — Lord, Father, and pronouns used for God
25. Titles of school course offerings — English 101, Geology 203
26. The first word of a direct quotation — Ms. Jones said, "We will help you."

Do not capitalize the following:

1. Games — football, baseball
2. Seasons — summer, winter, fall, spring
3. School subjects unless they are names of languages or titles of specific course offerings — geometry, English, history, biology, French, geography
4. Names of relatives, unless they are used as part of a person's name — aunt, uncle, cousin, Aunt Jane
5. A direction unless it names a definite area or is part of a name — north, east, North America
6. Words that are used in a general sense rather than as a name or part of a title — general, president, highway
7. Titles used alone unless they stand for a specific person of high rank

CASE. Case shows the relationship between a noun or pronoun and the other words in the sentence. Case is shown by a change in the form of the word or by the position of the word in a sentence. (See Pronoun Case.) *Examples:* The cat's fur turned green from the shampoo. (*Cat's* is in the possessive case.) The cat scratched the child. (*Cat* is in the subjective case; *child* is in the objective case.)

CLAUSE. In a sentence, a clause is a group of words that contains both a subject and a predicate. (See Dependent Clause and Independent Clause.)

CLOSED SYLLABLE. (See Syllable.)

COMBINING SENTENCES. Two or more sentences joined together are said to be combined. *Examples:* 1. Jack is friendly. Arthur is friendly. Seth is friendly. Jack, Arthur, and Seth are friendly. 2. The man watched the child play. The man was old. The man saved the child's life. The old man, who watched the child play, saved the child's life.

COMPOUND WORD. A compound word is made up of separate words that combine to form a new word. Compound words may appear as one-word compounds, as two-word compounds, as multiword compounds, or as hyphenated compounds. *Examples:* grandfather, river bank, maid of honor, man-of-war.

CONJUNCTIVE ADVERB. (See Adverb and Linking Word.)

CONJUNCTION. (See Linking Word.)

CONNOTATIVE MEANING. A connotative meaning goes beyond the direct, specific definition of a word. *Connotative* refers to the emotional sense of a word. It is the meaning associated with the word. *Examples:* She is a lamb. He is a pig. (The word *lamb* refers to *gentle* and influences the reader to react in a positive way. The word *pig* brings not very complimentary images to mind and influences the reader to react in a negative way.)

CONTEXT. The words surrounding a particular word that can shed light on its meaning.

CONTRACTION. A contraction is usually a combination of two words or a shortening of a compound word. The apostrophe is put in place of the omitted letter or letters. *Examples:* Let us go. Let's go. Who is he? Who's he? It is Jennifer. It's Jennifer.

Do not confuse the possessives such as *whose, its,* and *theirs* with the contractions *who's, it's,* and *there's.*

COORDINATE CONJUNCTION. (See Linking Word.)

CORRELATIVE CONJUNCTION. (See Linking Word.)

DENOTATIVE MEANING. The denotative meaning is the direct, specific meaning of a word.

DEPENDENT CLAUSE. A dependent clause is a group of words that contains both a subject and a predicate but cannot stand alone as a sentence because it does not express a complete thought. A dependent clause, which may also be referred to as a subordinate clause, is introduced by a subordinate conjunction. (See Linking Words.) *Examples:* Although he is kind; When I arrive; Because I need you; That he was going; Since a week has passed.

FIGURES OF SPEECH. Word usages that give color, decoration, and life to verbal expression. 1. Hyperbole — The use of excessive exaggeration for effect. *Example:* I walked a million miles today. 2. Oxymoron — The combining of opposites to convey a particular image or to produce a striking effect. *Example:* A loud silence. 3. Metaphor — A comparison between two unlike objects without the use of *like* or *as*. *Example:* He is a jellyfish. 4. Personification — The giving of human characteristics and capabilities to nonhuman things such as nonliving objects, abstract ideas, or animals. *Example:* Winter's icy breath. 5. Simile — A comparison between two unlike objects using *like* or *as*. *Example:* Her disposition is like glass; it breaks easily, and when it breaks, it cuts.

HOMOGRAPH. A homograph is a word that is spelled the same as another word but has a different meaning. *Examples:* He is a *mean* man. I *mean* that. *Mean* in statistics means "average."

HOMONYM OR HOMOPHONE. A homonym or homophone is a word that sounds like another word but is spelled differently and has a different meaning. *Examples:* one — won; meet — meat; hour — our; write — right; red — read; sew — so; weigh — way; too — two — to; piece — peace.

IDIOM. An expression peculiar to a people or to a district, community, or class.

INDEPENDENT CLAUSE. An independent clause is a group of words that can stand alone as a simple sentence. Each clause contains a subject and a predicate and expresses a complete thought. An independent clause may also be referred to as a principal or main clause. (See Sentence.) *Examples:*

The bride is wearing a beautiful white dress, but the groom is wearing jeans and a sweatshirt. (*The bride is wearing a beautiful white dress* and *the groom is wearing jeans and a sweatshirt* are both independent clauses. As independent clauses, they can stand alone as complete sentences. *The bride is wearing a beautiful white dress. The groom is wearing jeans and a sweatshirt.*)

INTERJECTION. An interjection is a word usually used with an exclamation mark to express an emotion. It is independent of the rest of the sentence. *Example:* Oh!

INTRANSITIVE VERB. An intransitive verb is a verb that cannot take an object; that is, it cannot carry over an action from a subject to an object. It is a verb expressing a state that is limited to the subject of the sentence. *Examples:* She jogs every morning. They are happy. He swims.

LINKING VERB. Verbs such as *be, become, smell, sound, taste, feel, look, seem,* and *appear* are called linking verbs because they often link a subject with a word that in effect renames the subject or describes the subject. An adjective should be used rather than an adverb after linking verbs. (See Adjective.) *Examples:* She is my teacher. She is nice.

LINKING WORD.

1. Coordinate (equal) conjunctions — The most often used linking words that join simple sentences are *and, but,* and *or. Nor, for* and *yet* are also used as coordinate conjunctions. *Examples:* My friend likes history the best of all her subjects, but she doesn't do very well in it. Try to do your best in it, or you will have regrets later on.

The linking words *and, but, or* are most commonly used to connect words as well as groups of words. *Examples:* I like to eat fruit, candy, and anything else that is sweet. I will take Jennifer and Sharon with me on the trip. Joe or Jerry can go.

2. Sometimes pairs of words called *correlative conjunctions* (linking words that show a one to one necessary relation between two sets of things) connect simple sentences. *Examples of correlative conjunctions:* either . . . or; neither . . . nor.

3. Subordinate (dependent) conjunctions — The most often used linking words that introduce a dependent clause (words that cannot stand alone as a sentence) are *although, as, because, before, if, since, that, unless, until, after, as if, as though, as soon as, in order that, even if, so that.* Other words such as *where, when,* and *while* often function as subordinate conjunctions. Pronouns such as *who, which, that,* and *what* also function as subordinate conjunctions. *Examples:* Before he went away to school, he was disrespectful, wild, and insensitive. I like her because she is a kind, considerate person.

4. Conjunctive adverbs such as *however, therefore,* and *nevertheless,* connect two simple sentences to form a compound sentence. (See Adverb.)

5. Linking words such as *however, therefore, nevertheless,* and *then* act as transitional words between sentences. They are usually called adverbs rather than conjunctive adverbs when used in this way.

MAIN CLAUSE. (See Independent Clause.)

MODIFIER. A modifier is a word that describes or limits another word or a group of words. (See Adjective and Adverb.)

1. A word can modify a noun, a verb, an adjective, or an adverb. *Examples:* She is a *charming, friendly,* and *pretty* girl. (adjectives modifying a noun) He runs *fast.* (adverb modifying a verb) He runs *very fast.* (adverb modifying an adverb) She is *very* charming. (an adverb modifying an adjective).

2. Modifiers can consist of phrases or dependent clauses. *Examples:* A *machine that doesn't work* is worthless. (The dependent clause *that doesn't work* limits *machine* to a particular one.) My sister, *a genius,* always gets everything right. (The phrase *a genius* describes sister.) We went *for our mother's sake.* (The phrase *for our mother's sake* describes *went.* It tells why we went.)

3. If the additional information is not necessary to the thought of the sentence, it is set off by commas. This modifier is called a nonrestrictive modifier. If the additional information is necessary to the thought of the sentence, it is not set off by commas. This modifier is called a restrictive modifier.

4. Modifiers should be placed next to or near the word or words that they modify. *Examples:* Mary, eating a sandwich, told her story. (correctly placed modifier) Mary told her story eating a sandwich. (incorrectly placed modifier)

5. A modifier can be a noun or pronoun with or without its own descriptive words that follows a noun or pronoun and gives additional information that identifies the noun or pronoun. This kind of modifier is called an appositive. An appositive that is a nonrestrictive modifier is set off by commas. An appositive that is a restrictive modifier is not set off by commas. *Examples:* The singer Ray Charles is blind. Margaret, my girlfriend, is very moody. (The first example is a restrictive appositive because the name *Ray Charles* restricts the noun *singer* to one particular person. In the second example, the appositive *my girlfriend* is not restrictive because it is giving additional information about Margaret that is not necessary to the meaning of the sentence.)

6. A modifier can be a word such as *however, then, also,* or *nevertheless.* (See Adverb and Linking Word.)

NONRESTRICTIVE MODIFIER. (See Modifier and Punctuation.)

NOUN. A noun is a word such as *hat, baby, money, goodness,* or *truth.* A noun names a person, an animal, a place, a thing, or an idea. (See Case.)

1. A proper noun names a particular person, place or thing. Proper nouns are capitalized. *Examples:* Anthony, Karen, India, Grand Canyon, Empire State Building.

2. All other nouns are common nouns. Common nouns are not capitalized. *Examples:* man, country, place, building.

3. A collective noun names a group, a class, or a collection and is considered as a unit or whole. *Examples:* crowd, class, jury, gang, group.

NOUN PLURAL.

1. An *-s* is added to nouns such as *cat, book, plum,* and *paper.* *Examples:* cats, books, plums, papers.

2. An *-es* is added to nouns that end in *-s, -ss, -sh, -ch,* or *-x.* *Examples:* buses, glasses, bushes, peaches, foxes.

3. Proper nouns (names) follow the regular rules for *-s* and *-es* plurals. *Examples:* Bob — four Bobs; Mrs. Smith — the Smiths; Mr. Jones — the Joneses.

4. Nouns that end in *-y* with a vowel before the *y* add *-s* to make the word plural. *Examples:* toy — toys; day — days.

5. Nouns that end in *-y* with a consonant before the *y* change the *y* to *i* and add *-es.* *Examples:* cherry — cherries; baby — babies.

6. Nouns that end in *-o* with a consonant before the *o* usually add *-es* or *-s* to make the word plural. *Examples:* domino — dominoes; piano — pianos; auto — autos; solo — solos; dynamo — dynamos.

7. Nouns that end in *-o* with a vowel before the *o* add *-s* to make the word plural. *Examples:* radio — radios; cameo — cameos.

8. The plural of some nouns ending in *-o* may be formed with either *-s* or *-es.* *Examples:* halos or haloes; volcanoes or volcanos.

9. Nouns that end in *-f* or *-fe* usually are made plural by changing the *f* or *fe* to *ves.* *Examples:* knife — knives; wife — wives. Some nouns ending in *-f* or *-fe* form the plural by adding *-s.* *Examples:* chief — chiefs; roof — roofs; safe — safes. The plural of some nouns ending in *-f* may be formed by either *fs* or *ves.* *Examples:* hoofs — hooves; scarves — scarfs.

10. Nouns that end in *-ff* usually add *-s* to the word to form the plural. *Examples:* staff — staffs; sheriff — sheriffs.

11. Following are exceptions ro rule patterns for plurals: foot — feet; man — men; child — children; ox — oxen; goose — geese; tooth — teeth; mouse — mice.

12. Following are some nouns that are the same in both the singular and plural: deer — deer; salmon — salmon; sheep — sheep; fish — fish.

13. Hyphenated compound words form their plurals by adding *-s* or *-es* to the important word in the hyphenated compound word. Usually, the first word is the important word in the compound. *Examples:* mother-in-law — mothers-in-law; attorney-at-law — attorneys-at-law.

OPEN SYLLABLE. (See Syllable.)

OVERWORKED PHRASE. A phrase that has been used over and over again to describe something is called an overworked phrase. *Examples:* pretty as a picture; hungry as a bear.

You should try to avoid using overworked phrases in your writing.

PARALLEL CONSTRUCTION. (See Sentence.)

PASSIVE. (See Verb Voice.)

PARTICIPLE. The present participle and the past participle are the two forms of the participle. A participle may be used as a modifier or as a verb. When a participle is used as a verb, it is used with an auxiliary. When a participle is used as a modifier, it is used alone. (See Adjective.)

1. *Present participle* — The present participle of regular and irregular verbs is formed by adding *-ing* to the verb. *Example:* running; crying; coughing. The present participle is used with some form of the auxiliary *be* to produce the progressive verb forms. (See Progressive Verb Form.) *Examples:* She is going; they are returning; we have been studying.

2. *Past Participle* — The past participle of regular verbs is formed by adding *-ed* or *-d* to the verb. *Examples:* climbed; described. The past participle of irregular verbs does not follow a regular pattern. *Examples:* broken; rung; torn. The past participle is used with some form of the auxiliary *be* to

form the passive voice. (See Verb Voice.)   *Examples:* was eaten; is played; is sung; should have been won.

PAST PARTICIPLE. (See Participle.)

PHRASE.   A phrase is a group of related words having either no subject or no predicate; it may lack both. A phrase cannot stand alone as a sentence. *Examples:* in the yard; at the door; have been going; for you; to me.

POSITIVE DEGREE.   (See Adjective and Adverb.)

POSSESSIVE.

1. When singular nouns or proper nouns show ownership, an apostrophe (') and *-s* are usually added to the nouns.   *Examples:* James's dog is a collie. The man's letter gave the reasons for his resignation.

2. Most biblical and classical names form the singular possessive by adding the apostrophe and *-s.*   *Examples:* Jupiter's lightning; Job's hardships. *Exceptions:* Jesus' words; Moses' words.

3. To show ownership for plural nouns ending in *-s* or *-es*, an apostrophe is added after the *s.*   *Examples:* our parents' property; the girls' activities; the cherries' pits; the Joneses' business.

4. To show ownership for plural nouns not ending in *-s* or *-es,* an apostrophe and *-s* are added.   *Examples:* the women's room; the children's playhouse; the mice's tails.

5. The possessive form is usually added to the last word of a hyphenated compound word.   *Examples:* brother-in-law's house; attorney-general's decision.

6. To show ownership by two or more persons as a group, the last proper noun is put in the possessive.   *Examples:* Joseph and Joan's child; Maria and Mike's house.

7. To show individual ownership, not group ownership, each proper noun is put in the possessive.   *Examples:* Margaret's and Tony's businesses are going very well. George's and Jim's activities are very exciting.

8. Indefinite pronouns such as *any, each, all,* and *some,* when combined with *body, one, other,* or *else*, add *-s* to form the possessive to show ownership.   *Examples:* anybody's, another's, someone's.

9. The pronouns *his, hers, mine, ours, theirs, its,* and *whose* do not need an apostrophe to form the possessive to show ownership.   *Examples:* This is mine. (This belongs to me.) Whose is that? (To whom does that belong?)

PREDICATE OF A SENTENCE.   The predicate of a sentence is a word or group of words that tells something about the subject of the sentence.

1. Simple predicate — A simple predicate is the verb alone. The verb is a telling word. It expresses an action, existence, or an occurrence. It can be one word such as *go, jump,* or *cook* or a group of words (verb phrase) such as *am going, have jumped,* or *will cook.*

2. Compound predicate — A compound predicate consists of two or more simple predicates (verbs).   *Example:* The children ran and played.

3. Complete predicate — The complete predicate consists of the simple predicate (verb) and the words that modify (describe or limit) the predicate.   *Examples:* John's father *is a lawyer.* George *asked for help.* (*Is* and *asked* are the simple predicates. *Is a lawyer* and *asked for help* are the complete predicates.)

PREPOSITION. A preposition shows the relation or connection between a noun or pronoun and another word in the sentence. Words such as *about, above, across, against, beyond, over,* and *under* are prepositions.

PREPOSITIONAL PHRASE. The prepositional phrase consists of the preposition, the noun or pronoun, and any word or words that describe the noun or pronoun. The noun or pronoun in the prepositional phrase is the object of the preposition. Prepositional phrases are used as adjectives or adverbs. *Examples:* My mother-in-law lives *near us.* (adverb) Let's go *with them.* (adverb) The child *on the rocking horse* is cute. (adjective)

PRESENT PARTICIPLE. (See Participle.)

PRINCIPAL CLAUSE. (See Independent Clause.)

PROGRESSIVE VERB FORM. The present participle with some form of the auxiliary *be* forms the progressive verb form. The progressive verb form is used to show that an action is continuing. It occurs in all tenses. *Examples:* She is playing; we were studying; I will be playing; he has been playing; we had been studying. (See Participle.)

PRONOUN. A pronoun is a word used in place of a noun. *Example:* Jennifer is a happy child. *She* likes to play ball with her friend. *Examples of pronouns:* I, you, he, she, we, this, that, who, what, any, anyone, herself, himself, each, one, another.

1. Pronouns and their antecedents — The word for which a pronoun stands is called its antecedent. *Example:* The book is excellent. It is excellent. (*Book* is the antecedent of *it.* The pronoun *it* refers to *book. It* is used in place of *book.*)

2. Agreement of pronouns with their antecedents — A singular antecedent requires a singular pronoun. *Example:* Anita is going away to school. She is looking forward to it.

3. Such words as *each, every, any, man, woman, person, either, neither, anybody, everybody,* and *anyone* require a singular pronoun. *Examples:* Each person does what he or she thinks is best. Everybody is practicing on his or her own.

4. A plural antecedent requires a plural pronoun. *Example:* Some parents are overprotective of their children.

5. If a pronoun has two or more antecedents connected by *and,* the pronoun referring to them is plural. *Examples:* My friend's brothers and sisters are planning a party for their parents. Juan and Anna are visiting their friends.

6. If a pronoun has two or more singular antecedents connected by *or* or *nor,* the pronoun referring to the antecedent is singular. *Examples:* Either James or Mike does his own work or we do not go. Neither Susan nor Cynthia has her own car.

7. If the antecedent of a pronoun is a collective noun, the pronoun is singular or plural depending on the meaning of the collective noun in the sentence. *Examples:* The crowd cheered their champion on to victory. The crowd screamed as one when its idol made the touchdown.

8. Indefinite pronouns such as *any, each, all,* and *some* do not refer to anything definite and may not have a definite antecedent.

9. Following are some different kinds of pronouns and examples of each.

Personal pronouns — These pronouns indicate the speaker, the person spoken to, or the person or thing spoken about (*I, you, he, she, it*).

Demonstrative pronouns — These pronouns point out the specific person or thing that is referred to (*this, that, these*).

Interrogative pronouns — These pronouns are used in asking questions (*who, which, what*).

Relative pronouns — These pronouns introduce a clause modifying an antecedent (*who, which, that*).

Indefinite pronouns — These pronouns refer to persons or things not easily identifiable. (*any, anyone, some*).

Reflexive pronouns — These pronouns are used as the object of a sentence. They point out or refer to the same person as the subject (*myself, yourself, oneself*).

Intensive pronouns — These pronouns are identical to the reflexive pronouns, but they tend to emphasize the noun that they are used with (*myself, yourself, oneself*).

PRONOUN CASE. The personal pronouns *I, you, he, she, it, we,* and *they* and the relative pronoun *who* have different forms in the possessive case (showing ownership): *my (mine), your (yours), his, her (hers), its, our (ours), their (theirs), and whose.* *Examples:* That is *my* book. (*My* functions as an adjective modifying book.) That book is *mine*. (*Mine* functions as a subject complement, that is, as the renamed subject, *book*.) She found *her* keys. Juanita is a friend of *hers*. Whose car is that? It is theirs.

The personal pronouns *I, he, she,* and *they* and the relative pronoun *who* also have different objective forms (forms used when the pronouns are objects): *me, him, her, us, them,* and *whom.* *Examples:* They took *me* for a drive. (direct object of *took*) The guard showed Art and *her* where to park. (direct object — with *Art* — of *showed*) Please take *us* to *them*. (*Us* is the direct object of *take*; *them* is the object of a preposition.) Paul gave *him* the money. (indirect object of *gave*) To *whom* shall I send this? (object of preposition)

PROOFREADING. Proofreading has to do with the correction of technical writing errors such as punctuation errors, capitalization errors, spelling errors, and so on.

PUNCTUATION.

1. Brackets — Brackets ([ ]) are used to enclose your comment, explanation, definition, and so on in quoted material that is being reported or edited. *Example:* "The author [Samuel Clemens] in his book *Huckleberry Finn* explores the theme of man's inhumanity to man."

2. Colon — A colon (:) is used in a formal sense to show that something is to follow. Following are examples of when a colon is used.

　　a. To introduce a list. *Example:* The laundry list includes these items: pillows, sheets, and towels.

　　b. After a formal heading. *Example:* Dear Sir:

　　c. In writing time. *Example:* 3:00 P.M.

　　d. To introduce a long quotation. *Example:* The judge made the following statement: "Based on all the evidence presented here, it seems that the jurors have but one verdict that they should bring in. However. . ."

　　e. In a title to separate parts of the title. *Example:* "Hallucinatory Drugs: Their Effects on Drivers"

3. Comma — The comma (,) is the most often used punctuation mark. A comma signals a slight pause. This pause is not as strong as the stop signaled by a period (.) or a semicolon (;).

a. The comma helps writers shorten sentences. It replaces *and* in a series.

Examples:

The cake is good and the ice cream is good and the soda is good.
The cake, ice cream, and soda are good.

The men swam and hiked and hunted.
The men swam, hiked, and hunted.

The child is well mannered and smart and pretty.
The well mannered, smart child is pretty.

b. The comma is usually used in a compound sentence to separate simple sentences joined by such conjunctions (linking words) as *and, but, for, or, yet,* and *nor.* *Examples:* Sharon is a good swimmer, but she doesn't like to dive. Seth is a good swimmer, and he likes to dive.

c. A comma is *not* used in a simple sentence to separate two different predicates. *Example:* They went to a movie and then to a restaurant.

d. A comma is usually used after a dependent clause (a group of words that cannot stand alone as a sentence) when it comes before an independent clause in a complex sentence. *Example:* Although she married a wealthy man, she continued to work.

e. A comma is *not* used in a complex sentence when the independent clause comes before the dependent clause and the dependent clause is restrictive. *Examples:* We felt badly that you could not come with us. We didn't go because it had started to rain.

f. A comma is usually used to set off such words as *also, moreover, therefore, then, nevertheless, likewise,* and *however* unless these words are used to join simple sentences. (See 11a under Semicolon in this section.) *Examples:* Nevertheless, you may stay here. However, that is not a good idea.

g. A comma is *not* used after *said* if there is no direct quotation. *Examples:* Direct quotation — She said, "Hello." Indirect quotation — She said that she was sorry.

h. A comma is *not* used between a subject and a verb. *Example:* They need money to pay the rent.

i. A comma is *not* used before the first item in a series. *Example:* I enjoy reading, writing, and athletics.

j. When two sentences are combined with only a comma and without a linking word, the writer is making a **run-on sentence error.** *Example:* It stopped raining, we went outside. *Correction:* It stopped raining; we went outside. When it stopped raining, we went outside. Since it stopped raining, we went outside. It stopped raining. We went outside.

k. A comma is *not* used between an adjective and a noun that acts as an adjective. *Examples:* big kitchen sink; pretty rose garden; large tea kettle.

l. Usually a comma is not placed before descriptive words that refer to size, color, or age.   *Examples:*   The nice little old lady.   The big brown dog.

   m.   Commas are used to set off nonrestrictive modifiers (modifiers that give additional or unnecessary information in a sentence) from the rest of the sentence.   *Example:*   Mr. Jones, *our physical education teacher,* gives us a tremendous workout each gym period.

   n.   Commas are *not* used to set off restrictive modifiers (modifiers that give essential information to the thought of the sentence.   *Example:* The student *who was cheating* was sent to the Dean's office.

   4.   Dash — The dash (—) is used to indicate some kind of break, and it is less limited than other punctuation marks.   Following are some uses of dash.

   a.   Used to show an abrupt shift in thought.   *Example:*   Yes, that is pretty—but did I tell you the news?

   b.   Used for suspense or emphasis.   *Example:*   The tapping of the cane came closer—closer.

   c.   Used to summarize or rephrase part of a sentence that came before.   *Example:*   The limping, frail old man in torn and tattered clothes staggered down the street—a sad sight to behold.

   d.   Used in place of parentheses.   *Example:*   Matricide—the killing of a mother by a son or daughter—is an especially horrible crime.

   e.   Used to show that a sentence is not finished.   *Example:*   I really can't say, but—

   5.   Exclamation mark — The exclamation mark (!) is used at the end of an exclamatory sentence.   *Example:*   That is beautiful! (See Interjection.)

   6.   Italics — Writers use a single straight line to show that something is to be put into italics.   Italics is a special kind of slant type that printers use. Items such as the following are usually put into italics: magazines, journals, newspapers, plays, movies, names of ships, foreign words, and words used as words or numbers used as numbers in a sentence.   *Examples: ibid.,* *Macbeth.*

   7.   Parentheses — Parentheses ( ) are generally used to enclose added material such as an explanation, a comment, or an elaboration of something in an already completed sentence.   Some other uses are to enclose numbers, symbols, or sums that are repeated in the sentence.   *Example:*   The check for three hundred dollars ($300.00) should arrive tomorrow.

   8.   Period — The period (.) is used at the end of a declarative (statement) sentence.   It is also usually used at the end of an imperative (command sentence.   *Examples:*   I am a college freshman.   Stop hitting him.

   9.   Question mark — A question mark (?) is used at the end of an interrogative (question) sentence.   *Example:*   What is his name?

   10.   Quotation marks — A direct quotation is always enclosed in quotation marks (" "); there is a comma after said, and the first word of the quotation is capitalized.   An indirect quotation is not enclosed in quotation marks.   *Examples:*   She said, "I'm enjoying myself here."   She said that she is enjoying herself here.

   a.   Separate sentences that follow one another and are part of the same speech should be enclosed in the same pair of quotation marks.   *Example:*   Mary said, "Please don't go yet.   Stay a little while longer."

b. Sentences that follow one another but are not part of the same speech should be enclosed in separate quotation marks. *Example:* The following questions were asked by the students: "When will we have our midterm?" "Will we have a final?" "Will you ask us to do a paper?"

c. If the words *she said* or *he said* occur in the middle of a quotation, *she said* or *he said* should not be included within the quotation marks. *Example:* "If that's true," he said, "I can't go with you."

d. If the quotation coming before *she said* or *he said* forms a complete sentence, a period should come after *she said* or *he said.*   *Example:* "That is a beautiful gown," she said. "I think that I'll get one just like it."

e. If the quotation comes before *he said* or *she said,* a comma usually separates the quotation from *he said* or *she said,* unless the quotation is a question or exclamation.   *Example:* "Oh no!" he exclaimed.

f. If the expression *he said* or *she said* comes in the middle of a question or exclamation, the exclamation mark or question mark is placed at the end of the quotation.   *Example:* "That is so marvelous," she exclaimed, "that I can't wait to hear all about it!"

g. If omitted material designated by ellipsis (...) is part of the quotation, the ellipsis should be included within the quotation marks.   *Example:* Alexander Pope said, "A little learning is a dangerous thing. Drink deep. . ."

h. A quotation within a quotation is designated by single quotation marks.   *Example:* The captain said, "When the shipwrecked man came aboard, he said, 'I never thought I'd see human beings again.' "

i. When you use an author's exact words in your writing, the author's words should be enclosed in quotation marks. If the quote is a sentence that comes in the middle of your sentence and it fits into what you are writing, the quote does not need a capital or a period.   *Example:* I agree with Sylvia Ashton-Warner when she says that "the mind of a five-year old is as a volcano with two vents, destructiveness and creativeness," but I'm not sure how many others do.

j.   Titles of poems (except long poems such as epics), stories, articles, and chapters are put in quotation marks.   *Examples:* "The Monkey's Paw"; "How to Study."

k. Quotation marks are used when defining a word.   *Example:* The word *animosity* means "hatred."

11. Semicolon — The semicolon (;) is a punctuation signal used to connect two simple sentences. However, the comma rather than the semicolon is usually used when two simple sentences are connected by such conjunctions as *and, but, for, nor,* or *yet.*

a. When linking words such as *nevertheless, however, then,* or *therefore* are used to join two simple sentences to form a compound sentence, a semicolon is usually used before the linking word.

b. A semicolon without a linking word is used if the simple sentences are closely related. If the simple sentences are not closely related, a period is usually used.   *Example:* The children played Monopoly for hours; it was their favorite game.

c. In special cases when a sentence has a long involved series that contains commas, a semicolon is used to separate the larger units of the sentence.

RESTRICTIVE MODIFIER. (See Modifier.)

REVISION. Revision refers to the creative improvement of an existing script.

RUN-ON SENTENCE. (See 3 j under Punctuation.)

SENTENCE. A word or group of words stating, asking, commanding, supposing, or exclaiming. It contains a subject and a verb that are in agreement with one another. It begins with a capital letter and ends with a period (.), question mark (?), or exclamation mark (!). *Examples:* They are friendly people. Go. Who are you? That is pretty!

1. Types of sentences.

a. Simple sentence — A simple sentence consists of one single statement, command, wish, question, or exclamation that can stand alone because it expresses a complete thought. A simple sentence contains only one independent clause. A simple sentence may have a single subject and verb or a compound (two or more) subject and compound verb. *Examples:* He won the tennis match. Jennifer and Sharon play together. The children went swimming and hiking. My mother and father jog and bicycle every day.

b. Compound sentence — A compound sentence is made up of two or more simple sentences. *Examples:* Jim studied very hard for his biology exam, but he did not do well on it. Maria likes to dance, but her boyfriend refuses to go dancing.

c. Complex sentence — A complex sentence is made up of one simple sentence and one or more dependent clauses (groups of words that cannot stand alone as sentences). *Examples:* She is very popular at school because she is a thoughtful, intelligent, and friendly person. Although he is not very strong, he tries to do his share.

d. Compound-complex sentence — A compound-complex sentence is made up of two or more simple sentences and one or more dependent clauses. *Examples:* He went to the food store, but he did not buy anything because he forgot his shopping list. When I need help with my homework, my father tries to help me, but he usually has difficulty figuring out the problems, also.

2. Declarative sentence — A declarative sentence is a statement. A period is used at the end of the sentence. *Examples:* My name is Ms. Smith. I am taking biology in the fall.

3. Exclamatory sentence — An exclamatory sentence expresses emotion or strong feeling. *Examples:* How lovely you look! What a horrible accident! (See Interjection.)

4. Interrogative sentence — An interrogative sentence is a question sentence. *Examples:* What is the average life span of a horse? Are you going to Yolanda's party?

5. Imperative sentence — An imperative sentence expresses a command. *Examples:* Come here. Do the work now.

6. Parallel construction — A sentence that has parallel construction is one in which the series of elements that have been combined are equal in importance. *Example:* During our college break we ate a lot, played a lot, and slept a lot.

SENTENCE PATTERNS. All writing in English is based on a few sentence patterns, that is, the way that words can be arranged and still make sense. Here are the most often used sentence patterns: Sentence Pattern 1

(N/P V) Birds fly. Sentence Pattern 2 (N/P V N/P) John hit Mary. Sentence Pattern 3 (N/P V N/P N) Jack read Mary a story. Sentence Pattern 4 (N/P LV N/P) John is a lawyer. Sentence Pattern 5 (N/P LV Adj.) Jennifer is pretty. Sentence Pattern 6 (N/P V N/P N) Dorothy considers Arthur a genius. Sentence Pattern 7 (N/P V N/P Adj.) The students found the lecture stimulating. (N/P means the word can be either a noun or a pronoun.)

SPELLING. (See also *Noun Plural.*)

1. Double consonant rule for closed syllables (one-syllable words) — One-syllable words that are closed syllables usually double the consonant before adding endings beginning with a vowel. (This rule does not apply to words that end in -*y* or -*w* because *y* and *w* act as vowels in such words as *say* and *saw*. *Examples:* canned, barred, running.

2. Double consonant rule for multisyllabic (having more than one syllable) words ending in closed syllables — A multisyllabic word that ends in a closed syllable usually doubles the consonant before an ending beginning with a vowel *if* the accent falls on the final syllable. *Examples:* occur — occurring; detain — detaining (not a closed syllable); reason — reasoning (accent on first syllable).

3. The final silent -*e* rule for adding the ending -*able* — Most words ending in a final silent -*e*, except those ending in -*ce* or -*ge*, drop the *e* before adding -*able*. Words ending in -*ce* and -*ge* keep the *e* to maintain the soft sound. *Examples:* change — changeable; love — lovable; sale — salable.

4. The final silent -*e* rule for adding the ending -*ing* — Most words ending in a final silent -*e*, including those ending in -*ce* or -*ge*, drop the *e* before adding the ending -*ing*. *Examples:* change — changing; rope — roping.

5. The final silent -*e* rule for adding endings beginning with consonants — Most words ending in a final silent -*e* retain the *e* when endings beginning with consonants are added to them. *Examples:* hope — hopeful; care — careful; encourage — encouragement; manage — management. *Exceptions:* judge — judgment; acknowledge — acknowledgment; nine — ninth; true — truly; whole — wholly; awe - awful.

6. The rule for adding endings to words that end in -*y* — When a word ends in -*y* and a consonant comes before the *y*, the *y* is usually changed to *i* before adding the ending. If a vowel comes before the *y*, the *y* is usually kept before adding the ending. *Examples:* beauty — beautiful; marry — married; say — saying.

7. The *ie* rule — a. In words having *ei* or *ie*, when the sound is long e, it's usually *i* before *e* except after *c*. *Examples:* shield, conceive. *Exceptions:* weird, protein, either, neither, leisure, seize, sheik, codeine. b. In words having *ei* or *ie*, when the sound is long *a*, it's *e* before *i*. *Examples:* neighbor, weigh.

SUBJECT OF A SENTENCE. A word or group of words about which something is said. The subject of a sentence can be a person, animal, place, thing, idea, and so on.

Simple subject — A simple subject is either a noun or a pronoun by itself. *Examples: Miss Smith* is my teacher. *She* is very strict. (*Miss Smith* and *she* are both simple subjects.)

Compound Subject — A compound subject consists of two or more simple subjects. The simple subjects may be two or more nouns or pronouns.

Examples: The *Smiths, Clarks,* and *Browns* are coming to my party. *Sharon, Seth,* and *I* are leaving for school tomorrow. (The italicized words in the sentences are compound subjects.)

Complete subject — The complete subject consists of the simple subject (noun or pronoun) and the words that describe or limit the subject. *Examples: The small, friendly dog* wagged its tail. *The juicy, ripe apple* tasted delicious. (The simple subjects are *dog* and *apple.* The complete subjects are *the small, friendly dog* and *the juicy, ripe apple.*)

SUBORDINATE CLAUSE. (See Dependent Clause.)

SUBORDINATE CONJUNCTION. (See Linking Words.)

SUFFIX. A suffix is a letter or a group of letters added to a root (base) word. *Examples: -less, -able, -ous, -ful, -ly.* (See Adjective and Adverb.)

SUPERLATIVE DEGREE. (See Adjective and Adverb.)

SYLLABLE. A syllable is a vowel or a group of letters that has one vowel sound. *Examples: a, bet, run, all, cle, bi.*

1. Closed syllables — Words or syllables that have only one vowel and end in a consonant are called closed syllables. The vowel sound in a closed syllable is usually short. *Examples:* got, man, hat.

2. Open syllables — Words or syllables that have a single vowel and end in a vowel are called open syllables. The vowel sound in an open syllable is usually long. *Examples:* go, we.

TOPIC SENTENCE. The topic sentence is that sentence, which states what the paragraph will be about by naming the topic.

TRANSITIVE VERB. A transitive verb is a verb that can take an object, that is, it can carry over an action from a subject to an object. *Examples:* The cat drinks milk. The man held the child. She threw the ball.

VERB. (See Predicate of a Sentence.)

VERB MOOD. The mood of a verb shows the way that the writer or speaker views the action of the verb. It expresses the writer's or speaker's mood or state of mind. Following are the three verb moods.

1. Indicative mood — Mood stating a fact or asking a question. Most verbs are in this mood. *Examples:* Are you going to the beach? I am not ready yet.

2. Imperative mood — Mood expressing a command, a desire, or an urgent request. *Examples:* Go. Don't do that.

3. Subjunctive mood — Mood expressing a condition contrary to fact (a condition that does not exist at the moment) or a wish. In the subjunctive, *were* is used in place of *was* for the past tense and *be* is used in place of *are* in the present tense. *Example:* If I were wealthy, I'd buy a new car and house. The subjunctive *be* is used in a dependent clause in a sentence expressing a demand, request, or requirement. *Examples:* It is important that you be present at the board meeting. He requested that you be present at the meeting.

VERB TENSE. Tense shows the *time* of the action of the verb.

1. Present tense — The present tense is used to show that action is taking place in the present and to show present facts. *Examples:* The students are studying for an exam. It is raining.

Generally, the present tense of a verb is used when discussing book reviews. *Example:* Charlotte in E.B. White's *Charlotte's Web* is given virtuous human characteristics.

Generally, the present tense of a verb is used when writing about general truths or statements that are permanently true.   *Examples:* One hundred centimeters equals a meter.   Geography is the study of the earth's surface.

2.   Past tense — The past tense of a verb is used to show that something has taken place in the past and that the action is completed.   *Examples:* Yesterday, I visited my uncle.   I wrote my composition two days ago.

3.   *Future tense* — The future tense of a verb is used to show actions that have not happened yet.   The actions will take place at a future time.   *Examples:* I will call you tomorrow.   He will become a father very soon.

4.   Present perfect tense — When an action that started in the past is going on or continuing at any time up to the present, the word *has* is used with the past participle of the verb.   *Examples:* He has been working for five hours on that project.   She has been gone for one week.

5.   Past perfect tense — When a tale of past events is interrupted with an event happening before the past event, the word *had* is used with the past participle of the verb.   *Examples:* She said that she had quit her job a week ago.   Our instructor told us that he had been a prisoner for four years in a concentration camp.

The word *had* is used with the part participle of the verb to describe an action that was completed before some other past action.   *Examples:* Before I traveled in Europe, I had toured the United States.   We had heard all about him before we met him.

6.   In writing sentences, the verb in the independent clause should be logically consistent with the verb of the dependent clause.   *Examples:* Although she receives very high grades, she claims that she never studies.   I was afraid of planes because ten years ago I had been in a plane crash.

7.   If the dependent clause is introduced by a verb of thinking, telling, or saying in the past tense, the verb in the dependent clause is usually in the past tense.   *Examples:* He said that he was pleased with my work.   He thought that I had a very important job.

8.   The tense used in a story should be consistent throughout.   *Example:* The man was old and poor.   He had nothing but the tattered rags on his back.

VERB VOICE

1.   If the subject in a sentence is doing the action, the verb is in the active voice.   *Examples:* Tony is writing a book.   Sharon typed the manuscript.

2.   If the subject in a sentence is receiving the action, the sentence is in the passive voice.   *Examples:* A book is being written by Tony.   The manuscript was typed by Sharon.

3.   A verb in the passive tense consists of some form of the auxiliary verb *to be* plus the past participle of the main verb.   *Examples:* The ball was thrown to me.   The cookie was eaten by the child.

4.   Only sentences that contain transitive verbs can be changed to the passive voice.   *Examples:* The cat drinks milk. (active voice) Milk is drunk by the cat. (passive voice)

5.   Sentences containing intransitive verbs cannot be put into the passive voice.   *Examples:* He is nineteen years old. Fish swim.

6.   The active voice is usually preferred.   However, the passive voice is necessary when the doer of an action is unknown or the mention of a specific subject is not desired.

Index